Ancient Teotihuacan

D0865328

This is the first comprehensive English-language book on the largest city in the Americas before the 1400s. Teotihuacan is a UNESCO World Heritage site, located in highland central Mexico, about twenty-five miles from Mexico City, visited by millions of tourists every year. The book begins with Cuicuilco, a predecessor that arose around 400 BCE, then traces Teotihuacan from its founding in approximately 150 BCE to its collapse around 600 CE. It describes the city's immense pyramids and other elite structures. It also discusses the dwellings and daily lives of commoners, including men, women, and children, and the craft activities of artisans. George L. Cowgill discusses politics, economics, technology, art, religion, and possible reasons for Teotihuacan's rise and fall. Long before the Aztecs, and 800 miles from Classic Maya centers, Teotihuacan was part of a broad Mesoamerican tradition but had a distinctive personality that invites comparison with other states and empires of the ancient world.

George L. Cowgill is Emeritus Professor of Anthropology in the School of Human Evolution and Social Change at Arizona State University. He is the director of the ASU-managed archaeological laboratory at Teotihuacan, Mexico. His work on Teotihuacan, anthropological theory, and quantitative methods in archaeology has been published in numerous major peer-reviewed journals. He is the coauthor, with René Millon and R. Bruce Drewitt, of *Urbanization at Teotihuacan, Mexico, Volume 1: The Teotihuacan Map, Part 2: Maps* (1973) and coeditor, with Norman Yoffee, of *The Collapse of Ancient States and Civilizations* (1988). He was the keynote speaker at the fifth Round Table on Teotihuacan at the Instituto Nacional de Antropología e Historia in Mexico in 2011.

Case Studies in Early Societies

Series Editor
Rita P. Wright, *New York University*

This series aims to introduce students to early societies that have been the subject of sustained archaeological research. Each study is also designed to demonstrate a contemporary method of archaeological analysis in action, and the authors are all specialists currently engaged in field research.

The books have been planned to cover many of the same fundamental issues. Tracing long-term developments, and describing and analyzing a discrete segment in the prehistory or history of a region, they represent an invaluable tool for comparative analysis. Clear, well organized, authoritative, and succinct, the case studies are an important resource for students, and for scholars in related fields, such as anthropology, ethnohistory, history, and political science. They also offer the general reader accessible introductions to important archaeological sites.

Other titles in the series include:

Ancient Teotihuacan

Early Urbanism in Central Mexico

George L. Cowgill

Arizona State University

CAMBRIDGE
UNIVERSITY PRESS

CAMBRIDGE
UNIVERSITY PRESS

University Printing House, Cambridge CB2 8BS, United Kingdom

One Liberty Plaza, 20th Floor, New York, NY 10006, USA

477 Williamstown Road, Port Melbourne, VIC 3207, Australia

314-321, 3rd Floor, Plot 3, Splendor Forum, Jasola District Centre, New Delhi - 110025, India

79 Anson Road, #06-04/06, Singapore 079906

Cambridge University Press is part of the University of Cambridge.

It furthers the University's mission by disseminating knowledge in the pursuit of education, learning and research at the highest international levels of excellence.

www.cambridge.org
Information on this title: www.cambridge.org/9780521690447

© George L. Cowgill 2015

This publication is in copyright. Subject to statutory exception and to the provisions of relevant collective licensing agreements, no reproduction of any part may take place without the written permission of Cambridge University Press.

First published 2015

A catalogue record for this publication is available from the British Library

Library of Congress Cataloging in Publication data
Cowgill, George L.
Ancient Teotihuacan : early urbanism in Central Mexico / George L. Cowgill, Arizona State University.
    pages   cm. – (Case studies in early societies)
Includes bibliographical references and index.
ISBN 978-0-521-87033-7 (hardback) – ISBN 978-0-521-69044-7 (pbk.)
1. Teotihuacán Site (San Juan Teotihuacán, Mexico) – History.
2. Teotihuacán Site (San Juan Teotihuacán, Mexico) – Excavations.
3. Teotihuacán Site (San Juan Teotihuacán, Mexico) – Antiquities.
4. Indians of Mexico – Mexico – San Juan Teotihuacán – Antiquities.
5. Indian architecture – Mexico – San Juan Teotihuacán.   6. Teotihuacán pottery.   I. Title.
F1219.1.T27C69   2015
972'.01–dc23   2014043711

ISBN 978-0-521-87033-7 Hardback
ISBN 978-0-521-69044-7 Paperback

Cambridge University Press has no responsibility for the persistence or accuracy of URLs for external or third-party internet websites referred to in this publication, and does not guarantee that any content on such websites is, or will remain, accurate or appropriate.

Contents

Figures

Tables

Boxes

Acknowledgments

In 1964, René Millon invited me to join his ambitious project to map the entirety of the great ancient city of Teotihuacan. That seemed like a fine idea, at least for a few years, during which I could think about what I might do next. But Teotihuacan has kept me busy ever since. My greatest debt in writing this book is to René. In the 1960s he was my principal mentor. He has not written much about theory. Most of what I have learned from him has come from conversations, often in the house he and the late Clara Millon occupied during many seasons at Teotihuacan. I have not agreed with all of René's ideas, but this book shows his influence in many ways.

Others to whom I am particularly indebted include Don Pedro Baños, who did a tremendous amount of fieldwork for the Teotihuacan Mapping Project in the 1960s and 1970s. He often independently led field crews, took perceptive notes, and subsequently devoted many years to classifying and tabulating the ceramic collections resulting from that project. Don Zeferino Ortega very ably aided in these ceramic analyses and in many aspects of later projects. The ceramic sequence itself, subsequently modified in some respects by Evelyn Rattray, was largely the creation of the late James Bennyhoff. Others who contributed especially to the work of the Mapping Project include Bruce Drewitt, Alicia Germán de Enciso, Michael Spence, and deceased colleagues Darlena Blucher, Paula Krotser, and G. Raymond Krotser. Former graduate students at Brandeis University, including Jeffrey Altschul, Miriam Chernoff, Michael Ester, Mary Hopkins, Emily McClung de Tapia, and Rebecca Sload, have helped in many ways. At Arizona State University, I have been greatly helped by Oralia Cabrera, Sarah Clayton, Destiny Crider, Tatsuya Murakami, Ian Robertson, Kristin Sullivan, and Nawa Sugiyama. Saburo Sugiyama has been a colleague and a steady source of challenging ideas.

In this book I synthesize the results of many projects carried out by U.S., Mexican, and other institutions, a few directed by myself, most directed by others. Support for projects in which I have been involved has come especially from a long series of grants from the National Science Foundation, and also from the National Endowment for the Humanities, the Wenner-Gren Foundation for Anthropological Research, the National Geographic Society, the American Council of Learned Societies, the Foundation for the Advancement of Mesoamerican Studies, Brandeis University, Arizona State University, and some other sources and private donors. Fieldwork permits and other assistance were provided by the Instituto Nacional de Antropología e Historia, and I am especially indebted to Arqlgo. Rubén Cabrera C. and the late Ing. Joaquín García-Bárcena. A year at the Center for Advanced Studies in the Behavioral Sciences in 1992–93 (aided by NSF grant SES 9022192 to the Center) offered an opportunity for reading that helped lay the groundwork for this book. Four anonymous reviewers of the initial outline and an anonymous reviewer of a later draft made useful and encouraging comments.

Rita Wright invited and encouraged me to do the book. She, Michael Smith, and Barbara Stark made comments on drafts of the entire book. Kelly Knudson provided information about uses of isotopes in archaeological research and saved me from some errors. Karl Taube was helpful about Teotihuacan imagery and notation, at home and abroad. Paul Schmidt provided data on Granular Ware in the state of Guerrero. Stephen Houston told me how to spell Tak'alik Abaj. Anastasia Graf, Beatrice Rehl, and Isabella Vitti of Cambridge University Press, as well as Nishanthini Vetrivel at Newgen, added encouragement and guided me through the publication process. Destiny Crider, Hannah Reitzel Rivera, Meagan Rubel, and Will G. Russell were immensely helpful with electronic aspects of the illustrations. Shearon Vaughn drew many of the figures and Table 1.1. Figures 3.2, 4.1, 5.1, 6.1, 7.1, 9.1, 9.2, 9.3, and 9.4 were modified from pictures derived from primitive computer graphics by Whitney Powell in about 1971. Only I am responsible for the uses I have made of all this assistance.

1   Preliminaries

Most English speakers have heard of the Aztec and Maya of Mexico and Central America and the Inka of South America, but other spectacular New World civilizations are less widely known. The ruins of Teotihuacan (Figure 1.1) are only forty-five kilometers (twenty-eight miles) from downtown Mexico City, and its immense pyramids are visited by hundreds of thousands every year, yet the distinctive nature of the culture that produced these monuments is often not recognized. Some tour guides say the city was built by the Aztecs, but their empire was a late development of the 1400s, resting on a long earlier tradition created by Teotihuacanos, Toltecs, and others. Tourists rarely see more than the restored central district of the city, and are given no idea of the vast extent of unexcavated surrounding ruins, most of which are today only gentle undulations in a surface largely covered by vegetation or, increasingly, by modern settlements.

Teotihuacan flourished in the highlands of Central Mexico between about 150/50 BCE and 550/650 CE. For much of this time, the city's population approached a hundred thousand, and in those days it was the largest city in the western hemisphere, with scores of great pyramids, richly frescoed elite dwellings, and thousands of residential compounds for the masses. It was more widely influential than any other civilization of its time in Mesoamerica – the region of politically complex societies that developed in the southern two-thirds of present-day Mexico and in northern Central America. Teotihuacan interacted with other Mesoamerican societies as far away as the Maya of Guatemala and Yucatán, some 1,100 km (700 miles) to the east (Figure 1.2). Their culture shared some general features with Teotihuacan but was quite distinct in language, political systems, and styles.

In this book I try to distill what I have learned from 50 years' study of the great ancient city. But the literature on Teotihuacan is so vast that, in order to ever finish, I could not read everything important ever written about the city. I concentrate on an outline of Teotihuacan's history,

1

Figure 1.1. Aerial photograph of the central part of Teotihuacan, looking south along the Avenue of the Dead in 1965.
Courtesy of René Millon (1973).

on issues raised by contemplation of a society so different from ours,
and on unanswered questions calling for further research. I focus on
the city itself and deal briefly with events leading up to Teotihuacan,
Teotihuacan's interactions with its neighbors, and the aftermath of its
collapse.

I hope the book will appeal to a wide audience, but I have provided
enough detail to make it useful for students and professionals concentrating on ancient civilizations elsewhere throughout the world. I have
tried to tell a story about all aspects of Teotihuacan society, including
technology, politics, economics, environmental interactions, religion,
and what we can infer about the texture of life – both everyday and on
exceptional occasions. I deal, insofar as possible, with all kinds of people in Teotihuacan society, inconspicuous commoners as well as the elite
and powerful, men, women, and children. I avoid a static picture and
discuss changes over time. For a society that had no full-blown writing,
all this is a daunting challenge, and we cannot trace the life history and

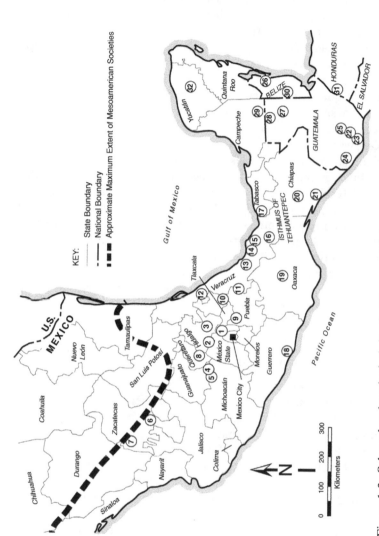

Figure 1.2. Selected archaeological sites in Mesoamerica.

1: Teotihuacan, 2: Tula, 3: Sierra de las Navajas, 4: Chupícuaro, 5: Ucareo, 6: La Quemada, 7: Alta Vista, 8: San Juan del Río, 9: Cholula, 10: Cantona, 11: Maltrata Valley, 12: El Tajín, 13: Cerro de las Mesas, 14: Tres Zapotes, 15: Matacapan, 16: San Lorenzo, 17: La Venta, 18: Acatempa, 19: Monte Albán, 20: Mirador, 21: Los Horcones, 22: Balberta, 23: Montana, 24: Tak'alik Abaj, 25: Kaminaljuyú, 26: Altun Ha, 27: Tikal, 28: Nakbé, 29: Calakmul, 30: Caracol, 31: Copan, 32: Chichén Itzá. By S. Vaughn.

3

deeds of any single individual. Nevertheless, there is much that we can say with some confidence.

To a degree, each person creates the past that he or she expects or wants or can imagine, but there are limits to how far one can go with this. There are real constraints on what one can reasonably believe about the past. One merit of continued research is that we can more sharply distinguish what is reasonable to think from what is not reasonable. Furthermore, we are constantly finding unexpected things that require us to revise our ideas drastically. Research on Teotihuacan is still in an early stage, and this book is a report of work in progress. It will be disappointing if little needs changing in another ten or twenty years.

Knowing about Teotihuacan is worthwhile for its own sake, as a society that was in many ways unique, and as an important part of the Mexican past, and that may be enough to satisfy many readers. Yet Teotihuacan was not so unique as to prevent useful comparisons with other ancient and modern societies. I try to do justice to what was special about Teotihuacan, but I also offer some comparisons and discuss how knowledge of Teotihuacan bears on some broad issues in anthropological theory, as well as concerns of today. I avoid presenting Teotihuacan as merely one example of some oversimplified and unduly homogenized abstract type, a defect of many comparative studies. However, claims that any specific society is too different from any other to permit meaningful comparisons are never convincing. It is a matter of method. Insights that can lead to better theory depend on nuanced comparisons among specific dimensions and aspects of variation, rather than on defining categories, although categorization can be a useful first step.

Pronunciations and Names

The name Teotihuacan is a tongue-twister for English speakers. We do not know what the ancient inhabitants called themselves or their city. Teotihuacan is the Spanish spelling of the name the much later Aztecs used for it in their language (Náhuatl, a language spoken today by about a million people). The meaning of this word is debated, but the most likely interpretation is something like "where divinity comes into being" (Ian Robertson, personal communication). In Spanish "hu" represents the same sound as "w" in English. The Náhuatl pronunciation is something like Tay-o-tee-WAH-kan, with stress on the next-to-last syllable, but in modern usage in Mexico the stress is often shifted to the final syllable: Tay-o-tee-wa-KAN (Teotihuacán in Spanish spelling). Here I follow the practice of many Mexican archaeologists in putting the stress on the next-to-last syllable, in the indigenous way, indicated by dropping the accent mark over the final syllable. I refer to occupants of the city as "Teotihuacanos." Pronunciation of other non-English words is generally as in modern Mexican Spanish, except that "x" often has the sound of English "sh," and "tl" represents a single Náhuatl sound that has no equivalent in either Spanish or English and is said to resemble the "ll" of Welsh (not much help if your Welsh is rusty).

Theoretical Standpoint

My theoretical standpoint has been influenced by sociologists Anthony Giddens (1979, 1984, 1991) and Pierre Bourdieu (1977, 1990; Jenkins 1992), but I use their ideas more as points of view than as full-blown theoretical systems (Cowgill 2000c). My discussion of craft production, exchange, and consumption in Chapter 7 has profited from the lucid overview of the topic by Schortman and Urban (2004). I believe material circumstances are important but they are not all-important, and too much is left out by "processual" and other approaches that fail to give enough weight to human motivations and emotions. I am highly dissatisfied with the notion that change is primarily driven by societies' adaptive responses to stresses, as if societies behaved like knowledgeable individuals. Something a little like biological selection can occur among societies, but the mechanisms of selection and transmission are so different that biological analogies do not get us very far. Likewise, so-called neo-evolutionary approaches, much in vogue among anthropological archaeologists in the United States in the 1960s and 1970s, are unsatisfyingly simplistic, with their tendency (in spite of disclaimers) to categorize societies according to universal developmental stages or types such as "bands," "tribes," "chiefdoms," and "states." They also tend to put unwarranted trust in archaeologically discernible features that are supposedly diagnostic of the distinct types, such as the number of tiers in site sizes within a region – whether three tiers (large, intermediate, small) or four or more such tiers. Supposedly the tiers are determined objectively, but usually a large unacknowledged subjective element is involved. And even if the tiers were unambiguously present, their interpretation in terms of sociopolitical types is ambiguous. Recent critics of neo-evolutionary approaches include Norman Yoffee (2005), Adam T. Smith (2003), and Jeffrey Quilter and Michele Koons (2012). I see far more explanatory promise in considering the actions of multiple individuals as they seek to pursue their goals in interaction with their social, institutional, and natural contexts, and in light of their attitudes about what is most desirable and their beliefs about what will work best to attain what they desire. I see value in much of what has been labeled "agency theory," although I avoid that term because it has been used to mean too many different things.

I have been influenced by some of the diverse archaeological literature labeled "postprocessual," especially in thinking that beliefs, states of mind, and emotions are important. However, I believe in a real past, and I believe archaeologists can and should achieve fuller and less ambiguous knowledge of that past (Cowgill 1993a). I am a philosophical realist (cf. Wylie 2002). I believe falling trees make noises even if no one is there to hear them. Some archaeologists see coexistence of multiple incompatible stories about the past as a refreshing kind of diversity that should be accepted and enjoyed, but I consider it a stimulating challenge that should be addressed. Different stories can be serviceable in different contexts and for different purposes, but I would like to "get it right" about a real past. For that reason, I sometimes say "clearly" this or that, but, more often than readers may like, I qualify statements with "probably," "perhaps," "possibly," or "conceivably." This isn't timidity. It's intended as a nuanced scale of the state of evidence, and a challenge to improve that state by further research.

"Dual-processual" theory (Blanton et al. 1996) has had a good effect in raising awareness that early complex polities differed considerably among one another. The theory postulates that there are two major political strategies in early polities: the "corporate" strategy emphasizes collective action within the polity, while the "exclusionary" strategy places more emphasis on individual rule and networking among the heads of different polities. But polities that differ greatly among themselves in scale and in other features share primarily corporate aspects, while in a wide variety of other societies exclusionary aspects predominate, so the distinction should not be used simply to pigeonhole cases. Additionally, I am troubled by treating the distinction as a matter of strategies. To me, the central distinction is in institutional structures. In some polities, institutions provide for strong centralization of power and authority, which are concentrated in a single individual or at most a very few top authorities. An extreme example might be Old Kingdom Egypt. In other polities, such as that specified by the U.S. Constitution, powers are more widely separated and shared among larger groups. In either case, *strategies* are pursued by individuals or interest groups, acting within a political arena that is shaped by the prevailing institutions. Strategies involve working within the institutional system, but also manipulating it, resisting it, or even subverting it. A simple corporate/exclusionary dichotomy does little justice to the various and changing institutions and strategies likely in play at Teotihuacan. Blanton and Fargher (2011) carry these issues further in their discussion of the collective logic of pre-modern cities.

Societies vary widely on several axes (dimensions) of sociocultural complexity (Nelson 1995). Those with a high degree of complexity and differentiation, and codification of institutions and political offices, are deservedly called states. However, I am unpersuaded by the claim made by some archaeologists that there is a clear threshold that makes all states qualitatively different from all non-state polities. I am especially skeptical of claims that there are readily discernible and reliable archaeological diagnostics of such thresholds. Many well-documented cases defy easy classification. For example, Charlemagne tried hard to create something enough like the defunct Western Roman Empire that it would have qualified as a state, but his success was limited and short-lived, and most of the polities of Western Europe between 500 and 1500 CE had mixes of state-like and chiefdom-like features. For these reasons, I often use the more ambiguous term "polity." The Teotihuacan polity can be called a state at least by 200 CE. It probably could be called that several centuries earlier, but I think it is unprofitable and unsound theory to try to specify an exact threshold date.

Box 1.1 The Metric System

As in other books in this series, I use "boxes" for information that is somewhat outside the main narrative, but too important to be relegated to an endnote.

I use the metric system for most measurements. One meter (m) is roughly three and a quarter feet, one kilometer (km) is about three-fifths of a mile, one mile is about 1.6 km, and one hectare (ha) is a square 100 meters on a side, that is, 10,000 square meters. There are 100 hectares in one square kilometer. One square kilometer is about two-fifths of a square mile. One cubic meter is about thirty-six cubic feet. One centimeter (cm) is 1/100 of a meter, and 1 millimeter (mm) is 1/10 cm.

Chronology

In the Maya lowlands, far from Teotihuacan, between about 250 and 1000 CE, inscriptions with "Long Count" dates (see Box 8.1) record the exact days, down to the day, of occurrence of many events. There are a few dated inscriptions elsewhere in Eastern Mesoamerica and in the Gulf Lowlands, one as early as 36 BCE. At Teotihuacan, and elsewhere in Mesoamerica, cross-ties with the Long Count chronology, based on datable imports from the Maya area or resemblances in ceramics or other objects, can be useful, but local chronologies depend mainly on sequences of stylistic and technological change in ceramics (broken pottery fragments, "sherds," survive in great numbers), architecture, and other durable materials, and absolute chronological estimates are mostly based on radiocarbon dates, with limited and often highly controversial uses of archaeomagnetism, obsidian hydration, and other methods.

Box 1.2 Radiocarbon Dating

The nuclei of atoms consist of protons (each with a positive electrical charge) and neutrons (electrically neutral). Surrounding the nucleus is a swarm of negatively charged electrons, just enough to balance the positive charges of the protons and make the atom neutral. The number of protons determines what element the atom is (hydrogen, oxygen, etc.) and its chemical properties are mainly determined by the electrons. The number of neutrons in the nucleus can vary, and atoms with the same number of electrons and protons (and hence similar chemical properties) but different numbers of neutrons are called "isotopes" of one another. Some isotopes are unstable, and decay by radioactive processes. Atoms of carbon have a nucleus with six protons and a variable number of neutrons. Nuclei with six or seven neutrons are stable (^{12}C or ^{13}C), but those with eight neutrons (^{14}C) decay radioactively. Decay occurs randomly, so it is impossible to tell when any specific nucleus will decay, but on average, half of a large number of nuclei will decay in about 5,730 years. Living plants and animals constantly absorb carbon atoms from their surroundings, a fairly constant proportion of which are ^{14}C. When organisms die, fresh carbon is not added, so the ratio of ^{14}C relative to stable carbon steadily declines. This means that the ratio in the remains of a once living thing can be used to estimate how long it's been dead. Radiocarbon dates suffer from several sources of uncertainty, including the intrinsically probabilistic nature of radioactive decay, the need to adopt a calibration curve in order to take account of slight variations over time in the $^{14}C/^{12}C$ ratio in the environment, issues about the relation between the dated object and its archaeological context, and errors such as contamination, mislabeling of specimens, and instrument malfunctions. For all these reasons, one or even a dozen radiocarbon dates can be quite misleading. Nevertheless, frequently that is all we have.

At present, units in many Mesoamerican chronologies come in chunks of two or three centuries, or even longer. Being able to deal with reliably identifiable periods of a century or less would not merely fill in minor details; it would transform our understanding of the past in the same way that the resolving power of microscopes and telescopes transformed biology and astronomy. With enough radiocarbon dates from good specimens, especially if combined with stratigraphic and other evidence from "Bayesian"[1] statistical analyses, such accuracy will be possible.

Two chronological systems have been widely used in Mesoamerica. Neither is satisfactory. One consists of broad stages or periods: Paleoindian, Archaic, Preclassic (or Formative), Classic, and Postclassic, sometimes with an "Epiclassic" period inserted between the Early Classic and the Postclassic. This system suffers from a tendency to mix pure chronology with developmental stages, so that a "Classic" stage may be reached several centuries later in one region than in another. In the 1970s, an attempt was made to introduce a developmentally neutral and purely chronological system of "Horizons" separated by "Intermediate Periods" (Millon 1976a; Price 1976) but this has not been widely adopted. It has proved less neutral than was hoped, because it induces one to think of cycles of greater and lesser pan-Mesoamerican unity (Rice 1983).

Neither scheme is well suited for Teotihuacan because major breaks in both systems (between the Late or Terminal Preclassic and the Early Classic, and between the First Intermediate Period and the Middle Horizon) do not correspond well to major changes at Teotihuacan. It is better to think of a Teotihuacan Period, from the beginning of Teotihuacan somewhere around 100 BCE to the violent destruction of the city's civic-ceremonial core, around 600 CE. To subdivide the Teotihuacan Period, I use the local relative chronology of ceramic phases. Most of these names derive from polysyllabic Náhuatl terms that English speakers must learn by rote. Numbered phases may seem more logical. However, numbered systems can become cumbersome and hard to learn when chronologies are revised and refined, especially if what was once thought to be Period III is subsequently found to be earlier than Period II. Table 1.1 shows my current chronological estimates for Teotihuacan, as well as for the Valley of Oaxaca and for Mesoamerica in general.

The absolute dates I use for Teotihuacan are estimates based on calibrated radiocarbon dates and any other relevant evidence I could find. They differ somewhat from those in earlier publications, including my own. I have taken into account the recent Bayesian statistical analysis

Table 1.1. Chronological estimates for Teotihuacan, Valley of Oaxaca, and Mesoamerica

Years	Mesoamerica General	Basin of Mexico	Valley of Oaxaca Blanton et al, 1993	Valley of Oaxaca Urcid, 2003	Southern Lowland Maya
1500	Postclassic	Late Aztec	Monte Albán V	Chila	Postclassic
1400		Late Aztec		Chila	
1300		Early Aztec	Monte Albán V	Chila	Postclassic
1200		Early Aztec	Monte Albán V		
1100				Late Liobaa	
1000		Mazapan	Monte Albán IV	Early Liobaa	Terminal Classic
900		Mazapan	Monte Albán IV	Early Liobaa	Terminal Classic
800	Late Classic	Coyotlatelco		Xoo	Late Classic
700	Late Classic	Early Epiclassic	Monte Albán III-B	Xoo	Late Classic
600		Metepec	Monte Albán III-B	Peche	
500	Early Classic	Late Xolalpan	Monte Albán III-A	Pitao	Early Classic
400	Early Classic	Early Xolalpan	Monte Albán III-A	Pitao	Early Classic
300		Late Tlamimilolpa		Tani	Protoclassic
200	Terminal Preclassic	Early Tlamimilolpa	Monte Albán II	Tani	Protoclassic
100	Terminal Preclassic	Miccaotli	Monte Albán II	Nisa	
CE		Tzacualli	Monte Albán II	Nisa	Late Preclassic
BCE		Patlachique			Late Preclassic
100	Late Preclassic	Tezoyuca	Monte Albán Late I	Pe	
200	Late Preclassic	Tezoyuca	Monte Albán Late I	Pe	
300	Late Preclassic	Cuanalan/ Cuicuilco Ticoman	Monte Albán Late I	Danibaan	
400		Cuanalan/ Cuicuilco Ticoman	Monte Albán Early I	Danibaan	Middle Preclassic
500			Monte Albán Early I		Middle Preclassic

(The center column between "Basin of Mexico" and "Valley of Oaxaca" is labeled vertically: Teotihuacan Period)

Drawn by S. Vaughn.

Table 1.2. Estimated Teotihuacan dates of ceramic phases in calendar years

Cuanalán, about 500-200 BCE
Tezoyuca, 200-100 BCE
Patlachique, 100–1 BCE
Tzacualli, 1–100 CE
Miccaotli, 100–170 CE
Early Tlamimilolpa, 170–250 CE
Late Tlamimilolpa, 250–350 CE
Early Xolalpan, 350–450 CE
Late Xolalpan, 450–550 CE
Metepec, 550–650 CE

of thirty-three calibrated radiocarbon dates from specimens in strati-graphic context from the Teopancazco compound (Beramendi-Orosco et al. 2009), the main effect of which is to suggest a somewhat earlier date for the beginning of the Tlamimilolpa phase and, implicitly, an earlier date for the preceding Miccaotli phase. Given the quantity of Miccaotli sherds collected by the Teotihuacan Mapping Project, it has always seemed unlikely that that phase lasted only a half-century, as sug-gested in some chronologies. I would assign it at least 70 years. Table 1.2 is the chronology I use in this book.

I cannot emphasize too strongly that these are only my current guesses, and are open to significant changes. For simplicity and conve-nience I present them as if they were definite, but in fact all dates much before the 1519–1521 Spanish Conquest should be understood as hav-ing at least a 50 to 100 year 95 percent "confidence interval." It would be nice if an estimate of 650 CE meant it is reasonable to give 19 to 1 odds that the true calendar date is between 600 and 700 CE, but more realistic odds are 19 to 1 that it is somewhere between 550 and 750 CE. We need to work very hard on improving chronologies. Many more Bayesian analyses of multiple calibrated radiocarbon dates from solid stratigraphic contexts should be carried out, but radiometric dating can never do more than a part of the job. It must be combined with hard work to improve ceramic sequencing for relative dating, and perhaps with other methods of absolute dating.

Some Terms Defined

A *phase* is a stretch of time identifiable by prevalence of a specific com-plex of cultural objects, especially ceramics. "Phase" emphasizes the time dimension within a culturally fairly homogeneous region. A *period* is a more inclusive interval comprising more than one phase, and often a broader region. A *tradition* is a sequence of complexes largely derived from one another without much external input. A *complex* may be characterized by one or more decorative and technological *styles*. For example, the Teotihuacan Period is the interval from the Patlachique phase through the Metepec phase, and the Xolalpan phase is an interval within this period during which ceramics of the Xolalpan complex were produced.

Some archaeologists object to using "utilitarian" to distinguish certain kinds of ceramics, because all ceramics have utility of some sort. True, but nearly all Teotihuacan ceramics can easily be fitted into one of five broad categories. One consists of vessels with little or no decoration, which, by their size, shape, and other evidence, were clearly intended primarily for use in transport, storage, and cooking. I call these "plain" or "utilitarian" wares. A second category, with different shapes, more carefully finished, and often more elaborately decorated, appear to have been intended primarily for serving food and sometimes, I suspect, for displaying the wealth of their owners. I call these "serving wares." Still other ceramics look intended primarily for use as censers in rituals. I call these "ritual wares," although many serving ware vessels may have also sometimes been used in rituals. Figurines and small ornaments are a fourth category. A fifth category consists of ceramic tools, such as the "lunates" used in shaping pots.

I avoid the term "frequency" when I refer to the quantity of something or the proportion of something relative to something else. Frequency is a good word for things that recur repeatedly, such as cycles of an oscillator (e.g., MHz), or in phrases like "We frequently eat there." But archaeologists tend to use it also to refer to a quantity or a proportion (or percent). Often it is clear from the context whether quantity or proportion is meant, but not always, and using frequency to mean either or both is an invitation to sloppy thinking.

Two False Issues

With painful regularity, media accounts of Teotihuacan blow out of proportion two oversimplified and misleading questions: "Who were the Teotihuacanos?" and "Where did they go?" Journalists seem deaf to attempts to explain the questions that interest archaeologists more, perhaps in the belief that anything more complicated will lose most of their audience. But endlessly hyping the same pseudo-problems only perpetuates an "Indiana Jones" caricature of archaeological research.

I hope I can do better at getting across what is really interesting about Teotihuacan, and why it is worthwhile for people to know about it today.

As to origins, the people who first built and occupied Teotihuacan were simply some of the people whose ancestors had already lived for millennia in Mesoamerica. As to what brought about the decline and eventual collapse of the Teotihuacan state, one school of thought, which we might call the "continuity model," holds that, although the central part of the city was burned somewhere around 550/650 CE and its population sharply declined, this disaster was mainly due to internal factors and the surviving occupants were mostly descendants of those who had lived there before. In contrast, "migrationists" believe that the city, after its destruction, was reoccupied mainly by newcomers, probably from the northwest, and many suspect that these newcomers played a large role in the collapse of the Teotihuacan state.

If further evidence supports a migration model, the question would remain, "Where did the Teotihuacanos go after invaders took over?" Some may have stayed at Teotihuacan and mingled with newcomers, while others scattered. It is really a question of survival of a "Teotihuacan" *identity*. Some elements of Teotihuacan culture survived, but many features disappeared during the 600s. With ethnically different newcomers holding positions of prestige and power, many Teotihuacan survivors would have seen advantages in adopting new practices and a new identity; while those who struggled to transmit an unchanged Teotihuacan identity to their children would have found it increasingly difficult. It would likely have become only a fading memory after a few generations (Cowgill 2013).

Better Questions

More interesting issues include explaining the rise of the city in terms of "why?" and "how?" rather than "who?". Why did the city and the state it ruled flourish so long without major interruption before the collapse? What was its sociopolitical system and in what ways did that system change over time? Why did Teotihuacan eventually collapse? What were the roles of environmental factors, internal stresses, and external threats? Other topics include religion and ideology, on both state and household levels (and how they were used for political and other purposes); the relations between "top-down" impositions and "bottom-up" efforts (those of intermediate elites as well as commoners); possible resistance to authority; craft technologies and the organization of production, distribution, and consumption; long-distance movements of objects through elite gift exchange and as commercial enterprise; Teotihuacan's foreign impacts in cultural, economic, and political terms; Teotihuacan art, iconography, and aesthetics; environmental topics, including provisioning the city with food, fuel, and other needs; the issue of "sustainability"; and the heritage of Teotihuacan for the Aztecs and for Mexico and the world today.

An Outline of Archaeological Research at Teotihuacan

Unlike ruins hidden in tropical forests, Teotihuacan is perhaps the least lost prehistoric city in the world. It is hard to overlook something the size of the Sun Pyramid. Nevertheless, less spectacular parts of the city were surprisingly neglected until recently, and as late as the 1950s, it could be argued that Teotihuacan was a sparsely occupied ceremonial center, inhabited mainly by priests and their attendants, supplied with prepared food from the kitchens of rural villagers.

The history of Teotihuacan studies begins with the Aztecs in the 1400s. For them, Teotihuacan was already a mythical place created by the gods – the place where two gods immolated themselves in sacred fire and arose as the Sun and the Moon, in the most recent of several cycles of creation. There were sizable Aztec settlements around the edges of the ancient civic-ceremonial core, predecessors of present-day municipalities in the Teotihuacan Valley, but the Aztecs seem to have reserved the core itself mainly for ceremonies (attested by a few finds of censer fragments) and a few burials. They also did some digging. Teotihuacan objects have been found in offerings in the principal temple precinct of Tenochtitlan, the Aztec capital, and some small Aztec temples there are imitations of Teotihuacan-style structures rather than in the Aztecs' own style. Most notable is a stone carving modeled after the Teotihuacan "Old God" (or Fire God), but carved in a distinctively Aztec style and with attributes of the Aztec Rain God added. The Aztecs did not fully understand Teotihuacan symbolism and reinterpreted in their own terms the objects that inspired this carving (Umberger 1987; López Luján 1989).

Cortés and other early conquerors did not mention Teotihuacan. Fray Bernardino de Sahagún, writing in the mid-1500s, recounted Aztec myths about Teotihuacan, but he does not describe the actual site. However, as early as the 1580s, a sketch of the principal Teotihuacan pyramids appears in the *Relaciones Geográficas* prepared for Philip II of Spain (Nuttall 1926). Around 1675 Carlos de Sigüenza y Góngora excavated a short tunnel atop the fore-platform of the Moon Pyramid (Schávelzon 1983). Sugiyama and Cabrera (2007) say it was left open

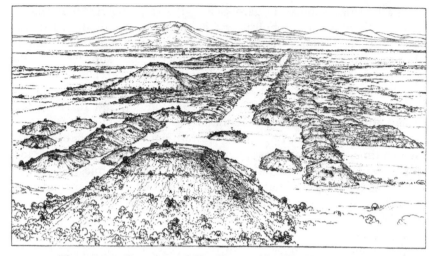

Figure 1.3. Drawing of Teotihuacan by W. H. Holmes, ca. 1895.
Compare with Figure 1.1.
After Schávelzon (1981).

for several centuries, then refilled, probably in 1924, when consolidation
work was undertaken by a Mexican project. There is no solid information about materials recovered. In the nineteenth century, various travel-
ers mentioned the ruins. Ramón Almaraz mapped the main pyramids
in 1864 and made a small excavation (Millon 1973: xi; Almaraz 1865).
The French explorer Désiré Charnay (1887) reported sketchily on his
diggings near the Avenue of the Dead. In the 1800s, José María Velasco,
W. H. Holmes (Figure 1.3), and others made very useful drawings,
paintings, and photos that show the city before excavations had taken
place. Antonio García Cubas discovered Teotihuacan murals in the residential compound called Teopancazco (tract 1:S2E2 of the Teotihuacan
Mapping Project).

Leopoldo Batres (1906) excavated at the "Temple of Agriculture"
on the northern Avenue of the Dead, uncovering now lost murals. He
removed much of the outer layer of the Sun Pyramid, creating a spurious
fifth level (earlier photos and drawings show that this stepped pyramid
originally had only four bodies). He reconstructed the fore-platform[2]
attached to its front about seven degrees off its true orientation. He published little information about his finds. However, to be fair to him, the
quality of his work was comparable to much other archaeology of the
time, and even later.

The German scholar Eduard Seler (1915) pioneered the detailed study of Teotihuacan symbolism and iconography, although he believed that little time separated Teotihuacan from the Aztecs (a reasonable assumption, given the state of archaeological knowledge at the time), and this led him to interpret Teotihuacan materials in the light of ethnohistoric data on the Aztecs more freely than seems warranted today. Manuel Gamio (García Chávez 1995) and Alfred Tozzer (1921) excavated at the important Teotihuacan Period regional center of Azcapotzalco (Figure 1.4/8),[3] in the western part of the Basin of Mexico. By that time, Teotihuacan was attributed to a pre-Aztec "Toltec" period, but Tozzer failed to distinguish Teotihuacan Period ceramics chronologically from the later Coyotlatelco style ceramics that he also encountered, and he did not recognize that Teotihuacan was not only pre-Aztec, but pre-Toltec as well.

A new era in Teotihuacan studies began with the work of Manuel Gamio, Ignacio Marquina, and others between 1917 and 1922 (Gamio 1979[1922]). Involving extensive excavations, ethnography, ethnohistory, and environmental studies, it was multidisciplinary and ahead of its time. They excavated in the Ciudadela, where they uncovered the extraordinary stone sculptures on the front façade of the Feathered Serpent Pyramid (also known as the Temple of Quetzalcóatl, or FSP, Figure 1.5). They drove a tunnel into the Sun Pyramid, running from its east side to the center, at the level where its second body begins. Pedro Dozal (1925) found sacrificed individuals in pits at each corner of the FSP. In 1931–32 George Vaillant dug in the triadic group called Five-Prime, about a hundred meters west of the Moon Pyramid, where ceramics in the earliest layers were like those in the interior of the Sun Pyramid. Vaillant and others considered them transitional between the ceramics of what was then called the Upper Archaic (now Late Preclassic) of Ticomán (Figure 1.4/7) and those of Teotihuacan itself. Vaillant also found, in a plot called Las Palmas, in the village of San Francisco Mazapan, east of the Sun Pyramid, a post-Teotihuacan style of ceramics called Mazapan. Much of Vaillant's work remains unpublished (Elson and Mowbray 2005 is a recent exception). In 1933 José Pérez, under the direction of Eduardo Noguera, dug a second tunnel into the Sun Pyramid, from west to east at ground level, in the center joining the earlier tunnel by a stairway.

Reports of the tunnel excavations and their finds, by Marquina (in Gamio 1979[1922]), Kroeber (1925), Noguera (1935), and Vaillant (1935a, 1938), indicated that there were no major earlier structures in the interior of the Sun Pyramid (recent work has found a walled enclosure preceding the pyramid [N. Sugiyama et al. 2013]) and that

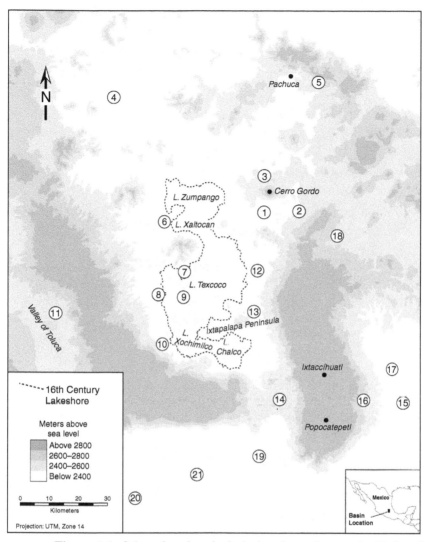

Figure 1.4. Selected archaeological sites in and near the Basin of Mexico.

1: Teotihuacan, 2: obsidian source east of Otumba, 3: Maquixco Alto (TC46), 4: Tula, 5: Sierra de las Navajas obsidian source, 6: Cuauhtitlán, 7: Ticomán, 8: Azcapotzalco, 9: Tenochtitlan, 10: Cuicuilco, 11: Calixtlahuaca, 12: Texcoco, 13: Cerro Portezuelo, 14: Amecameca, 15: Cholula, 16: Tetimpa, 17: Cacaxtla/Xochitécatl, 18: Calpulalpan/Las Colinas, 19: Chalcatzingo, 20: Xochicalco, 21: Yautepec.

By S. Vaughn, base map courtesy of Larry Gorenflo.

Figure 1.5. Façade of the Feathered Serpent Pyramid (Temple of Quetzalcoatl).

Photo by author.

the ceramics in the pyramid fill pertained to an "Archaic" stage (now called Tzacualli) known elsewhere in the Basin of Mexico but not previously recognized at Teotihuacan. It was generally believed, however, that the Sun Pyramid itself was built somewhat later, by people who incorporated debris from an earlier settlement into the fill of the pyramid (Millon 1960).

In the 1930s, the Swedish archaeologist Sigvald Linné (2003a[1934], 2003b[1942]) studied sites in the states of Puebla and Tlaxcala and excavated at two apartment compounds within Teotihuacan, called Xolalpan and Tlamimilolpa. His reports are sketchy about stratigraphy and ordinary potsherds, but they include important architectural data and illustrations and descriptions of grave lots and other special finds that have rarely been surpassed in Teotihuacan research. Linné's are the first major publications on Teotihuacan multi-apartment compounds. In 1939, Pérez dug a pit in front of the stairway of the FSP and another under the stairway of its fore-platform, about which he wrote a brief unpublished report. The only publication of the finds, by Daniel F. Rubín de la Borbolla (1947) fails to distinguish the contents of the two pits.

Pedro Armillas, a Spanish expatriate who had fought against the fascists during the 1936–39 civil war, excavated in several Teotihuacan apartment compounds in the 1940s, including the "Viking" group (so named because work was supported by the Viking Fund, predecessor of the Wenner-Gren Foundation), Tetitla, Tepantitla, Zacuala, and Atetelco, partly in collaboration with Pérez, Rafael Orellana, Carlos Margáin, and others, including artist Agustín Villagra, who skillfully restored fragmentary murals. At Atetelco, they found two meters of debris with post-Teotihuacan Coyotlatelco-style ceramics above the floors. Armillas published on the deities of Teotihuacan, made major contributions to the ceramic chronology, and emphasized the distinction between Teotihuacan and "Toltec" cultures (Armillas 1944, 1945, 1947, 1950). This distinction was confirmed in excavations by Jorge Acosta (1940, 1964a) at the site of Tula (Figure 1.4/4) in the 1940s and later, which showed that the ceramics there were post-Teotihuacan, and by the ethnohistorical work of Wigberto Jiménez Moreno (1941), which indicated that many sixteenth century references to "Tollan" applied to Tula rather than to Teotihuacan.

Most Teotihuacan research before the 1950s was in a descriptive vein, although Vaillant (1935a: 304) expressed discontent with this neglect of explicit theory and urged a closer collaboration between archaeology and sociology. Armillas (1948, 1951) introduced a somewhat Marxist cultural-ecological outlook in Mesoamerican studies. A review by Armillas (1950) is a landmark in Teotihuacan studies. Among other things, he used names rather than numbers for phases: Tzacualli, Miccaotli, Xolalpan, and Tlamimilolpa. He stated firmly that the city covered at least 750 ha. By 1963, Millon's careful survey of the perimeter showed the actual area to be about 2000 ha, a fact to be pondered for sites whose limits have never been carefully studied.

In the 1950s and 1960s, the French scholar Laurette Séjourné (1959, 1966a, 1966b, 1966c) dug further at several Teotihuacan apartment compounds, including Zacuala, Tetitla, and Yayahuala, concentrating on art and religion. Her publications are weak on stratigraphy and context, but important for somewhat inaccurate plans of buildings and abundant illustrations of murals, ceramics, figurines, and lithic artifacts. Frank Moore (1966) excavated further at Tetitla. In the 1950s Paul Tolstoy (1958) made surface collections at a number of sites in the Teotihuacan Valley and elsewhere in the Basin of Mexico and applied seriation methods developed by James Ford, in another step toward an adequate ceramic chronology. William Mayer-Oakes (1959) made a test pit at El Risco, near Mexico City. These projects still left many aspects of the chronology unclear. René Millon, with James Bennyhoff and others,

studied early stages of Teotihuacan's development in stratigraphic excavations at Plaza One, a triadic group nearly a kilometer west-northwest
of the Moon Pyramid (Millon 1960; Millon and Bennyhoff 1961),
where Carmen Cook de Leonard (1957) also excavated. With Bennyhoff
and Bruce Drewitt, Millon closely reexamined the previously made tunnels in the Sun Pyramid (Millon, Drewitt, and Bennyhoff 1965). As a
result of their work, it became clear that ceramics as early as those in
the pyramid could be found in quantity over a large area in the northwestern part of Teotihuacan, and this, plus the absence of later ceramics
in all but the uppermost and outermost additions to the Sun Pyramid,
indicated that the pyramid had been constructed during this early phase
(Tzacualli), rather than later, as earlier investigators had thought.

Between 1960 and 1964, extensive clearing and restoration work
along the Avenue of the Dead was carried out by the Instituto Nacional
de Antropología e Historia (INAH), under the direction of Ignacio
Bernal. Bernal (1963) summarized this work, Jorge Acosta (1964b)
reported on the Quetzalpapalotl Palace, and Eduardo Matos (1980)
described work on a platform within the Avenue of the Dead complex.
Florencia Müller's (1978) ceramics volume is based largely on finds by
this project. Other reports from this project exist as manuscripts. Except
for whole vessels, most ceramics from this project have been discarded
for lack of adequate storage space, with little or no analysis.

By the early 1950s, the broad outline of a ceramic sequence for
Teotihuacan had taken shape, although estimates of absolute dates
still depended heavily on ceramic crossties with the Maya area. It was
still believed that Teotihuacan covered only a few square kilometers,
and little was known of the archaeology of the Teotihuacan Valley outside the city itself. The true extent and nature of the city first became
clear from the detailed mapping and intensive surface collecting of the
Teotihuacan Mapping Project (TMP), which began in 1962, directed
by Millon (Millon 1973; Millon et al. 1973; Cowgill, Robertson, and
Sload, in preparation; Millon and Altschul, in preparation). The combination of scale and intensity of this survey is probably without precedent in archaeology. Among other things, it revealed that Teotihuacan
had covered about twenty square kilometers. The TMP also carried out
28 stratigraphic excavations intended to solve a number of problems,
including the need for data that could further improve the ceramic chronology. Most remain unpublished, although a report on Excavation 28
in the ancient tunnel underneath the Sun Pyramid is in preparation
by Rebecca Sload. Some profiles appear in Millon (1992) and Rattray
(2001); the latter also tabulates counts of ceramic categories. Except
for one brief article (Bennyhoff 1967), the extensive work on ceramic

chronology by James Bennyhoff, as part of the TMP, remains unpublished. However, building on Bennyhoff's accomplishments, Evelyn Rattray (2001) published what is, to date, the best available study of Teotihuacan ceramic chronology, in spite of some ambiguities and inconsistencies. Other major recent publications on Teotihuacan ceramics include Smith (1987) and Sanders (1986, 1995).

At the time that Millon was conducting the survey and mapping of the city itself, William T. Sanders complemented this with a regional settlement pattern survey of the rest of the Teotihuacan Valley. This became the first stage of a massive series of settlement surveys of most of the Basin of Mexico (Sanders et al. 1979; Sanders 1981; Parsons 1971, 2008; Parsons et al. 1982; Parsons et al. 1983; Blanton 1972). This great undertaking remains critical for providing a regional context for Teotihuacan and for knowledge of the overall history of the Basin from the earliest pottery-using societies until the 1970s. For many sites in the Basin, these surveys tell us all we will ever know, since many sites have since been destroyed by modern developments, and others very badly damaged.

Between 1980 and 1982, the INAH Proyecto Arqueológico Teotihuacán, directed by Rubén Cabrera Castro, dug extensively in the Ciudadela and along the Avenue of the Dead, especially in and near the Avenue of the Dead Complex (Cabrera, Rodríguez, and Morelos 1982a, 1982b, 1991). Other notable field projects at Teotihuacan since 1980 include excavations by Rebecca Storey and Randolph Widmer at Tlajinga 33, an apartment compound of potters in the southern part of the city (Sheehy 1992, 1998; Storey 1991, 1992; Widmer 1987, 1991; Widmer and Storey 1993) (Figure 1.6/7); several projects in an enclave with strong Oaxacan ties (Palomares 2006, 2013); by Sergio Gómez in a compound just east of the Oaxaca Enclave with strong ties to sites in the west Mexican state of Michoacán (Gómez Chávez 2002; Gómez Chávez and Gazzola 2007); by Linda Manzanilla (1993) in a residential complex in the far northwestern part of the city (Oztoyahualco 15B) (Figure 1.6/8); by Manzanilla and others in caves east of the Sun Pyramid (Manzanilla et al. 1996); by Manzanilla at Teopancazco (Manzanilla 2009, 2012); by Manzanilla and Leonardo López Luján (López Luján et al. 2006) in the Xalla complex; by Rattray at the Hacienda Metepec in the far eastern outskirts of the city (Rattray 1983); by Rattray in an enclave with Gulf Lowlands and Maya ties (the Merchants' Enclave) (Rattray 1989, 1990a); by Millon in Techinantitla, a very large compound noted for its murals, located about 500 m east of the Moon Pyramid (Berrin 1988; Millon 1991); by Cabrera, Sugiyama, and Cowgill at the FSP, where mass human sacrifices were found

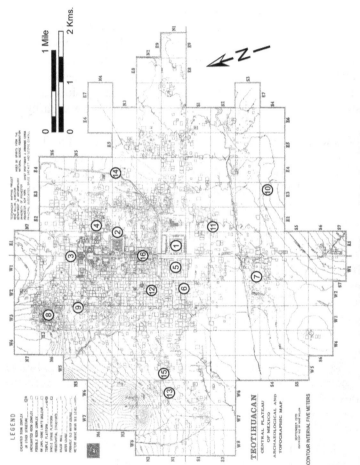

Figure 1.6. A reduced version of the Teotihuacan Mapping Project map.

1: the Ciudadela, 2: the Sun Pyramid, 3: the Moon Pyramid, 4: Xalla, 5: the Great Compound, 6: the La Ventilla district, 7: Tlajinga 33, 8: Oztoyahualco 15B, 9: Cosotlán 23, 10: San José 520, 11: Teopancaxco, 12: Tetitla, 13: the Oaxaca enclave, 14: the Merchants' enclave, 15: a compound of West Mexicans (19:N1W5), 16: the Avenue of the Dead complex.

By S. Vaughn, base map courtesy of R. Millon (1973).

(Cabrera, Sugiyama, and Cowgill 1991; Sugiyama 2005); by Cabrera and others in several residential and civic-ceremonial compounds in the La Ventilla district (Gómez 2000; Cabrera and Gómez 2008); by Eduardo Matos at and near the Sun Pyramid and in Group Five-Prime; and a series of tunnels that found further sacrificial burials in the Moon Pyramid by Sugiyama and Cabrera (2007). Fieldwork at Teotihuacan continues very actively. An incomplete list includes unpublished work by Rodolfo Cid in a small temple complex on the western outskirts (1:N3W6), and elsewhere (Torres Sanders 1995), Oralia Cabrera (2006, 2011) in a pottery-making workshop on the southeastern periphery (Figure 1.6/10), Ian Robertson at 15:N1E6, an insubstantial structure (Robertson 2008), intensive surface collection by Kristin Sullivan at 23:N5W3 (a figurine workshop, Figure 1.6/9) (Sullivan 2005, 2007) and excavations at the Sun Pyramid (N. Sugiyama et al. 2013; Sarabia 2013). Even today, however, less than 5 percent of the city has been excavated by archaeologists. Unfortunately, much of Teotihuacan lies outside the protected archaeological zone, and is being rapidly lost to urban growth and looters.

Besides these field projects, there have been many studies of Teotihuacan art, iconography, and symbolism, and of various classes of Teotihuacan artifacts. Recent edited volumes include McClung de Tapia and Rattray (1987), Berlo (1992a), Berrin and Pasztory (1993), Brambila and Cabrera (1998), Manzanilla and Serrano (1999), Ruiz Gallut (2002), Ruiz Gallut and Soto (2004), and Ruiz Gallut and Torres (2005). Among innumerable other publications, especially outstanding are long articles by Millon (1974, 1976b, 1981, 1988a, 1992, 1993) and books by James Langley (1986), Hasso von Winning (1987), and Annabeth Headrick (2007). Publications by myself not otherwise cited herein include (Cowgill 1974, 1977, 1979, 1987, 1992a, 1992b, 1993b, 2000a, 2000b, 2002, 2003a, 2003b, 2005, 2008).

The Teotihuacan Mapping Project

During the 1960s, the TMP, directed by Millon (Millon 1973; Millon et al. 1973), intensively surveyed about thirty square kilometers, somewhat more than the maximum extent of the ancient city. Besides mapping ruins, about 634,000 rim and feature sherds of the Teotihuacan Period were collected, as well as about 3,000 sherds from pre-Teotihuacan periods and 196,000 from post-Teotihuacan periods, nearly 61,000 other ceramic objects (mostly fragments of figurines and *candeleros*), 230,000 fragments of obsidian (volcanic glass), and about 25,000 fragments of other worked stone objects. These came from the surfaces of over 5,000 spatial units, which I call collection tracts. I and others have often referred to these collection tracts as "sites," but, to reduce confusion, I reserve "site" to refer only to the entire city or to settlements outside the TMP survey area. Tracts refer to the actual spatial units covered by the survey. Since the survey was "full coverage" except in cases where modern construction made this impossible and in a very few cases where permission to survey was denied, survey tracts usually are contiguous, without separating gaps. This means that areas of tracts are generally somewhat larger than the structures or other features within them. Structures are fairly well separated in many parts of the city, and even in the most densely occupied parts they are usually separated by streets three or more meters wide. The tracts vary in size and shape and correspond insofar as could be determined to distinct Teotihuacan structures or meaningful spaces between structures, such as plazas. The mean size of collection tracts is about 0.36 ha (about 60×60 m), although some were considerably smaller and a few were much larger. The size of residential compounds is quite variable and the average is smaller than 60×60 m, as I will explain in Chapter 7. Within each tract, team members usually walked about two meters apart, collecting all visible feature sherds and ancient objects of other materials.

Figure 1.6 is a version of the TMP map, at a reduced scale. Numbers highlight some notable places. I refer to it often in discussing neighborhoods and specific structures at Teotihuacan, so it is worth spending some time learning how to use it. Most of the tiny rectangles represent the approximate outer limits of multi-apartment residential compounds, limits mostly estimated by surface survey of low mounds and visible traces of walls, rather than by excavation. Fortunately, clear traces of plastered outer walls, barely poking above the ground, were often visible even without excavation. Other features represented include pyramids, platforms, free-standing walls, major and minor thoroughfares, and watercourses. The full map (Millon et al. 1973) consists of 147 bound sheets, at a scale of 1:2000, showing topography and cultural and natural features as they existed in 1962, with transparent plastic overlays showing archaeological interpretations. Larger unbound sheets show parts of the city at scales of 1:2000 or 1:10,000. Millon (1973), and Millon and Altschul (in preparation) provide fuller accounts of how the map was created.

Millon subdivided the mapped area into arbitrary 500 by 500 meter squares. Following R. Cabrera (1982), I refer to these arbitrary squares as "sectors." Since one hectare is a square 100 by 100 m, each sector covers 25 ha, or one fourth of a square kilometer. Starting from a base point slightly southwest of the southwestern corner of the Ciudadela complex, each sector is labeled by a number and the designation W for west or E for east. Similarly, north and south designations are labeled N or S. Thus, the sector that is the third one north and the fifth one west of the starting point is labeled N3W5. The north-south designation always comes first and is followed by that for east-west. Within each sector, collection tracts were numbered in approximately the order in which they were surveyed. Some tracts were subdivided, as indicated by a letter or letters following the numerical designation. In a few cases, tracts not considered to have been occupied during the Teotihuacan Period were labeled by a number preceded by the capital letter L. The full label of a collection tract precedes the sector label and is separated from it by a colon. Thus, 15B:N6W3 is part B of the 15th tract surveyed in sector N6W3, while 33:S3W1 is the 33rd tract in sector S3W1. A few collection tracts overlap two or more sectors. These are labeled as pertaining to a single sector, usually the sector within which most of the tract lies.

Figure 1.6, rather than being oriented to true (astronomic) north, the direction toward the north pole, is oriented about 15.5 degrees east of true north, because that is the orientation of the Avenue of the Dead, as well as most other north-south features at Teotihuacan. This is significantly different from magnetic north, the direction in which a compass points. Today, that difference at Teotihuacan is about 6 degrees. It was different at different times in the past because (unlike true north) magnetic north changes over the centuries.

Organization and Scope of the Book

In describing many aspects of a society that changed markedly over time, one faces the dilemma of whether to organize the book in terms of topics, tracing each topic over time, or in terms of time chunks, discussing each topic for each period. Neither way is entirely satisfactory. For better or worse, I organize my story primarily by periods, usually of about two centuries, which is about the finest time-resolution currently possible (Chapter 8, dealing with imagery, is an exception). This means that to trace any one topic through time, the reader must skip from one chapter to another. But I don't recommend that, for no single topic can be understood if it is extracted from its wider context. The Teotihuacanos, whatever their memory of the past or anticipation of the future, necessarily lived in what was for them the present, and experienced all topics at once. By organizing my book by periods, I can present a story closer to their lived experiences. For readers who want to pursue a specific topic through time, I have made their job easier by providing subheadings.

We cannot begin to understand Teotihuacan's rise without a sketch of what is known of the few centuries prior to its beginning, especially developments at the site of Cuicuilco, about 50 km to the south (Figure 1.4/10). However, to keep this book within bounds, I have focused on the city in the centuries during which it flourished, from about 150/100 BCE to 550/650 CE. Teotihuacan's external political, economic, and cultural relations are intensely interesting, but too little is known of them to make a well-rounded picture possible, so my coverage of that topic is selective and incomplete. It would take another book as long as this one to do justice to Teotihuacan's distant presences. Similarly, the very complex period following the collapse of the Teotihuacan state is extremely interesting and controversial, but most of that has to be left for other occasions.

Even so, my story bristles with ambiguities and unanswered questions – I offer few neatly packaged answers. This may create the impression that after more than a century of archaeological research we have made little progress. In fact, a tremendous amount has been learned, and the past century has seen vast improvements in archaeological techniques and some improvements in archaeological theory. But if I were to say we have many tidy answers it would give a highly unrealistic picture of the way archaeological knowledge advances. It would also make for a less interesting book. The story I tell abounds with challenges and opportunities for the next generation of researchers. Many of the questions I leave open are answerable – it just takes imagination, adequate techniques, respect for data, and the financial resources to carry out the needed work before too much of the rapidly disappearing archaeological record is lost forever.

Mesoamerica

The region of ancient complex civilizations in Mexico and Central America does not correspond neatly to modern political boundaries, so it is useful to label it by a special term. "Mesoamerica" is the word introduced by ethnohistorian Paul Kirchhoff (1943). Although its boundaries shifted somewhat over time, Mesoamerica includes all but far northern Mexico, and the northern parts of Central America covered by the countries of Guatemala, Belize, El Salvador, western Honduras and Nicaragua, and the northwestern tip of Costa Rica (Figure 1.2). North of Mesoamerica there were farming towns and villages whose cultures were generally related to those of the southwestern United States, and, in the more arid areas, bands of mobile hunter-gatherers. South of Mesoamerica, in southern Central America and northern South America, politically somewhat less complex societies occupied a large region that stretched southward to the states and empires of the central Andes – the Inkas and their numerous predecessors.

Societies within Mesoamerica tended to share a number of cultural features, perhaps most notably an intricate system of intermeshing sacred calendars. However, it is not useful to try to list a set of defining features that every society must have in order to be deemed truly "Mesoamerican." It is better to say that while not all societies shared all the features, enough were shared to give Mesoamerican societies a recognizable "family resemblance." In spite of these broad similarities, Mesoamerican societies were diverse in many ways. For example, there were hundreds of distinct languages, belonging to several families that are only remotely (if at all) related to one another. Within individual families, the diversity is comparable to that within the Indo-European family, which includes languages as different as English, Spanish, Russian, and Hindi. Regional styles of art and architecture were also markedly different. Mesoamerica was never politically unified before the Spanish Conquest, and it is not clear that the pre-Conquest inhabitants ever had any concept of a shared "Mesoamerican" identity overarching more local identities. This diversity about specifics within a broad general unity means that it is difficult to fill in gaps in our knowledge of one cultural tradition, such as that of Teotihuacan, with data on some other Mesoamerican society. Nevertheless, modern scholars have found Mesoamerica a very useful concept.

Because the general trend of the land linking North and South America is southerly, it is easy to think of Mesoamerica as running more north-south than east-west. Actually the trend is northwest-southeast (northern Yucatán is a bit north of the Basin of Mexico). The Isthmus of Tehuántepec marks a broad division between "Eastern" and the rest of Mesoamerica. Eastern Mesoamerica is predominantly Maya country, although it includes a number of other indigenous groups. West of Tehuántepec, major regions include the uplands and Pacific lowlands of the state of Oaxaca (primarily occupied by speakers of Zapotecan and Mixtecan languages), the lowlands along the Gulf of Mexico in the state of Veracruz, and the highlands of Central Mexico, centered on the Basin of Mexico (which includes Mexico City and Teotihuacan). Farther west is a large area of mountains and valleys reaching to the Pacific coast, an area sometimes dismissed as peripheral to Mesoamerica, but that in fact contained many complex and vigorous polities.

Throughout Mesoamerica, the lowlands are generally humid and hot, although some parts of the lowlands are rather arid. Highlands tend to be arid or semi-arid and mostly mountainous, but there are some plateaus and broad valleys, generally in the range of 1,200 to 2,500 m above sea level. A few snow-covered volcanic peaks rise above 5,000 m. Few agricultural settlements are higher than about 2,800 m.

Irrigation is useful or indispensable for agriculture in the highlands. There were many small or medium-sized water management systems, but no great rivers such as the Nile, Tigris, Euphrates, Indus, Ganges, Yellow River, and Yangtze of the Old World. Rainfall in the highlands is generally sharply seasonal, with a summer rainy season and a winter dry season. Highland temperatures can be hot in the summer (especially before the onset of the rains) but are cool or even cold in the winter. Snow is rare except at very high altitudes, but winter frosts are a serious threat above about 2,000 m.

The Central Highlands and the Basin of Mexico

The Basin of Mexico, in the Central Mexican highlands, is a broad plain that slopes gently upward from a floor about 2,240 m (7,350 feet) above sea level (Figure 1.4). It is limited on the west, south, and

Figure 2.1. Popocatépetl (right) and Ixtaccíhuatl (center) volcanoes seen from near Xaltocan, northwest of Teotihuacan.
Courtesy of Christopher Morehart.

east by mountains that rise above 3,000 m, including, in the southeast, the volcanoes Ixtaccíhuatl and Popocatépetl (5,452 m above sea level, Figures 1.4 and 2.1). The northwestern margin of the Basin is not well marked, and a low divide leads to the drainage of the Tula region (Figures 1.2/2 and 1.4/4), whose streams flow into the Gulf of Mexico. In the northeastern part of the Basin, the Teotihuacan Valley runs by a gentle gradient into the plains of Tlaxcala and central Puebla. These plains stretch east and northeastward and then drop precipitously toward the Gulf lowlands. Southeastward they slope gradually to southern Puebla and Oaxaca. Defined by watersheds, the Basin of Mexico extends into Tlaxcala-Puebla and covers about 12,000 square km, but from a cultural point of view, it is better to define the Basin as a more compact area ringed by the mountains, running about 110 km north-south by 80 km east-west, covering about 8,000 square km (about 3,000 square miles) (J. Parsons 2008: 9). This more compact area is often called the Valley of Mexico, but I use "Basin" here to avoid confusion with other spatial units called valleys.

Interconnected shallow lakes occupied the central part of the Basin; Xaltocan and Zumpango to the north and Xochimilco and Chalco to the south, with the somewhat lower Lake Texcoco in the middle. Lake

Texcoco was moderately salty because of its lack of exterior drainage. The principal Aztec cities, Tenochtitlan and Tlatelolco, were built on low islands in Lake Texcoco (Figure 1.4/9). For the Aztecs the lakes were sources of fish, waterfowl, and edible insects, and a major means of transport by raft and canoe. Especially in the southern lakes, the Aztecs practiced wetland "chinampa" agriculture[1] on plots artificially raised above the water level, using techniques that were labor intensive but highly productive per unit area. These are the inaccurately labeled "floating" gardens. Remnants still exist in the southern suburb called Xochimilco. In Teotihuacan times, much of the Basin's population was concentrated in the Teotihuacan Valley, where only about 100 ha are suitable for wetland agriculture, and chinampa methods were perhaps little used by Teotihuacanos.

In the centuries after the Spanish Conquest in 1521, the lakes were mostly drained. The Mexico City metropolitan area, much of it sprawled over the former lake beds, now houses more than 21 million people. It is the world's fifth-largest city.

West of the Basin of Mexico lies the Valley of Toluca (Figure 1.4), whose floor is also relatively flat, at around 2,600 to 2,700 m (Sugiura 1990: 192). East of the Basin, the plains of Tlaxcala and central Puebla are slightly lower except near La Malinche, whose peak rises to 4,461 m. South of the Basin, in the state of Morelos, the land is significantly lower, ranging between 1,000 and 1,500 m (Grove 1987a: 6). At these lower altitudes, frost is not a hazard, rainfall is somewhat higher, and crops that could not be grown in the Basin, such as cotton, were important.

Rainfall is seasonal in the Central Highlands, mostly from June to October (Sanders et al. 1979: 82). Precipitation tends to be higher in the south and lower in the north. It averages more than 1,000 mm per year in parts of Morelos and the southern Basin of Mexico, around 600 mm in the Teotihuacan Valley (Sanders et al. 1979: 83), and only 400 to 600 mm in the region around Tula (Diehl 1989a: 8). However, these are only averages. Actual precipitation varies greatly from year to year and over short distances. Much of it occurs in the form of localized storms that can be violent, with lightning and sometimes strong winds that drop heavy rain along a narrow path and leave lands to either side untouched. Agriculture would not be possible without these rains, but sometimes the storms bring hail and leave devastated crops in their wake. With precipitation both indispensable and unpredictably destructive, it is no surprise that the Storm God was one of Teotihuacan's principal deities.

In many parts of the Central Highlands, including the Basin of Mexico, rainfall alone can yield a fair harvest of maize in some years. Everywhere, however, irrigation makes harvests larger and more secure. No large streams are available in the Central Highlands, and floodwater irrigation from rainfall is feasible only in limited areas. Irrigation from permanent year-round springs is better because it is affected much less by annual fluctuations in rainfall and because it permits earlier planting, before the rains begin, which improves chances that crops will mature before the autumn frosts. However, outside the Teotihuacan Valley, perennial springs are few and scattered, and they do not provide enough water to irrigate very large areas (Sanders et al. 1979: 270).

There is evidence in the Basin of Mexico and other parts of the Central Highlands for all these types of water management – wetland farming, floodwater irrigation, and spring-fed canals – at least as early as Teotihuacan times. It is virtually certain that all were well developed several centuries before the beginning of the city (Nichols 1982).

The Teotihuacan Valley

The Teotihuacan Valley is the broad and gently sloping northeastern part of the Basin of Mexico, framed on the north by hills and an extinct volcano (Cerro Gordo), the Patlachique range on the south, and more distant mountains on the east (Figures 2.2 and 2.3). To the southwest, the Teotihuacan Valley widens and opens onto the former bed of Lake Texcoco. To the northeast, it is separated by an almost imperceptible divide forming an easy route into Tlaxcala and central Puebla. A series of Teotihuacan sites, notably Maquixco Alto (TC-46) (Figures 1.4/3 and 2.3/9), run along the north slope of Cerro Gordo, in the next valley to the north, confusingly termed part of the Teotihuacan Valley by Sanders et al. (1979) because it was part of their Teotihuacan Valley survey area. Maquixco Bajo is a modern town just west of San Juan Teotihuacán. TC-8 is a small site just north of this town (Figure 2.3/1).

The ruins of Teotihuacan lie in the middle section of the valley, at altitudes ranging from 2,265 m near the springs to 2,350 m in its most uphill parts, a vertical span of about 85 m over a horizontal distance of several kilometers. Most of the city is on nearly flat land; none of it is really steep. In this respect, it contrasts markedly with many other large settlements of its time in Western Mesoamerica, such as Monte Albán in the Valley of Oaxaca, which were placed on hilltops. Whatever the reasons to settle on flat land, the choice facilitated the extraordinarily regular layout of the city. In the Colonial era, most of the ruins were

Figure 2.2. A panorama of the Teotihuacan Valley, looking north from the Patlachique range. Cerro Gordo is in the background. Major pyramids are in the middle distance.

Photo by author.

used for rainfall agriculture until the land was taken for archaeology early in the 1900s. Much of the northwestern part (the "Oztoyahualco" district) lies over old lava flows. These flows extend under and somewhat east of the Sun Pyramid. Today, much of this region has quite broken terrain – probably the result of Teotihuacano mining for building materials.

The Teotihuacan Valley is about 35 km long – an area of about 500 square km (Sanders 1965: 22). In the lower valley, up to about 2,265 m, approximately 3,650 ha (36.5 square km) were irrigated in 1954 from year-round springs, mostly located near the present parish church of San Juan Teotihuacán, with an average flow of about 590 liters (156 gallons) per second (Sanders et al. 1979: 258), using a technically simple system of small canals. As recently as 1922, the flow seems to have been nearly twice as much (Sanders et al. 1979: 256), but this may not mean that twice the area was ever irrigated, since a limit is set by the land area

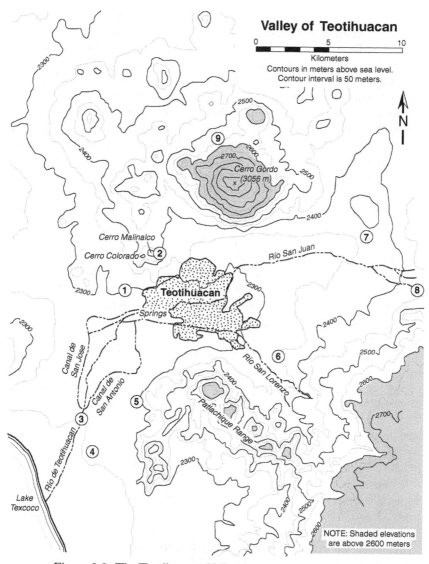

Figure 2.3. The Teotihuacan Valley.

1: TC-8 (Maquixco Bajo), 2: Tlachinolpan, 3: Cuanalán, 4: Cerro Tezoyuca, 5: TT-21 (Xometla), 6: TT-82 (Oxtoticpac), 7: TC-83 (San Bartolomé el Alto), 8: Obsidian source east of Otumba (approximate), 9: TC-46 (Maquixco Alto).

By S. Vaughn, after Sanders et al. (1979).

reachable by gravity flow from the springs. The water in these springs derives ultimately from rainfall that soaks into the earth, which absorbs it like a sponge and then releases it gradually, so that the flow varies little from season to season. Subsoil in most of the Teotihuacan Valley consists of agriculturally sterile compacted volcanic ash, mostly air-deposited, called *tepetate*. Its hard, almost rocky texture and yellowish-brown color distinguish it sharply from the dark fertile soil above it. In Teotihuacan times, the water table in much of the city was not far below the ground surface, as demonstrated by finds of Teotihuacan Period wells that are only a few meters deep. The springs occur where the water table reaches the level of the ground surface. In recent decades, the water table has dropped considerably, probably as a result of increasing use of deep-drilled wells, and the flow of water from the springs has decreased dramatically.

Surface streams in the Teotihuacan Valley – the Río San Juan, the Río San Lorenzo, and their tributaries – are short and have small and seasonally highly variable flows from rainwater runoff. Flash floods can occur, but most of the year they carry almost no water. Today, they are mostly in deep ravines and are far less important than the springs as a source of irrigation water. It is unlikely that they were ever of any value for transportation.

At least until recently, wetland agriculture was practiced in a naturally swampy district of about 100 hectares in the *barrio* of Puxtla, one of the modern *barrios* in the municipality of San Juan Teotihuacán, just down-valley from the major springs in sectors S1W4 and S1W5 of the TMP map (Figures 1.6 and 2.4) (Sanders et al. 1979: 273–281). It may have originally been reedy, and it is possible that Teotihuacan was named "place of reeds" – Tollan in Náhuatl. This small patch of highly productive land may have helped give Teotihuacan an early edge over other settlements in the northern Basin of Mexico, although it does not explain the subsequent immense expansion of the city. Produce from these drained fields could not have fed more than a small fraction of Teotihuacan's population.

Much of the middle stretch of the Teotihuacan Valley is covered by ruins of the ancient city. Fields in this and the upper Valley depend mainly on rainfall and floodwater irrigation. Today much of the agricultural land consists of orchards of *nopales* (prickly pears), valued for their tasty fruit (Figure 2.5), and fields of *magueys* (century plants), whose sap is fermented to make a mildly alcoholic beverage called *pulque* (Figure 2.6). North of the city, the valley floor slopes up through a piedmont zone to Cerro Gordo, presently largely covered by forest, and to lower hills northwest of the city, Cerro Malinalco and Cerro Colorado.

Figure 2.4. Recent wetland agriculture in the Teotihuacan Valley, just downstream from the perennial springs southwest of ancient Teotihuacan.

Photo by author.

South of the city, piedmont leads to the Patlachique range. Today, especially in piedmont zones, there are many areas where erosion has exposed sterile *tepetate*. It is hard to say if climatic change and human environmental impacts had any role in the collapse of the Teotihuacan state, discussed in Chapter 9.

A deposit of gray obsidian (with occasional red streaks), about 18 km east of Teotihuacan and a few kilometers east of the town of Otumba, was a major source for the Teotihuacan obsidian industry, especially for making bifacial points and knives (Figures 1.4/2 and 2.3/8). About 55 km to the north, outside the Basin of Mexico and near Pachuca, the Sierra de las Navajas (Figures 1.2/3 and 1.4/5) is a source of distinctive high-quality greenish obsidian that was favored for prismatic blades (long thin blades with extremely sharp edges, removed from prepared cores by pressure flaking). Obsidian from more distant sources was also used to some extent, especially that from Ucareo (Figure 1.2/5).

Most ceramics were made from clay deposits within the Teotihuacan Valley. Some grinding implements were made from local exposures of dense basalt, while others came from farther away. There are no significant local deposits of the limestone needed in great quantities for

Figure 2.5. Prickly pears (*nopales*) in the Teotihuacan Valley.
Photo by author.

Figure 2.6. Agaves (*magueys*) in the Teotihuacan Valley.
Photo by author.

making lime for mortar and plaster. The nearest sources are in the northwestern Basin, 30–40 km away (Parsons 2008), and still farther to the northwest, near Tula, about 55 km away, and more than 100 km to the southeast, south of the city of Puebla. Limestone was probably burned near its sources to make quicklime, but trees and other vegetation closer to Teotihuacan would have supplied fuel for cooking and heating. Wood was used sparingly for beams and poles in flat roofs of buildings and door lintels.

Local lava flows from extinct volcanoes were mined to obtain unworked rocks for building materials and for fine gravel (*cascajo*) added to Teotihuacan concrete. The lava deposits are more friable on their lower side, so miners dug underneath the layer of lava, creating what now appear to be natural caves but which are in fact human-made tunnels. Cut stone, often called ashlar by Old World archaeologists and locally called *cantera*, was used abundantly at the FSP and to some extent elsewhere (Murakami 2010). This stone is mostly light-colored andesite from nearby sources, including the Texcoco area about 20 km to the south (Figure 1.4/12).

Lapidary materials were imported from greater distances and include several kinds of greenstone (mostly fuchsite and serpentine), jadeite, mica, iron pyrites, slate, cinnabar, and shells from the Pacific and Gulf coasts. Very little, if any, turquoise has been found in Teotihuacan contexts, though in later times it was imported in quantity to Central Mexico, from as far as the southwestern United States. Some textiles and cordage were made from the fibers of locally grown *magueys*, but the climate is too cold for cotton, which would have come from Morelos and the Gulf Lowlands.

3 Urbanism Begins in Central Mexico: 500–100 BCE

Prelude

This book is about Teotihuacan, rather than all of Mesoamerica, but a brief historical overview can put Teotihuacan into context. Humans were in Mesoamerica by at least 11,000 BCE, having come from northeastern Asia. For millennia they lived as hunter-gatherers, collecting a variety of wild plant foods, hunting and trapping small game, and occasionally dining on very large animals, such as extinct kinds of elephants. We still know little about these early people because most Mesoamerican research has focused on later, pottery-making societies. Hunting and gathering ways of life were evidently quite satisfactory for a long time, but eventually, for reasons still not well understood, people in some parts of Mesoamerica began to spend part of their time not only harvesting wild plants, but also intervening in the life cycles of some species, most fatefully, into that of a grass called *teosinte*, the wild ancestor of maize (corn). These interventions amounted to domestication processes that led to new varieties or even new species that provided more food or other useful products per unit area, at the expense of greater human labor devoted to them and less time spent on wild resources. Besides maize, domesticated plants in Mesoamerica included various kinds of squashes and gourds (used for containers as well as for food), manioc from South America, beans, tomatoes, and less well-known grains such as the tiny but nutritious seeds of amaranths (a wide variety of leafy herbs). An early tree domesticate was the avocado. Many varieties of peppers were used for seasoning, and cacao "beans" for chocolate were highly prized. *Magueys* were used for food and other purposes, and their fermented sap made *pulque*. Prickly pears (*nopales*, genus *Opuntia*) provided tasty fruit and their leaves, stripped of spines, could also be prepared as food. Many other kinds of plants were used as vegetables, seasonings, and as medicines. Tobacco and other hallucinogenic substances were used for religious purposes.

Cotton and agaves were the main sources of fibers for nets, bags, cordage, and textiles.

The list of domesticated animals is much shorter. Dogs were important, probably brought from Asia by early migrants. Turkeys were kept for eggs as well as meat. At least in the Maya area, peccaries (a pig-like animal), white-tailed deer, and bees may have been semi-domesticated. Honey was used as a sweetener and for fermented drink. Notably absent were domesticated species that could serve as draft or pack animals or as major sources of meat (although some varieties of dogs were eaten). Farming, transport, and all other work depended entirely on human muscle and sweat.

Further developments in Mesoamerica included the increasing prevalence of life in permanent settlements and (to the delight of future archaeologists) the use of ceramic vessels for storing, preparing, and serving food and drink. By 2000 BCE, all this was present in several regions of Mesoamerica. Just how it all came about poses fascinating problems, but it happened so long before the beginnings of Teotihuacan that, for the Teotihuacanos, these practices had long been taken for granted, and their origins were part of myths about how their world was created.

The earliest farming settlements were so small and scattered that it is safe to assume that political systems were small and relatively egalitarian. Undoubtedly, individuals and households sometimes competed for high status within their community, but status was probably largely achieved through the efforts and skills of individuals, and not easily transmitted from parents to children. Many of the concepts prevalent in later Mesoamerican religions were probably already taking shape.

By 1400 to 1000 BCE, the situation had changed dramatically in some parts of Mesoamerica. This is especially clear in sites of the "Olmec" culture in the southern Gulf Lowlands, such as San Lorenzo (Figure 1.2/16), notable for great earthen platforms, colossal basalt stone heads, and other carvings. By this time, there were large inequalities in the statuses of individuals in this area, and elites were able to mobilize the labor of large numbers of lesser people. Some monumental Olmec sculptures look like portraits of specific individuals, whose facial expressions convey an attitude of command. These portrayals of specific individuals contrast markedly with the impersonal content and style of most Teotihuacan imagery.

Signs of increased sociocultural complexity occur by this time in other parts of Mesoamerica, notably in the Mazatán area of Pacific coastal Chiapas (Clark 2007), and in the highland Valley of Oaxaca (Marcus and

Flannery 1996, 2000; Blanton et al. 1999). In far western Mesoamerica, impressive shaft tombs appear to be this early. Archaeologists argue heatedly about whether the Gulf Olmec were enough ahead of other regions to merit the label of a "mother culture" (Sharer and Grove 1989; Blomster 2010; Cheetham 2010). In any case, a thousand years before the beginning of Teotihuacan, there were already Mesoamerican societies that had developed great art styles whose symbolism helped legitimize the institutionalized power of a few individuals over the mass of the population. Techniques of statecraft were perhaps not yet highly developed, but notions that some persons had god-given rights to rule others had been created.

In the Central Mexican highlands, Chalcatzingo (Figure 1.4/19), in the state of Morelos, just south of the Basin of Mexico, had strong iconographic ties with the southern Gulf lowlands (Grove 1984, 1987a). In the southern and better-watered part of the Basin of Mexico, Tlatilco, not far from Azcapotzalco, surely at least a good-sized town, has yielded numerous graves with Olmec-related ceramics, and there are other Olmec-related sites, such as Coapexco, in the southeastern Basin (Tolstoy 1989), but there is no evidence of monumental art or architecture, and the Basin looks somewhat marginal to developments elsewhere, rather than the key area it later became. In the northern part of the Basin, including the Teotihuacan Valley, there were only a few small settlements (Sanders et al. 1979: 96–97).

By 400 BCE, the "Olmec" culture of the southern Gulf lowlands had run its course, although "Epi-Olmec" styles continued in the lowlands for several centuries. In highland Central Mexico and Oaxaca, local societies developed their own styles. Hieroglyphic writing, possibly present earlier, is evident on stone monuments in lowland Epi-Olmec sites and in the Valley of Oaxaca. In the Pacific coastal lowlands of Chiapas and Guatemala, the Izapa culture drew in part on Olmec antecedents but showed many stylistic and iconographic innovations. In the Maya area, major centers such as Tak'alik Abaj (Figure 1.2/24) and Kaminaljuyú (Figure 1.2/25) in the highlands and Nakbé (Figure 1.2/28) and other sites in the lowlands were developing distinctively Maya styles of art, architecture, and writing.

Metals were another story. Throughout all these times, and even much later, they were essentially unused in Mesoamerica. Only at the very end of the Teotihuacan Period, or a little later, metal working began in far western Mesoamerica, with techniques derived from Central and South America (Hosler 1994). Teotihuacan's predecessors and neighbors and Teotihuacan itself used only stone tools, a fact that makes their achievements all the more impressive.

Cuicuilco and Its Neighbors, 500–100 BCE

During this period, called Late Preclassic in pan-Mesoamerican schemes, it looks as if new concepts and practices of statecraft were widely shared in Mesoamerica, even as regions preserved their strong individuality. Major centers became more populous and their principal monuments more ambitious. The Basin of Mexico, hitherto rather marginal, became a player in these developments.

In what are now the southwestern reaches of Mexico City (Figure 1.4/10), about seventy square kilometers of barren and nearly lifeless rock cover the earth in twisted and tormented shapes. This is the *Pedregal*, remains of a lava flow from a small volcano called Xitle, probably only about 1700 years ago, so recent that nature has had little time to soften its stark consequences. Urbanism in the Basin of Mexico began in this now seemingly unpromising area. Before the eruption, it was one of the most lush and fertile zones in the entire Basin. Given the favorable environment, it seems logical that the largest settlement in the Basin should have arisen somewhere in this area, and that is what happened. The settlement, which we now call Cuicuilco, eventually grew so large, and its major monuments so tall, that even today a huge circular pyramid, about 130 m in diameter and sixteen to twenty m high, rises above the lava that engulfed it. Byron Cummings (1933) excavated here in the 1920s. Unfortunately, his excavations took place before modern methods of excavation and recording were in use. Because the lava is virtually impenetrable solid rock, unlike the much softer volcanic ash that preserved Pompeii and other sites, we still know desperately little about Cuicuilco. Yet, what we do know makes it clear that it had achieved fully urban status long before the eruption (Heizer and Bennyhoff 1958).

There is evidence for a sedentary community at Cuicuilco at least as early as anywhere else in the Basin of Mexico, if not all of Mesoamerica. Heizer and Bennyhoff (1972) describe a "Tlalpan" ceramic phase, the earliest evidence of occupation at the site, with uncalibrated radiocarbon dates around 2000 to 1800 BCE. The ceramics, with deep, open, thin-walled bowls, few *tecomates* (nearly globular bowls with restricted orifices and no necks), and decoration limited to red paint (often highly polished) and wide channeling, show little indication of any ancestral relationship to later ceramic traditions in the Basin. Two variants of "Type M" figurines are diagnostic. Now that far more is known about very early ceramics elsewhere in Mesoamerica, Tlalpan materials should be restudied and compared with early ceramics elsewhere.

Heizer and Bennyhoff (1972) say that the great circular pyramid began as a modest structure and was enlarged in five stages to reach its final size. They also briefly describe a long series of post-Tlalpan ceramic phases, both at the major pyramid (Cuicuilco A), and in an area called Peña Pobre, about 500 m to the west (Cuicuilco B), where an additional eleven mounds were partially explored. The ceramics of these phases generally closely resemble those already known from smaller sites in the Basin, especially those excavated by George Vaillant (1930, 1931, 1935a, 1935b) in the early 1930s. Further salvage operations were carried out at Cuicuilco B by INAH in 1967. Florencia Müller (1990) provides numerous drawings and photos of ceramics and architectural features. Pastrana and Ramírez (2012) summarize further excavations.

Heizer and Bennyhoff (1972) postulate some periods of possible abandonment, and a series of possible sources of external influences, including "Olmec" (perhaps related to Chalcatzingo in Morelos, Figure 1.4/19); the Chupícuaro tradition 200 km to the west, in Guanajuato (Figure 1.2/4); and the Gulf lowlands. The strength and even the existence of these external influences need further investigation.

We have little sense of the processes of Cuicuilco's growth; whether it was slow or rapid, whether a single small village grew slowly larger, or whether several villages abruptly amalgamated in the process called synoecism, as sometimes happened in other parts of the world. However, there is good evidence that, at its height (around 400 to 100 BCE), Cuicuilco covered at least 400 ha (four square kilometers) with a population that Sanders et al. (1979: 99, 193) estimate to have been at least 20,000. Some rectangular structures hint at an orthogonal layout. In 1956, Angel Palerm and Eric Wolf (Palerm 1972) conducted a brief reconnaissance in areas not covered by lava and found evidence for irrigation canals earlier than the volcanic eruption, implying that water from small local streams was already being diverted for agriculture.

During its height, Cuicuilco was by far the largest settlement in the Basin of Mexico. Like Teotihuacan, but unlike Monte Albán and many other politically important sites in Mesoamerica, Cuicuilco was situated on relatively flat ground rather than on a hilltop. It must have politically dominated at least a sizable part of the southwestern Basin of Mexico, and ceramic uniformity throughout the Basin suggests that its influence was strong everywhere in the Basin. Whether it ever politically controlled the entire Basin is unclear – the rise of Teotihuacan, apparently coeval with its final occupation, suggests a degree of independence in the northeastern Basin.

Geologic information about the volcanic eruption has been conflicting, especially as to the number and date or dates of eruptions. The most important point is that there is archaeological evidence that the ash deposit and lava covered structures that were already in disrepair

(Heizer and Bennyhoff 1958, 1972; Córdova et al. 1994). Müller (1990) believed that Cuicuilco was abandoned as a direct result of a heavy ash fall, and that the lava flow occurred after a considerable interval during which structures eroded. But Claus Siebe (2000) argues for a single explosive ash eruption, probably sometime between 200 and 400 CE, followed within a few days or at most a few years by the lava. This would place this volcanic event somewhere in the Tlamimilolpa ceramic phase at Teotihuacan, when that city was already highly developed, and long after Cuicuilco had declined for other reasons.

Most of the ceramics associated with Cuicuilco in its last centuries are quite similar to those of the phases called Ticomán I, II, and III, about 500–100 BCE, named after a village on the northwestern shore of Lake Texcoco where the tradition was first well described (Figure 1.4/7), (Vaillant 1931). Bennyhoff (1967) aptly pointed out that it would be better named the Cuicuilco tradition, since Cuicuilco was its major center. The local variant in the Teotihuacan Valley is called Cuanalán. Serving vessels of the Cuicuilco tradition tend to have relatively simple decoration in a red slip over the natural surface, but are often remarkably graceful in form (Figure 3.1). Bowls with medial or shoulder breaks in profile, often with large hollow supports, are common. Many are as pleasing as any ceramics ever produced in the Basin of Mexico.

However, ceramics resembling those of the Patlachique phase of Teotihuacan (currently estimated to date around 100–1 BCE, but possibly as late as 1–100 CE) also occur below the lava. In some earlier publications, before the Patlachique phase was defined at Teotihuacan, these were referred to as Tzacualli, the subsequent phase in the Teotihuacan sequence. But Heizer and Bennyhoff (1972: 101–02) are emphatic that there are no middens with ceramics of the Tzacualli or any later phase below the lava, although they found a few Tzacualli "trade" sherds in the final structure in Mound 2 at Cuicuilco B. Bennyhoff and Heizer (1965), based on petrographic study and instrumental neutron activation analysis (NAA) of a single element (manganese), identified a small sample of these Tzacualli resist-decorated sherds as from Teotihuacan. There is little doubt that these sherds were imports to Cuicuilco. Now that much more is known about compositions of clays and tempering materials in the Basin of Mexico and at least five provenance subareas can be distinguished, it is extremely desirable to carry out compositional studies of a much larger sample of Cuicuilco materials. Müller (1990) agrees about the lack of evidence for a Tzacualli phase occupation, although ceramics of many later periods have filtered into cracks and holes within the lava, some apparently having arrived as offerings deposited by visitors.

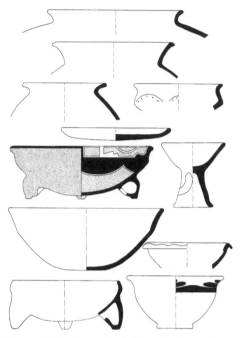

Figure 3.1. Cuicuilco/Ticomán/Cuanalán tradition serving vessels. From Sanders et al. (1979), with permission of Academic Press. Courtesy of Jeffrey Parsons.

Box 3.1 Neutron Activation Analysis

Bombardment of materials by neutrons can knock particles out of the nuclei of some atoms, leading to different isotopes, some of which are unstable (radioactive). The emissions from different elements are known, and their strengths can be used to determine the proportion of different elements in a sample, including trace elements. Proportions of as many as 20 or 30 different elements can be identified in each specimen. Minerals from different sources are unlikely to have highly similar proportions of all elements studied, so this is often a good way of identifying specific sources. The method is often called NAA, or INAA (instrumental neutron activation analysis).

Putting all this together with Siebe's geologic evidence, it appears that Cuicuilco was still flourishing during the Patlachique phase of Teotihuacan but had been abandoned by the onset of the Tzacualli phase, for reasons other than the eruption of Xitle several centuries later. But Teotihuacan's explosive growth began in the Patlachique phase, apparently during the last century or so of Cuicuilco's prominence. This suggests that there was a period of rivalry between the two centers for dominance in the Basin of Mexico. We can no longer look to Xitle for an easy explanation for the decline of Cuicuilco and the rise of Teotihuacan. But, as discussed below, ash fall from Popocatépetl around 200–1 BCE was devastating in the southeastern Basin and probably had effects as far west as Cuicuilco. Teotihuacan, at the northeastern extreme of the Basin of Mexico, would have been far less affected. It may also have been important that Teotihuacan was on an easy route to the Tlaxcala/Puebla plains and beyond to the Gulf Lowlands and to south-Central Mexico, while Cuicuilco was less well situated for exchange.

Cuicuilco's urban experiences were available as models for Teotihuacan's creators. Teotihuacan was the continuation and elaboration of an urban tradition already developed at Cuicuilco. This helps us to understand why Teotihuacan developed its urban character so rapidly. The impression that urbanization in the Basin of Mexico was something of a late starter in Mesoamerica overlooks the fact that Teotihuacan was the direct heir of urbanization practices already well underway in the southern Basin and going back to 400 BCE or earlier, not long after the beginning of Monte Albán in Oaxaca, currently estimated at around 500 BCE (Marcus and Flannery 1996; Blanton et al. 1999).

The sheer size of Cuicuilco and the number and scale of its civic-ceremonial structures leaves no doubt that during this period it became a politically complex society, in which a few individuals exercised strong power over the multitudes. Sanders et al. (1979: 97–105) see Cuicuilco as growing from a population of 5,000–10,000 early in this period to at least 20,000, by which time they think there was a four-tiered settlement hierarchy in the Basin of Mexico, composed of hamlets, small villages, large villages, and 13 small regional centers that were dominated at least to some extent by two much larger centers, Cuicuilco and Teotihuacan, which they see as competing to expand their spheres of influence.

Does this mean that the Cuicuilco polity qualifies as a "state," or only a "complex chiefdom"? I believe this is an ill-framed question, partly because I am very skeptical of simply counting "tiers" (sites of more or less the same size, separated by apparent gaps in the range of site sizes) as an index of political type. To be sure, in any region there are usually a few large sites and a number of smaller sites of varying sizes. But the existence of well-defined discrete tiers is often problematic, because those who rely on this approach usually determine significant gaps in the size range intuitively and on the basis of too few cases (Drennan and Peterson 2004). Even where gaps are unambiguous, it is a leap of faith to assume that the difference between three and four tiers is reliably diagnostic of a qualitative change in the political system. Others who have problems with this assumption include Elizabeth Brumfiel (1995: 127) and Robin Yates (1997: 81). Furthermore, there are reasons to doubt whether there is a clear demarcation between "complex chiefdoms" and "simple states," even when ample historical information is available, as I explained in Chapter 1.

The Tezoyuca Puzzle

Somewhere around 200 BCE, a new ceramic complex called Tezoyuca strongly influenced the Cuicuilco tradition in the Basin of Mexico. The Tezoyuca complex was once thought to overlap in time with the Patlachique phase, but Bennyhoff (1967) emphatically questioned this, and Sanders et al. (1979: 98–105) agreed that it represents a phase, perhaps quite brief, prior to Patlachique. Ceramics of this complex are especially notable at 13 small sites, each with estimated populations of no more than 300–600, consisting of well-defined precincts of public architecture, all situated atop isolated steep-sided hills – locations notable for wide viewsheds and defensive possibilities. One is the "type site" of Cerro Tezoyuca, situated on the southwestern margin of the Teotihuacan Valley, where it opens out onto the central Basin (Figure 2.3/4). Another eight are around the edges of the Patlachique hills on the southern flank of the Teotihuacan Valley. Two more are a few kilometers farther south, in the central and south-central parts of the Texcoco region. Finally, two are on the east side of the Guadalupe range, near the far northwest corner of Lake Texcoco. It appears that at least many of these hilltop sites were abandoned in the Patlachique phase.

However, Tezoyuca ceramics are not limited to hilltop sites. Within the later city of Teotihuacan itself, the TMP found at most a handful of Tezoyuca sherds, but Harold McBride (1974) says they are well represented in a large site at Cuauhtitlán (Figure 1.4/6), in the flat alluvial plain in the northwestern Basin of Mexico. Considerable numbers of Tezoyuca sherds were found in surface collections dominated by Patlachique ceramics at sites in gently sloping terrain in the Texcoco region. Sanders et al. (1979: 98–105) found so few Tezoyuca sherds in the southern Basin that they think they are likely trade pieces.[1] They interpret the evidence as suggesting warfare among perhaps as many as six competing small polities in the Basin, which implies that Cuicuilco's political control did not extend into the northern Basin.

The Tezoyuca complex seems derived from the Cuicuilco tradition, but with the addition of certain elements, notably a distinctive style of white-on-red painting, slant-eyed figurines, and various vessel forms that Bennyhoff (1967) thought were derived from the Chupícuaro tradition, some 180 kilometers to the west, (Figure 1.2/4) (Porter 1956; Florance 2000). Müller (1990) sees some Chupícuaro influences at Cuicuilco (as well as possible influences from Oaxaca). These comparisons have raised the possibility that westerners invaded the Basin of Mexico and established hilltop centers from which they dominated the locals. However, Bennyhoff did not believe the ceramic influences were strong enough to indicate any sizable migration of people. Moreover, recent work on Chupícuaro pottery, figurines, architecture (Darras and Faugère 2007), and mortuary practices (David, Platas, and Gamboa 2007) finds little evidence of any close connection between Chupícuaro peoples and those in the Basin of Mexico.

If the Tezoyuca complex really represents an incursion of outsiders, it could have a bearing on the issue of languages prevalent at this time in the Basin of Mexico. In particular, it could conceivably represent the first arrival of substantial numbers of Náhuatl speakers from a homeland farther to the west or northwest. That might possibly be the case, but the Chupícuaro region seems well within the plausible range of Otomanguean speakers. Given that, and the questionable evidence for any significant migration at all, the case for substantial movement of Náhuatl speakers into the Basin at this time looks weak.

Teotihuacan

Seen in the narrow context of the Teotihuacan Valley, the explosive growth of Teotihuacan in the last century BCE looks surprising. But this would be too myopic a view. To even begin to understand what was happening at this time in the Teotihuacan Valley, one has to look at developments throughout the Basin of Mexico, especially at Cuicuilco; elsewhere in Central Mexico; and throughout Mesoamerica.

Too little of Cuicuilco architecture and its layout is known to say how closely it foreshadowed Teotihuacan in detail, except that circular pyramids are unknown at Teotihuacan. At least in ceramics, however, there is considerable continuity between Cuicuilco and Teotihuacan. Smaller settlements in the Basin of Mexico during Cuicuilco's dominance include Ticomán in the northwest (Vaillant 1931), and two sizable nucleated villages in the Teotihuacan Valley. One is called Cuanalán (Figure 2.3/3), in the lower valley, in the region probably already watered by spring-fed canals. The other, on the dry ground in the middle valley, near these springs, was labeled TF-35 in Sanders' survey of the valley. It is described as a "large dispersed village" (Sanders et al. 1979, Map 12), a category with an estimated population of "500–1000+" (Sanders et al. 1979: 56). TF-35 was resurveyed more intensively by the TMP, and its actual area was found to be about 20–30 hectares. I estimate its population as 1000–2000, a sizable village, although much smaller than Cuicuilco. It is centered in dry land in sector S1W6 of the TMP map (Figure 3.2). Just down valley from the springs, which are in sector S1W5, is an area of about 100 hectares in which wetland agriculture is practiced today. I suspect this was already the case during the Cuanalán phase. Both of the large Teotihuacan Valley villages of this period are in or adjacent to land watered by the springs, either as wetlands (TF-35) or by canals a few kilometers long (the Cuanalán site). Proximity to prime agricultural land was probably a major consideration in their location. A kilometer or two to the north of TF-35, scatters of Cuanalán phase ceramics on the east and north slopes of Cerro Malinalco represent dispersed dry land settlement, including the excavated site of Tlachinolpan (Figure 2.3/2), in sector N7W8, somewhat northwest of the area shown on the TMP map (Blucher 1971). A thin scatter of Cuanalán sherds in sector N5W2 includes the later triadic group called Plaza One. The TMP also found a much smaller compact Cuanalán phase village several kilometers to the southeast, in sector S3E6, not reported by Sanders. Sanders's survey located 21 additional sites that he calls hamlets and six trace occupations of this period in the Teotihuacan Valley, mostly in hilly terrain. Sites were larger and more numerous in the southern Basin.

Given the evidence for continued occupation at Cuicuilco into the Patlachique phase, it seems unlikely that refugees from Cuicuilco contributed much to the initial growth spurt of Teotihuacan. But there is little doubt that a different kind of volcanic damage in the southern Basin gave Teotihuacan a significant edge in political competition. Siebe (2000) dates a major cataclysmic eruption of Popocatépetl to around 200–1 BCE. It caused an extensive ash fall to the east in Puebla that completely devastated several settlements. This has been especially well documented at Tetimpa (Plunket and Uruñuela 1998, 2002; Uruñuela and Plunket 2002, 2007). The northwestern slopes of Popo were also devastated by pyroclastic flows. Survivors in the Amecameca-Chalco region in the far southeastern Basin of Mexico would have had to migrate to other places. Siebe feels that this eruption (not the much later Xitle eruption) must have played a role in the concentration of a large proportion of the Basin of Mexico's population at Teotihuacan. Parsons et al. (1982: 265–266) see a modest but noticeable population decline in the Chalco-Xochimilco region in the Patlachique phase. This is followed

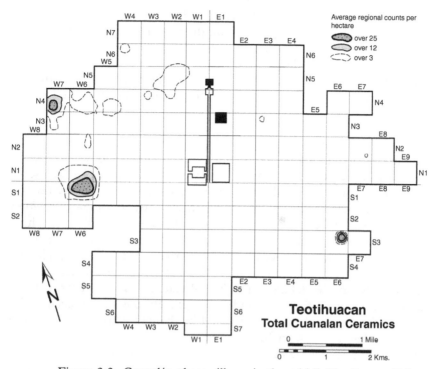

Figure 3.2. Cuanalán phase villages in the middle Teotihuacan Valley, a smoothed contour map of sherd densities per hectare collected by the TMP.

By S. Vaughn after original by author & W. Powell.

by an apparent near-depopulation of that entire region in the Tzacualli phase. Tzacualli pottery is scarce in the adjacent Ixtapalapa Peninsula (Figure 1.4) and in most of the Texcoco region to the north. In the Texcoco region, Tzacualli material is abundant only in the northernmost part, just south of the Teotihuacan Valley. Another growth cycle in the Chalco-Xochimilco region begins in the Miccaotli and Tlamimilolpa phases, although the population level attained seems to have been only about a fifth of that during the Cuicuilco (Ticomán) period. This demographic pattern may well be explained by the eruption of Popocatépetl described by Siebe. No sites buried in ash, comparable to Tetimpa, have been reported for the southeastern Basin of Mexico, but even a lighter ash fall might have spurred abandonment.

The fact that serious ash fall from Popocatépetl did not reach as far as the Teotihuacan Valley could help explain migration into the city of Teotihuacan in the Patlachique and Tzacualli phases. Perhaps the Teotihuacan leadership capitalized on the fact that the Volcano God had spared the Teotihuacan Valley in order to bolster their claim to a special connection with that powerful deity. I discuss some iconographic evidence in support of this conjecture in Chapter 8. The ability of such ideas to have concrete consequences should not be underestimated.

Outside the Basin of Mexico

In thinking about Teotihuacan's wider impacts, I have not found "World Systems" concepts derived from Immanuel Wallerstein (1974) useful. For a range of views on their utility, see Parkinson and Galaty (2010). I find it better to distinguish four concepts. By Teotihuacan *culture*, I refer to sites where the full repertoire of material remains may have been made of local materials but are only minor variants of those in the city. Probably their occupants recognized a shared ethnic identity and most spoke the same language. Given good archaeological data, it is relatively easy to delineate the spatial extent of Teotihuacan culture, although it can be fuzzy around the edges. By the Teotihuacan *polity*, I mean the areas politically controlled by the city. This is much harder to determine: places with Teotihuacan culture may have been politically independent, and some culturally different places may have been politically controlled. By *presence*, I mean places where there is evidence that people of Teotihuacan affiliation were physically present, although not necessarily as representatives of the state. By *influence*, I mean places where locals adopted stylistic elements derived from Teotihuacan, perhaps in emulation inspired by Teotihuacan's prestige.

The extent of Teotihuacan culture, polity, presence, and influence varied considerably over time, and archaeologists often disagree about which concept is most applicable in a specific case. At its height, the Teotihuacan polity almost certainly covered enough territory and embraced a sufficient variety of peoples to merit the term "empire." There is increasing evidence that agents of the Teotihuacan state controlled key outposts up to 200 km to the west and as far southeast as Guatemala. But often we know little more than that objects have been found that were imported from Teotihuacan, or locally made objects are so similar to Teotihuacan styles that they must be related.

Interaction can take many forms. Politically, it ranges from direct political administration, to "hegemonic" rule through control of local elites, to less direct influence over nominally autonomous polities by means of the potential to intervene in situations not to Teotihuacan's liking, backed by superior military and other resources. Exchange relations include gift-giving as part of elite diplomacy, commerce carried out by merchants, and "down-the-line" trading from region to region, in which the final recipients may have little or no idea of the original source. Besides political outposts, Teotihuacan-related settlements may have included enclaves of merchants, migrants, and even dissident émigrés.

Religious or ideological relations include the spread of appealing cults and the movement of prestigious symbols whose meanings may have changed considerably in the course of their travels, which may be freely adopted by local elites for their own purposes. Interactions went both ways; foreign objects and foreign enclaves occur in Teotihuacan. Visitors to Teotihuacan may have returned home with new ideas and/or objects acquired during their visit.

It seems unlikely that the Cuicuilco polity had much impact outside the Basin of Mexico. Ceramics possibly imported from Chupícuaro are reported from the site of Cerro del Tepalcate, a few kilometers west of Tlatilco, but otherwise Chupícuaro influences in the Basin of Mexico do not seem strong. Teotihuacan influences in the Chupícuaro region may have been somewhat stronger (Florance 2000), but others see them as very limited (Darras and Faugère 2007; David et al. 2007). At this time, people in the Basin of Mexico shared a broad redware ceramic tradition that was widespread in western Mesoamerica. Teotihuacan had less in common, in terms of ceramics, with people in Veracruz and farther to the southeast. In later periods, this redware tradition evolved and proliferated in far western Mesoamerica, while Teotihuacan, without wholly breaking with it, began to acquire a number of ceramic features derived from the east and south. Ceramic changes in the Epiclassic Period, following the collapse of the Teotihuacan state, mark a reappearance in the Basin of Mexico of the western redware tradition.

There were probably closer affinities with people in parts of Tlaxcala and Puebla. Cholula may have already covered 2 square km (Geoffrey McCafferty, personal communication, 2007) and a number of other centers had developed (Carballo 2012). In Morelos, just south of the Basin of Mexico and at a lower altitude, the Early and Middle Preclassic site of Chalcatzingo, with its strong Gulf Olmec ties, had declined. Ceramic traditions, especially in the eastern part of the state, share some similarities with the Cuicuilco tradition, but not enough to suggest any strong political or economic ties (Cyphers and Hirth, 2000). Eastern Morelos is connected with the Basin of Mexico by a broad pass that runs through the modern town of Amecameca, and is the part most easily reached from the Basin, while the route to western Morelos runs through higher ground and is more difficult.

The Valley of Oaxaca, about 375 km southeast of the Basin of Mexico, covers about 2,500 square km, at an altitude of about 1,500 m (Blanton et al. 1999: 29, 31). It is smaller and lower than the Basin of Mexico. It has a milder climate, although it is also semiarid and, except in a few favored locations, irrigation is important for agriculture. For many centuries independent polities had been developing in the Valley of Oaxaca and in some of the smaller valleys and mountainous areas elsewhere in what is now the state of Oaxaca. By 700 BCE it seems that polities in the Valley of Oaxaca tended to be in conflict, with sparsely occupied buffer zones between settlement clusters centered on head towns (Blanton et al. 1999: 42). Then, around 500 BCE, a new settlement called Monte Albán was created on a 400-meter high hill, in a previously sparsely occupied and agriculturally marginal central part of the valley. The new center's location on a high, steep hill and the scarcity of nearby good farm land contrast with Cuicuilco and Teotihuacan. It rapidly became by far the largest settlement in Oaxaca, covering about 320 hectares, soon had an estimated population of 5000, and grew to about 17,000 by about 150 BCE (Blanton et al. 1999: 53). Such a rapid growth rate implies considerable in-migration. Monte Albán quickly reached an "urban" scale and complexity at least comparable to and perhaps exceeding roughly contemporary developments in the Basin of Mexico. Little is known about civic-ceremonial structures at this time because they are obscured by later buildings, but there seems to have been nothing like the largest Cuicuilco pyramids. However, over 300 carved stone slabs show nude and mutilated male bodies. They are called *danzantes*, dancers, but they are clearly victims, probably war captives (Blanton et al. 1999: 62). Several lines of evidence strongly suggest that Monte Albán was the political capital of the Valley of Oaxaca region, the largest polity in the southern Mexican highlands in this period.

In the Gulf lowlands there were important sites, such as epi-Olmec Tres Zapotes (Figure 1.2/14) (Stark and Arnold 1997). Major centers flourished in the Maya lowlands and highlands and in Pacific coastal Guatemala (Demarest 2004), and there was a somewhat different tradition at Izapa in coastal Chiapas.

4   Teotihuacan Takes Off: 100–1 BCE

It has been difficult to get people to recognize that the Patlachique phase (c. 100–1 BCE) was more than a prelude to the development of Teotihuacan. Art historian Esther Pasztory (1997) doesn't even mention it. Yet it was during the Patlachique phase that, in one or two centuries, Teotihuacan grew from almost nothing to become a large city. The area of fairly dense Patlachique sherd cover extends over 6 to 8 square km (Figure 4.1). By the end of this phase, the population was likely at least 20,000. Teotihuacan was now comparable to the population of Cuicuilco at its peak, if not larger. The TMP ceramic analysis, carried out in the 1960s, classified about 27,500 sherds from the surface collections as Patlachique. A reanalysis supervised by Evelyn Rattray in the 1970s classified about 42,300 as Patlachique – a 61% increase, but this is probably in error. Only another analysis of a selected sample (possible only because Millon insisted on saving all the TMP collections) can resolve this discrepancy. Fortunately, Sugiyama and Cabrera (2007) recovered a large quantity of stylistically homogeneous ceramics from the fill of Stage One of the Moon Pyramid, enabling a much clearer definition of the Patlachique ceramic complex, which can be the basis for this re-reanalysis.

Highest densities of Patlachique ceramics were collected by the TMP in a broad area around the eastern and northern slopes of Cerros Colorado and Malinalco. Patlachique sherd cover, probably light, extends an unknown distance west and north beyond the TMP map. Millon was constrained by NSF reviewers in the 1960s who did not recommend funds to extend his map beyond the limits of the Early Classic city.

This western Patlachique-phase settlement might be seen as a logical development from the sparse Cuicuilco tradition occupation on these hill slopes. However, the Cuicuilco tradition village near the wetlands below the springs (TF-35) was nearly abandoned. Conceivably, this shift to hill slopes might be due to greater emphasis on defense, but the slopes do not seem steep enough to have offered much difficulty to

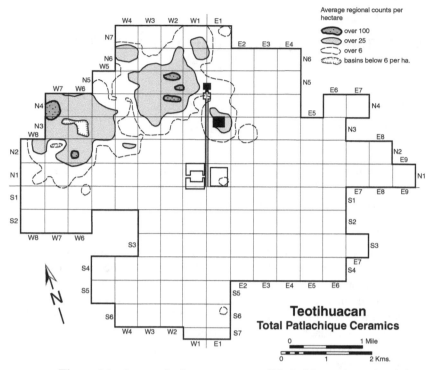

Figure 4.1. A smoothed contour map of Patlachique phase sherd densities per hectare collected by the TMP.

By S. Vaughn after original by author & W. Powell.

attackers, the summits of the hills were not occupied, and no evidence of fortifications survives.

Another broad zone of heavy Patlachique sherd cover is centered in TMP map sectors N5W2 and N4W2 (Figure 4.1), in relatively flat land considerably farther from the wetlands or any irrigable areas than was the Cuicuilco tradition village. It is unclear why this region was selected for settlement. Neither defense nor close proximity to the best agricultural land explain it, and it now seems that supposed caves in this area are results of later mining for building materials, rather than possible sacred localities. The Moon Pyramid is near the eastern margin of this zone, instead of near its center. Likewise sector N6W3, although labeled "Old City" on the TMP map (Millon et al. 1973) is marginal to this zone. There is a probable Patlachique sherd concentration near the Sun Pyramid. The location of the future Ciudadela complex, in TMP sector N1E1, is nearly a kilometer south of the zone of dense Patlachique sherd cover, and significant occupation in this district is doubtful. A small concentration several kilometers to the south, in sector S6E1, looks like a separate settlement, although its location near what would become the southern terminus of the Avenue of the Dead suggests that this place already had symbolic meaning.

Whatever the outcome of further ceramic analysis, the Patlachique-phase settlement surely qualifies as urban in size. Nevertheless, there is little evidence of monumental structures at this time in Teotihuacan, and the extent to which the settlement was "urban" in terms of practices, institutions, and function remains to be determined. The Patlachique phase polity must have been quite complex, with a variety of institutionalized offices and wide hereditary differences in status and power. Whether it qualifies as the capital of a state depends on one's definition of "state" and also on what one believes are valid and reliable archaeological clues of statehood, as I discussed in Chapter 1.

The clearest evidence of Patlachique civic-ceremonial construction is from the earliest of the seven stages of construction at the Moon Pyramid, where Sugiyama and Cabrera (2007) found a square pyramidal platform that measures 23.5 m on a side. Its height is unknown because of later disturbance. The façade on all sides is a sloping apron (*talud*) made of small pink cut stones set in mud mortar. There is no surviving evidence of ornamentation, burials, or offerings. The orientation is 11–12 degrees east of astronomic north, which differs by about four degrees from the orientation that later became canonical at Teotihuacan. Ceramics in the fill of this structure are almost entirely of the Patlachique complex, although about 2.5 percent have been assigned to the Tzacualli complex in preliminary analysis. These may be intrusive or misidentified. Stage One of the Moon Pyramid was probably built toward the end of the Patlachique phase or very early in the Tzacualli phase.

Box 4.1 Triadic Groups (Three-Pyramid Complexes)

There are many single pyramids at Teotihuacan, but pyramids sometimes occur in groups of three: one on each of three sides of a rectangular plaza, often with a low transverse platform along the fourth side (Headrick 2001). This arrangement suggests their dedication to a triad of deities, but it is not clear what deities they might be. Triadic groups also appear at many other sites in Mesoamerica.

Stage One of the Moon Pyramid is perhaps not the only Patlachique phase civic-ceremonial structure at Teotihuacan. Even so, there was nothing on the scale of the largest pyramids at Cuicuilco. Several of the triadic groups in the northwestern quadrant of the city have above-average surface densities of Patlachique sherds in their vicinities, although their visible features are later. Plaza One (1:N5W2) is the best example. Excavations there in the 1950s (Cook de Leonard 1957; Millon 1960; Millon and Bennyhoff 1961) found evidence of Tzacualli construction and possibly a Patlachique occupation. Further work is needed at Plaza One, and the other triadic groups in this northwestern district remain to be explored by excavation. All these groups, as well as the Moon Pyramid, face southward, suggesting an early religious emphasis on this direction. Whether any of the platforms and pyramids that now face east and west on both sides of the Avenue of the Dead has Patlachique antecedents remains to be determined.

A tunnel at ground level into the Sun Pyramid, excavated by José Pérez in 1933 under the direction of Eduardo Noguera (Pérez 1935: 91; Noguera 1935: 5–6), revealed remains of a small structure faced with stone cobbles (Millon et al. 1965). Within it was an offering that included a small obsidian human effigy, surrounded by nearly 40 tiny obsidian points. The contents and their arrangement are reminiscent of those in the considerably later Tombs 2 and 6 in the Moon Pyramid, but on a much smaller scale. This suggested that a small structure of ritual importance existed here prior to the massive Sun Pyramid construction event during the Tzacualli phase. Renewed excavations in the Sun Pyramid in 2008–2011 (N. Sugiyama et al. 2013) revealed burials, offerings, and traces of structures predating the pyramid. Most notable is what seems to have been a free-standing wall more than 13.5 m long, too large for an ordinary residential room, and not a pyramid. It probably was part of a civic-ceremonial enclosure, such as existed elsewhere in Central Mexico in Late Preclassic times (Carballo 2012), suggesting a relatively egalitarian society. Dates of these pre-pyramid features are unclear, perhaps Tzacualli but possibly Patlachique.

Although Stage One of the Moon Pyramid was likely the single largest structure in Teotihuacan in the Patlachique phase, it is on the edge of the districts of heavy Patlachique sherd cover. There is no clear single center for the settlement, which seems incongruous in view of its size and the rapidity of its growth. It is unlikely that low Patlachique sherd densities east and south of the Moon Pyramid are due to incorporation of Patlachique phase debris in later structures, because the quantity of Patlachique ceramics in these later structures (including the Sun Pyramid) is small. Perhaps at this time the city had multiple centers. Lack of a single preeminent civic-ceremonial core would suggest a coming-together of several relatively autonomous and, in terms of politics, relatively equal groups, rather than a strong central authority, a possibility also suggested by Tatsuya Murakami (2010). But if that was the case, why did independent groups choose to settle in close proximity to one another and attract such a flow of immigrants? Patlachique Teotihuacan was probably politically unified but perhaps without a single monarch. Excavations testing the dates and sizes of the earliest stages of later civic-ceremonial complexes with heavy Patlachique sherd cover (including further work at Plaza One) are badly needed.

We still have no data on Patlachique phase residential architecture within the city. Probably it was of perishable materials, perhaps much like the structures of adobes and stones set in mud mortar that are well preserved at Tetimpa, about 90 km to the southeast, in the state of Puebla (Figure 1.4/16) (Uruñuela and Plunket 2002, 2007; Plunket and Uruñuela 1998, 2002). At Tlachinolpan, only a kilometer or two northwest of the later city of Teotihuacan, on the northeastern slopes of Cerro Malinalco (1:N7W8, Figure 2.3/2, TF-39 in the Teotihuacan Valley survey) Darlena Blucher (1971) found abundant Cuanalán phase ceramics, but no evidence of Cuanalán structures. She excavated several structures that seem to have been built in the Patlachique phase and rebuilt in the Tzacualli phase. They appear to be civic (rather than residential or religious) buildings – small, partially roofed, rectangular stone-walled enclosures unlike anything else known for Teotihuacan, although somewhat like slightly earlier structures found at Nativitas in Tlaxcala (Hirth et al. 2009). The largest is a low rectangular building about 15 by 10 m, its long axis oriented approximately to astronomic north. These structures were enlarged in the Tzacualli phase, and then abandoned.

The rapidity of growth of the city during the Patlachique phase suggests strong, although possibly collective, leadership. The city may have grown in periodic spurts, but the average rate of population growth must have been at least 1.5 percent per year. Part of this exceptionally high growth rate may have been due to unusually high fertility, but death rates were so high everywhere in the world before the twentieth century that high fertility alone probably could not account for this growth rate. Archaeological and historical evidence suggests that, before the twentieth century, rates of natural increase that were this high only occurred when people moved into territory previously unoccupied by humans or when, as in North America, they often could easily remove former occupants. Neither of these situations was the case in the Basin of Mexico in Patlachique times. Much of the rapid increase probably was due to in-migration, from elsewhere in the Teotihuacan Valley and from somewhat beyond, although Parsons et al. (1982) see only a modest decline in population in the southeastern Basin of Mexico, and Cuicuilco was apparently still quite large. According to Siebe (2000) the Xitle eruption was still several centuries in the future. There is no good evidence of much migration from far beyond the Basin.

Why, then, did Teotihuacan grow so rapidly in this period – from nearly nothing to the largest settlement in Central Mexico, outstripping its rival, Cuicuilco? It was probably a combination of several factors, including successful warfare, a good location for trade, perhaps compelling new religious ideas, and very possibly the sheer luck of having a few unusually able and ambitious leaders. Irrigation can hardly be the sole explanation, but being not too far from a small area of wetland farming and a larger region of irrigated agriculture should not be discounted. Yet it seems that Cuicuilco, not yet devastated by a volcanic eruption, was in a richer zone for irrigated farming. Perhaps several independent villages joined forces to resist Cuiculco expansion.

Patlachique Phase Ceramics and Lithic Artifacts

After the Tezoyuca ceramic complex, Bennyhoff (1967) saw the ensuing Patlachique complex as a return to the Cuicuilco tradition, after rejection of Chupícuaro influences, although with, in his opinion, other influences perhaps from the Cholula region. There is little to support Sanders's (2006: 184–186) belief that Náhuatl speakers might have entered the Basin of Mexico in numbers at this time. My discussion of Patlachique ceramics is based largely on a manuscript by Darlena Blucher (1983) and her dissertation (Blucher 1971). Ceramic forms that continue from the Cuicuilco/Cuanalán tradition include composite silhouette vessels with shoulder breaks, and ollas with "wedge" rims, usually less angular than those in Tzacualli. Tecomates are rare. Hollow supports continue but are less common and tend to be smaller. Bichrome and polychrome decoration includes combinations of red, white, and resist. Polychrome motifs include angular broad red geometric shapes with white borders. Incising is rare and includes hatched triangles. Figures 4.2 and 4.3 show Patlachique examples. Rattray (2001: 467, Figures 26 c and d) mislabels two good Patlachique sherds as "Early Tzacualli."

Obsidian implements were produced for local consumption. Less than one percent of sharp-edged lithic artifacts from all periods at Teotihuacan were made of chert or other materials. Spence (1984, 1987), using the surface collections of the TMP, identified nine possible Patlachique phase obsidian workshops on the western edge of the city, apparently intermittent and independent producers not specializing in

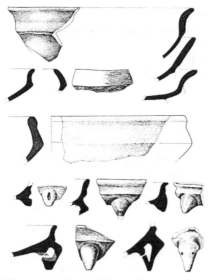

Figure 4.2. Patlachique phase serving wares.
After Blucher (1983).

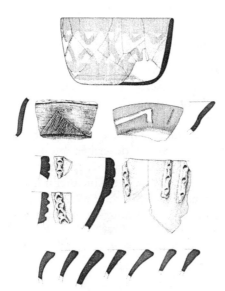

Figure 4.3. Patlachique ceramics. Upper two rows serving wares (top
is red-on-natural), third row matte censers, bottom row olla rims.
After Blucher (1983).

particular kinds of objects. Otherwise nothing is known about organization of production or mechanisms of distribution and consumption. Even less is known about production, distribution, and consumption of ceramics and other materials, although some objects are so skillfully crafted and sensitively designed that they must have been made by experienced and unusually talented artisans.

Elsewhere in the Basin of Mexico

Sanders et al. (1979: 98–105) see a four-tier settlement hierarchy during the Patlachique phase, with six principal spatial groups in the Basin, separated by zones of sparse occupation, probably buffer zones between hostile polities, a notion that seems inconsistent with the idea that, between them, Cuicuilco and Teotihuacan firmly controlled most of the Basin at this time. Yet the 13 other regional centers they identified in their surveys are so much smaller that "they must almost certainly have been to some extent subordinate to" Cuicuilco and Teotihuacan (Sanders et al. 1979: 102). They estimate that the Chalco, Ixtapalapa, and Texcoco clusters each had around 15,000 people. The southeastern Basin continued to be a major demographic focus, but there were also new foci in the Teotihuacan Valley and the Texcoco region.

Teotihuacan's More Distant Interactions

Robert Smith (1987: 26–29) found two Maya-style waxy ware sherds below the Sun Pyramid, in a layer described as 80 cm below the pyramid and above *tepetate* subsoil (Smith 1987: 4), which Smith thought likely dated to the Patlachique phase. Maya ceramics are drastically different from Central Mexican ceramics. These sherds are imports from somewhere in the Maya Lowlands. Smith describes one as "a bowl or dish with red slip and very much in the Chicanel tradition," while the other is a bowl, "which may also belong to the Chicanel horizon, but ... has more of a Mamomlike appearance" (Smith 1987: 29). Maya ceramics were already reaching Teotihuacan, although not in large numbers and possibly by way of intermediaries.

5   Teotihuacan Supremacy in the Basin of Mexico: 1–100 CE

During the Tzacualli ceramic phase (ca. 1–100 CE), the city of Teotihuacan continued its rapid growth. It expanded to cover about twenty square kilometers. I estimate its population by the end of this phase as perhaps around 60,000 to 80,000 – that is, three to four times the population at the end of the Patlachique phase. In absolute numbers, this is an increase of somewhere between 40,000 and 60,000 persons. But because the starting population was so much larger than at the onset of the Patlachique phase, it represents a considerable slowing of the growth rate. It had averaged at least 1.5 percent per year but now averaged not more than 0.9 percent. Probably much of the increase continued to be due to migration, since this is the time when population appears to have declined markedly elsewhere in the Basin of Mexico. Sanders et al. (1979: 105–108) found a dramatic decrease outside the city in this period, although probably not as great as the 80 to 90 percent once thought (Sanders, personal communication 2006; Parsons 2008). However, Tzacualli ceramics are derived from those of the Patlachique complex and do not differ enough to suggest any sizable influx from far outside the Basin.

The areas of highest sherd density in the city (Figure 5.1) remained in the northwest, although density decreased on the slopes of Cerros Colorado and Malinalco and increased in the zone centered on sectors N5W2 and N4W2, which expanded somewhat to the west and north to include sector N6W3. Density was only moderate along most of the northern Avenue of the Dead (possibly many of the sherds in this area were incorporated in the fill of the Sun Pyramid). There is a small density peak in the area of the later Ciudadela complex, where there are remains of pre-Ciudadela structures that were completely razed when the Ciudadela was built. Farther to the south and east, light to moderate Tzacualli sherd cover extends over most of the entire area of the later city. The scale of the great pyramids suggests powerful and highly centralized authority. During this period, Teotihuacan almost surely came

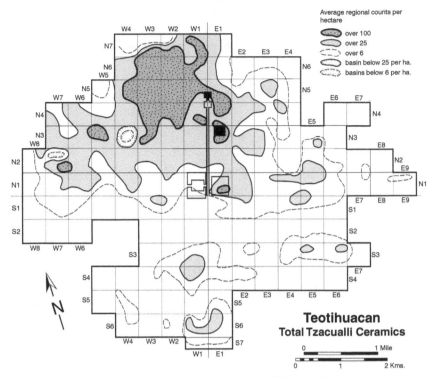

Figure 5.1. A smoothed contour map of Tzacualli phase sherd densities per hectare collected by the TMP.

By S. Vaughn after original by author & W. Powell.

to dominate the Basin of Mexico politically as well as demographically, and its rule may have reached farther.

The Sun Pyramid

Everything else at Teotihuacan, as well as at Cuicuilco and everywhere else in Central Mexico, was dwarfed by the Sun Pyramid, where small, earlier structures were superseded in a single prodigious effort by a great stepped pyramid that reached nearly its present height of about 63 m and basal dimensions of 216 m (later enlarged to 222.7 m) (Sugiyama 2005: 47), with a volume of about 1,175,000 cubic meters (Millon et al. 1965: 12) (Figure 5.2). While there was probably no single epicenter for Patlachique phase Teotihuacan, the Sun Pyramid and its immediate neighborhood were now unmistakably the epicenter. The Sun Pyramid was among the first Teotihuacan structures to be covered by Teotihuacan concrete. Few other structures built anywhere or at any

Figure 5.2. The Sun Pyramid.
Photo by author.

time in Mesoamerica exceeded or even approached it in size. The great pyramid of Cholula eventually became larger, but it was enlarged in a long series of stages, many of them post-Teotihuacan.

Box 5.1 Teotihuacan Concrete and Plaster

"Teotihuacan concrete" is composed of earth mixed with volcanic scoria crushed to the size of fine gravel (*cascajo*), and sand or other additives. Over time, this "concrete" tended to replace compacted earth as the surfacing for Teotihuacan structures. It appears in Tzacualli times in the civic-ceremonial core: on the Sun Pyramid, and on pre-Ciudadela structures. Later, it came into use for the majority of residential structures. Barba and Frunz (1999) estimate that eventually at least 12 million square meters of surfaces at Teotihuacan were covered by a thin layer of lime plaster over concrete. Lime for plaster is made by burning limestone, mostly calcium carbonate ($CaCO_3$), to drive off the carbon and produce quicklime, calcium oxide (CaO), a pasty material

(*continued*)

Box 5.1 (*continued*)

that reacts violently with water to generate considerable heat and form calcium hydroxide ($Ca(OH)_2$) that can be mixed with sand and gravel and solidifies, acquiring carbon from the surrounding air and returning to calcium carbonate. (This offers a tantalizing chance to date structures by radiocarbon, if contamination and other problems can be overcome.) In the Maya lowlands, where limestone is ubiquitous and fuel was abundant (at least early on), lime plasters and mortars had already been in use for some time. Teotihuacanos faced two problems. One is that suitable fuel was probably not abundant nearby; the other is that the nearest significant limestone deposits were 30–40 km to the northwest in the Zumpango region. Compositional studies by Barba et al. (2009) have established that lime for the plaster surface of the Xolalpan phase courtyard floor in the Teopancazco compound came from the Tula area, but more work is needed to see if other sources were used in different structures and/or at different times. Lime was hard to obtain until Teotihuacanos became wealthy enough to pay for it or, more likely, gained political control over one or more of the source regions and could demand quicklime as tribute. It would have made good sense to burn the limestone in the area where it was quarried, because quicklime is considerably less bulky than limestone, and because this would have left vegetation in the Teotihuacan Valley available for other uses.

Today, the Sun Pyramid has five levels or "bodies," each consisting of a sloping surface (*talud*) that ends in a horizontal terrace, so the overall effect is stepped. This is the result of faulty reconstruction by Leopoldo Batres in the early 1900s. Earlier pictures show it with only four bodies (Figure 1.3). Most smaller pyramids and platforms at Teotihuacan have "*talud-tablero*" profiles, in which a lower sloping panel (*talud*) is topped by a slightly overhanging recessed vertical panel (*tablero*).

Box 5.2 *Talud-Tablero* **Construction**

This is a style of construction in which long, low, rectangular panels (*tableros*) are set atop sloping aprons (*taludes*) (Figures 5.3 and 5.4). The style occurs earlier in Puebla-Tlaxcala, and it occurs elsewhere in Mesoamerica. At Teotihuacan, the *tableros* usually have projecting moldings on all four sides, giving the central part of the *tablero* a recessed appearance. Some Teotihuacan *tableros* lack a molding on the bottom margin, a style more typical of sites in Oaxaca.

Except at the FSP, where all its façades are composed of cut stone, the lower edges of Teotihuacan *tablero* moldings are supported by naturally tabular flagstones (*lajas*), while all other surfaces are made of Teotihuacan concrete.

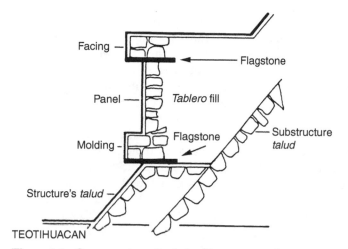

Figure 5.3. Cross section of *talud-tablero* construction. By S. Vaughn.

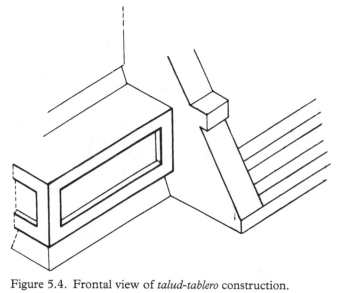

Figure 5.4. Frontal view of *talud-tablero* construction. By S. Vaughn.

The Sun Pyramid and the Moon have only *taludes*; *tableros* tall enough to have been proportional to the size of these pyramids would have been unstable. A few smaller pyramids, such as those in Group Five-Prime and those atop the outer platforms of the Ciudadela, have stepped *talud-tablero* profiles in front and only a single long *talud* in the rear.

In contrast to the south-facing Moon Pyramid, the Sun Pyramid faces west, where stairs lead to the top. An early free-standing fore-platform at the foot of the stairs (Millon et al. 1965: 25–31) may date to this time. The other three sides of the Sun Pyramid are surrounded at a distance by low platforms. These platforms, together with a plaza with smaller pyramids and room groups on the west, define a "Sun Precinct." On the south and north, the platforms are separated from the Sun Pyramid by about 30 m, and on the east by 45 m. The "House of the Priests" sits on the south platform. Little is known of it, but it was clearly an elite residence, perhaps for priests or early rulers, and it may date to this period.

Underneath the lava that underlies the Sun Pyramid, and quite distinct from the tunnels dug into the pyramid by modern archaeologists, a long and irregular tunnel ends in a four-lobed chamber (Figure 5.5) (Heyden 1975). Until recently, it was believed to be a natural cave, heavily altered by humans (e.g., Millon 1981). Given the importance of caves in Mesoamerican religions, it was thought likely to have been a sacred spot, where ancestors emerged and perhaps the very place where time itself began. But geological studies indicate that there are no natural caves at Teotihuacan (Manzanilla et al. 1994). Some other explanation is needed for the precise location of the Sun Pyramid. Nevertheless, much as Maya regarded pyramids as man-made mountains, it may be that the tunnel was created as the physical manifestation of a myth about a cave of origin.

The Sun Pyramid would have been readily visible from the flat roofs of houses everywhere in the city, and for many kilometers around. It can be seen, at least with low-power binoculars, from the hills ringing the southwestern Basin of Mexico, 50 or 60 km away. On a clear day, the viewshed atop the pyramid covers much of the Basin, although not all of it. Perhaps significantly, it does not include Popocatépetl or Ixtaccíhuatl. Sight of these volcanoes is blocked by the nearby Patlachique range of hills. Only three or four kilometers west of the Sun Pyramid, in the modern town of Maquixco Bajo, the tip of Ixtaccíhuatl is visible, so it would not have been difficult to have located the ancient city where it could have been glimpsed. Perhaps Teotihuacan was deliberately placed so as to be out of sight of the ever-threatening volcano gods. Whatever considerations determined location of the city's epicenter, connection with active volcanoes was not among them.

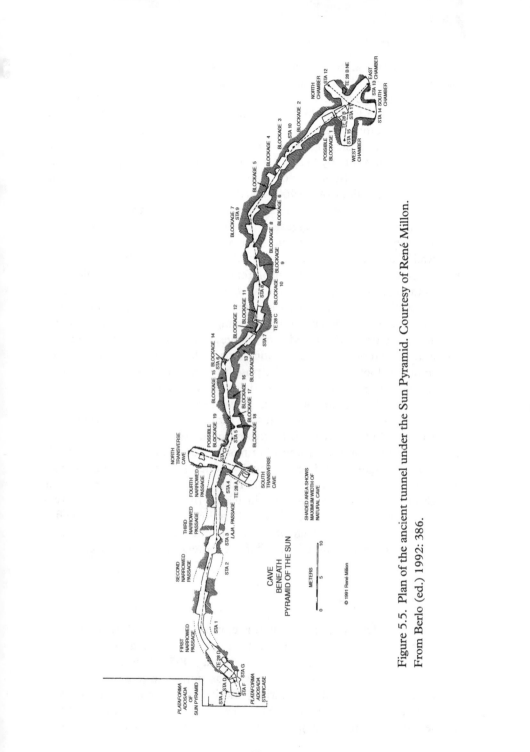

Figure 5.5. Plan of the ancient tunnel under the Sun Pyramid. Courtesy of René Millon. From Berlo (ed.) 1992: 386.

67

Minor sacrificial burials at the corners of the Sun Pyramid were sketchily reported by Batres, but no tombs have been found at the Sun Pyramid. Yet, in view of what we now know about major tombs in and atop the FSP and in the Moon Pyramid, it would be surprising if there was no great tomb within the Sun Pyramid. Millon et al. (1965: 18) saw hints of a tomb in sloping layers near ground level in the tunnel within the Sun Pyramid dug by Gamio, but recent work has found no evidence of a tomb there (N. Sugiyama et al. 2013). TMP Test Excavation 22, dug by Rattray in the floor of a 1960s INAH tunnel high up on the east side of the pyramid, came upon an apparent sloping earthen wall running east-west, which Millon suggested may have been the wall of one of a pair of temples atop the pyramid. But recent work finds no evidence of this wall (Sugiyama, personal communication, 2014). A few Aztec pyramids, notably the Templo Mayor of Tenochtitlan, have twin temples, but twin temples atop a single pyramid were not common even in Aztec times (Smith 2008: 101–103). Moreover, the square shape of the Sun Pyramid argues that it was topped by (at most) a single temple. Possibly the sloping wall found by Rattray is the edge of a huge tomb, filled in with rubble like those in the Moon Pyramid. S. Sugiyama (2005: 210) suggests another possibility: a looted major tomb, possibly royal, in the ancient tunnel underneath the Sun Pyramid. If so, the looters must have been very thorough, or INAH explorations would have recognized something special there. No sign of such a tomb in this tunnel was noted by subsequent excavations (Millon 1981; N. Sugiyama et al. 2013). These possibilities need further exploration. Tomb offerings, besides being spectacular finds in their own right, would reveal much about the symbolism of the Sun Pyramid. Most recently, Alejandro Sarabia (2013) reports a large looter trench at the top of the pyramid, in which the looters left behind two large smooth greenstone stelae, one 2.56 m long, fragments of a stone figure of an unknown personage 58 cm high, and smaller objects, including marine shells. There is no telling what the looters may have carried away.

The Moon Pyramid

At the Moon Pyramid, Stage One was completely covered by Stage Two, a pyramid 29.3 m east-west at its base and probably about the same length north-south (Sugiyama and Cabrera 2007). This was a considerable increase in size, but Stage Two was not as large as some of the Cuicuilco pyramids had been earlier, and it was far smaller than the Sun Pyramid. Ceramics in the fill of Stage Two indicate a probable Tzacualli phase date, although it is just possible that it was built in the ensuing

Miccaotli phase. Available radiocarbon dates are too inconsistent to be of much help. Stage Three is a modest further enlargement that probably also pertains to this period. Stage Four, discussed in the next chapter, may have been built at the very end of this period.

The Pre-Ciudadela

Excavations by Julie Gazzola and Sergio Gómez since 2002 have revealed remains of several large civic-ceremonial structures with rectangular layouts underlying three superposed concrete floors in the great plaza area of the later Ciudadela complex (Figure 1.6/1) (Gazzola 2012). These structures probably originated in the Tzacualli phase, although their later stages may date to early in the Miccaotli phase. Most of their walls and floors were faced with Teotihuacan concrete. It is unlikely that any ordinary Teotihuacan residences used concrete at this time. Lime for making concrete and plaster was probably still a costly material in short supply, yet some elements of Teotihuacan society had access to it. Some walls show traces of mural paintings with abstract designs using red, orange, yellow, green, and black pigments. Finds from these pre-Ciudadela structures include materials from distant regions, including greenstones, cinnabar, marine shells, Thin Orange Ware from southern Puebla, Granular Ware from Guerrero, and fine paste wares from Oaxaca and the Gulf Lowlands. Whether Teotihuacan already politically controlled any of the source areas or obtained these materials by exchange, the Teotihuacan elite were able to obtain materials from a few hundred kilometers away.

The walls of pre-Ciudadela structures are oriented about 11 degrees east of true north, like Stage One of the Moon Pyramid, built in the previous period. However, these pre-Ciudadela structures, to judge by the associated ceramics, more likely are coeval with Stages 2 and 3 of the Moon Pyramid and with the Sun Pyramid, where the canonical 15.5 degrees east of north was already in use.

We have no data on upper parts of these structures, because they were thoroughly razed when the Ciudadela itself was built. They were not an early phase of the Ciudadela, but were something quite different. However, their sizes, as well as the quality of materials and workmanship, show that they were the locus of important activities.

Further evidence about demolished pre-Ciudadela structures is provided by 46 large conical ground stone objects found dispersed in the fill of the FSP (Figure 5.6). They vary from 16 to 31 cm in length and from 15 to 18 cm in diameter. Nothing quite like them has been found anywhere else at Teotihuacan. Sugiyama (2005: 163–65) acknowledges

Figure 5.6. A large tenoned stone cone in fill of the Feathered Serpent Pyramid.
Courtesy of Saburo Sugiyama.

that they may have been architectural elements but thinks it more likely that they were the tips of hafted digging tools. But they seem extraordinarily unsuitable for digging implements, in their shape, dimensions, and raw material, which is the somewhat friable andesitic stone often used for sculptures and cut stone in Teotihuacan structures, rather than the denser and tougher basaltic stone used for grinding and other tools. It is implausible that a unique kind of digging implement was used in large numbers, only at this location. It is far more likely that they were decorative elements in a pre-Ciudadela structure. They are unique, but the Ciudadela itself is unique, so it would not be surprising if its predecessor was also unlike anything else at Teotihuacan.

Sergio Gómez is exploring an ancient tunnel that runs underneath the FSP, containing fragments of a stone frieze that belonged to the pre-Ciudadela structures. One shows a rattlesnake tail with rattles. Evidently the place was already related to the Feathered Serpent.

The large amount of Tzacualli ceramics found in surface collections and in the fill of later structures in the area of the Ciudadela complex adds to the evidence of a sizable Tzacualli phase occupation in this district. However, it is a southeastern extension of the contiguous zone of substantial Tzacualli sherd cover, although moderate densities of Tzacualli sherds spread throughout the southern part of the city. Another case in Mesoamerica of a major civic-ceremonial complex outside a city rather than within it is at Late Postclassic Tlaxcallan, which Lane Fargher et al. (2011) suspect was a republic rather than a kingdom. Still another, also Late Postclassic, is at Calixtlahuaca, in the Toluca Valley (Figure 1.4/11) (Smith et al. 2009).

One implication of something special, but unlike the Ciudadela, existing in this locality in Tzacualli times, is that the Ciudadela was not foreseen when the Sun and Moon Pyramids were built. I think the layout of the civic-ceremonial core of Teotihuacan evolved over time, *contra* Sugiyama's (2005) argument that a coherent master plan for the entire layout of the core was conceived from its beginning. The findings of Gazzola and Gómez do not suggest that the Ciudadela in its present form was already part of an early plan. Sugiyama (2013) now acknowledges the present layout probably came into being around 200 CE and early Teotihuacan was quite different.

Other Civic-Ceremonial Structures

Tzacualli ceramics are sparse on the surface of the Great Compound, just west of the Ciudadela. Probably that mega-complex belongs to the next period, discussed in Chapter 6. The large triadic group called Plaza One (1:N5W2), about 800 m west-northwest of the Moon Pyramid, which may have already existed in the Patlachique phase, was certainly in existence by this time. Carmen Cook de Leonard drove a tunnel into the central (northern) mound, finding 12 burials, possibly sacrificial victims, accompanied by Storm God jars of an early type (Figure 5.7). In 1957 and 1959 Millon found a long architectural sequence on the south transverse platform of this group (Millon and Bennyhoff 1961; Millon et al. 1965). Layers at least as early as Tzacualli and as late as Aztec were found. Several caches contained fine vessels, including a gorgeous resist-decorated vase (Figure 5.8). Some smaller pyramid groups in the northwestern part of the city also appear to have begun at least this early. The northern part of the Avenue of the Dead may have existed, represented by pyramids and platforms – earlier versions of those we now see – but excavations are required to confirm this and tell us their size, number, and stylistic features. Both the Sun Pyramid and the second stage of the Moon Pyramid had the distinctive 15.5 degrees east of astronomic north orientation that became canonical at Teotihuacan. The meaning of this orientation is controversial but it was probably of cosmological significance.

Figure 5.7. Early types of Storm God jars, from Plaza One (left) and the Moon Pyramid (right).

After Bracamontes (2001).

Figure 5.8. A Tzacualli resist-decorated vase, from Plaza One, with the "ojo de ave" motif.

©American Philosophical Society, permission of René Millon.

Ceramics and Lithic Artifacts

Some earlier writers believed that ceramics of the Tzacualli complex differed enough from their predecessors to imply strong outside influences, perhaps migrations, but Bennyhoff (1967) pointed out that they are a local development from the Patlachique complex. He also saw enough continuity between Tzacualli and the subsequent Miccaotli complex to suggest primarily local development. Nothing we have learned since then challenges Bennyhoff's opinion. Supports, present in some Patlachique serving wares, are absent in the Tzacualli complex. Serving wares are sometimes monochrome red, but often have polychrome decoration in soft glowing colors that include resist decoration (Figure 5.9). Reds are less brilliant than later, and specular red (slip to which tiny, shiny, hematite particles have been added) is rare or absent. Motifs are abstract but tend to be more curvilinear than those of Patlachique. Another decorative style consists of motifs in a viscous and somewhat fugitive white paint over a solid red slip. Serving ware forms include *cazuelas* (a type of cooking pot) and round-bottomed shouldered bowls, often with broad encircling channels between shoulder and lip, a development from earlier Patlachique and Cuicuilco forms (Figure 5.9). Flat-bottomed outcurving bowls, so typical of later periods at Teotihuacan, may begin to appear. Tall vases, very different from the later direct-rim cylinder vases, are another typical shape, decorated in resist polychrome or White-on-red. In contrast to Patlachique pastes, those of Tzacualli are usually a distinctive reddish brown with yellowish or whitish inclusions (Hopkins 1995). This composition extends into Miccaotli and even into some Early Tlamimilolpa vessels.

Storm God jars (Figure 5.7) (Bracamontes 2001) foreshadow later forms but have clay fillets suggestive of straps, suggesting that they are imitations (skeuomorphs) of vessels made of other materials (gourds?) tied with some kind of cordage. This is another sign that the Storm God has deep pre-Teotihuacan roots and that later Teotihuacanos (probably elites) significantly reinterpreted him. A ceramic cup with Storm God attributes found at the Sun Pyramid (Millon et al. 1965) is an atypical variant.

The rims of utility ware ollas, like those of most Patlachique ollas, have a "wedge" shape, thicker near the lip than lower down. However, Tzacualli olla rims are more angular. Their forms grade into those more typical of the ensuing Miccaotli complex. Coarse Ware censer vessels foreshadow those of later times but lack elaborate "theater" ornamentation. Warren Barbour (1976) describes handmade ceramic figurines.

There were probably more obsidian workshops than before, and more specialization in different kinds of obsidian implements (Spence 1984, 1987), but little can be said with any confidence about the organization of production, distribution, and consumption.

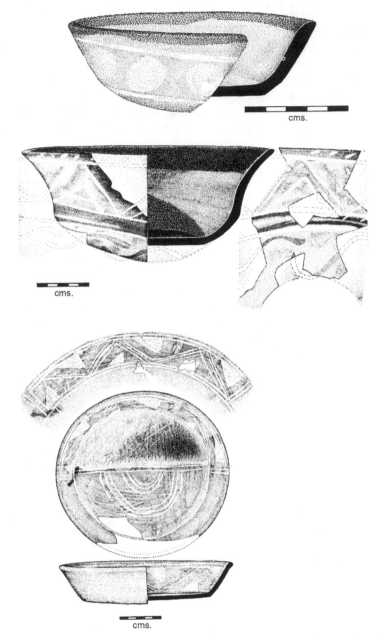

Figure 5.9. Tzacualli phase ceramics, including polychrome bowls, one is shouldered.

©American Philosophical Society, permission of René Millon.

The Early Teotihuacan Polity

Possibly, Teotihuacan began as a republic, run by a governing council, perhaps with representatives from the several districts of the Patlachique city. If so, republican institutions were likely subverted by strong and ambitious rulers who were responsible for the immense pyramids and other ambitious buildings of the Tzacualli and Miccaotli phases. It is tempting to compare it with the takeover of republican Rome and creation of an empire by Augustus, but the analogy may not be very close.

Where did the rulers of Teotihuacan live at this time, or the high priests who must have been associated with the massive Sun Pyramid, who may have in fact been the rulers? For a while it was thought that the Xalla complex, a configuration of pyramids, platforms, and large courtyards unlike any other structure at Teotihuacan, covering about four hectares and about 160 m north of the Sun Pyramid precinct (Figures 1.6/4 and 6.2/7), might have been an early royal palace. However, excavations by Linda Manzanilla and Leonardo López Luján (López Luján et al. 2006) discovered that its earliest construction stage dates to the next period. It is also unlikely that the residential complex known as the "Palace of the Sun" was begun this early. One other candidate is the "House of the Priests" (2:N3E1) (Figure 6.2/10), atop the southwestern end of the great platform that bounds the Sun Pyramid precinct. The House of the Priests was dug in the early 1900s by Batres, and I know of no materials suitable for dating. However, a large archaeological cut through the south platform surrounding the Sun precinct reveals its adobe construction and Tzacualli-phase ceramics. The House of the Priests faces south, away from the Sun Pyramid, toward an unusually large sunken court that is unlike any other feature at Teotihuacan (25:N3E1). Perhaps the House of the Priests is not a strong candidate for a royal palace, but it deserves testing by modern excavation techniques. Finally, we cannot rule out the Pre-Ciudadela complex, although its distance from the Sun Pyramid suggests that it housed a hierarchy distinct from that at the Sun Pyramid.

The area covered by substantial quantities of Tzacualli phase ceramics implies that there must already have been thousands of residential structures for commoners, perhaps much like those known from Tetimpa, in Puebla (Figure 5.10) (Uruñuela and Plunket 2007), although probably more closely spaced and more compact. Apparently many farmers lived in the city and continued to do so throughout Teotihuacan's history.

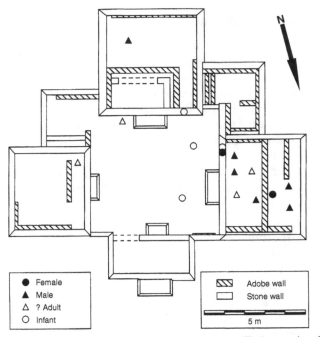

● Female		▨ Adobe wall	
▲ Male		▢ Stone wall	
△ ? Adult			
○ Infant		5 m	

Figure 5.10. Plan of a residential unit at Tetimpa, in the state of Puebla.
After Plunket and Uruñuela (2002).

Elsewhere in the Basin of Mexico

Cuicuilco was apparently not yet covered by volcanic ash or lava but was abandoned or nearly abandoned. Sanders et al. (1979: 105–108) estimated that 80–90 percent of the entire population of the Basin was now concentrated in Teotihuacan. But Parsons (2008) now thinks that the shift in population was less drastic, especially in the northern and western Basin, where the lakes made bulk transport by water feasible for much of the distance to Teotihuacan. Nevertheless, there is little doubt that population in most of the Basin declined, and this seems especially true of the southeastern Basin. A sizable rural population within 35 km of Teotihuacan could have provided much of the food and other staples for the city, and the relative neglect of the southern Basin seems reasonable. Nevertheless, from a purely utilitarian point of view, the concentration of population in the city does not seem optimal. Most of the residents must have been farmers, going outside the city to practice intensive wetland and canal irrigated agriculture in the lower Teotihuacan Valley and also using less productive lands nearby.

People may have been drawn to Teotihuacan partly by the attraction of its religious significance and possibly even by the appeal of an urban center, but probably a strong coercive element was also involved. Perhaps techniques and practices of statecraft were not well enough developed to permit firm control of sizable populations outside the capital city. It may have been hard to control subordinate elites not living close enough to be in almost daily contact with the heads of the polity. Also, although the amount of labor required for building the Sun Pyramid must have been immense (Tatsuya Murakami [2010: 490–91] estimates that it would have required nearly 12 million person-days), given the population of the city and assuming 50 years for its construction, the per capita burden per year would have been modest, something like fifteen days per year from each able-bodied adult male. People probably spent more time in rituals and festivals: creating costumes and learning, performing, and witnessing them; activities that leave few material traces.

Yet, assembling the labor force for building the Sun Pyramid could have been one reason for the continued growth of Teotihuacan. Subjecting people to the experience of sharing supervised labor on such a project could have been a means of altering consciousnesses to create a populace more amenable to being subordinated by a small elite. Such a strategy has been proposed for the pyramid-building projects of early Egypt. This, plus the labor involved in subsequent projects of civic-ceremonial building at Teotihuacan, would help explain the continuing concentration of population.

Teotihuacan's Foreign Interactions

The Basin of Mexico lacks fine clays, and Teotihuacanos tended more toward importing ceramics from other regions, rather than exporting them. Teotihuacan serving wares of this period are attractive, but not markedly more so than those being produced elsewhere in Mesoamerica. Rare and fine ceramic objects would have been exchanged as elite gifts, while larger quantities of less fine ceramics were more likely traded for other goods or demanded as tribute. Thin Orange Ware was already being imported in small proportions from southern Puebla (Rattray 1990b), and Granular Ware was arriving from Guerrero (Reyna Robles and Schmidt Schoenberg 2004). Sarah Clayton's (2005) NAA study of Maya-style sherds from TMP collections includes eleven sherds of Late Preclassic Maya types. Most were found in districts considerably east of the Patlachique phase settlement, and probably belong to this later period. Conceivably, they reached Teotihuacan through intermediaries, but more likely they reflect direct interactions between Teotihuacanos and Mayas. Another twenty to thirty Late Preclassic Maya sherds not available to Clayton will be discussed in a volume by Evelyn Rattray on foreign wares at Teotihuacan. I know of no evidence of Teotihuacan influences this early in the Maya area.

Outside the Basin, Tzacualli-like wedge rim ollas appear at many sites in eastern Morelos, and much less frequently at sites in western Morelos (Hirth and Angulo 1981). The fact that this is a utilitarian type of vessel, usually undecorated, suggests a migration rather than local emulation of anything prestigious. Nevertheless, Morelos was probably not under Teotihuacan political control at this time. Hirth (1978) interprets the settlement pattern in eastern Morelos as suggesting two autonomous chiefdoms, one with its head settlement in the north of the Amatzinac Valley and one, whose largest settlement was San Ignacio, in the south. Neither head settlement covered more than thirty to forty hectares. In western Morelos, where there is little evidence of Teotihuacan connections at this time, the site of Coatlán del Río grew to some hundred hectares, apparently the capital of a sizable independent regional polity.

6 Great Pyramids and Early Grandeur: 100–250 CE

This interval spans the Miccaotli and Early Tlamimilolpa ceramic phases, whose ceramics do not differ drastically from one another. Plainwares derive from those of the Tzacualli phase, while serving and ceremonial wares show some innovations. The city did not increase in area. Settlement withdrew from the slopes of Cerros Malinalco and Colorado in the northwest (Figure 6.1), while sherd densities increased in the eastern and southern parts of the city, and in and around sector N6W3, in what was now the far northwest of the city. The population of the city probably did not increase much, perhaps because of problems in provisioning a larger settlement. I estimate that it was around 80,000 to 100,000.

The rapid pace of civic-ceremonial construction continued or even accelerated. There was a vast program of civic-ceremonial building on an unprecedented scale – the great enlargement of the Moon Pyramid, razing of the pre-Ciudadela and putting something different in its place, the Five-Prime group (and presumably its unexcavated twin, Group Five), the Great Compound, the Xalla complex, and probably the Avenue of the Dead Complex. During this interval, the material form of the civic-ceremonial core assumed the basic configuration that it has had ever since, although in later times there were some significant modifications (Figure 6.2). It is hard to convey in words and pictures the scale of this central district, and it seems only the experience of actually being there can do this. But some comparisons may help. Along the Avenue of the Dead, from the top of the Moon Pyramid to the southern edge of the Ciudadela, the north-south distance is 2.15 km. This is just short of the distance from the dome of the capitol building in Washington to the Washington Monument, and a little more than three-fifths of the distance from the capitol dome to the foot of the Lincoln Memorial. It is not quite half the length of Central Park in New York City. It is about the distance in Mexico City from the Palacio Nacional to the Paseo de la Reforma. It is the distance (air line) in London from Trafalgar Square to St. Paul's

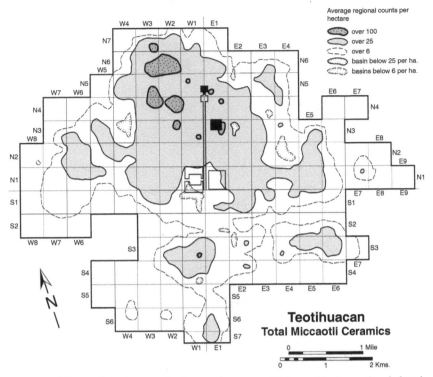

Figure 6.1. A smoothed contour map of Miccaotli phase sherd densities per hectare collected by the TMP.

By S. Vaughn after original by author & W. Powell.

Cathedral. Platforms and pyramid groups occupy a zone that extends 100 to 500 m on either side of the Avenue of the Dead, from the Moon Pyramid to Ciudadela. The total area of this civic-ceremonial core is about 150 ha (1.5 square km). The Avenue of the Dead is traceable for another 3.2 km to the south, although civic-ceremonial structures are sparse and widely spaced along this southern extension.

Elsewhere in Mesoamerica, the main plaza of Monte Albán was about 0.28 km long (0.6 km from the rear of the northernmost main plaza structure to the rear of the southernmost) (Blanton et al. 1993: 85). Most major structures at the more dispersed lowland Maya city of Tikal (Figure 1.2/27) are within a zone about 1.3 km wide in both directions (Blanton et al. 1993: 178).

The Sun Pyramid, already immense, was somewhat enlarged and reached its ultimate height early in this period. Its fore-platform was greatly enlarged in at least two stages that had cut stone facings and two

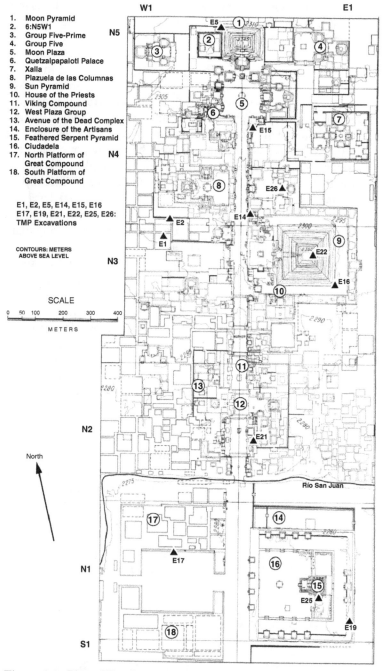

1. Moon Pyramid
2. 6:N5W1
3. Group Five-Prime
4. Group Five
5. Moon Plaza
6. Quetzalpapalotl Palace
7. Xalla
8. Plazuela de las Columnas
9. Sun Pyramid
10. House of the Priests
11. Viking Compound
12. West Plaza Group
13. Avenue of the Dead Complex
14. Enclosure of the Artisans
15. Feathered Serpent Pyramid
16. Ciudadela
17. North Platform of
    Great Compound
18. South Platform of
    Great Compound

E1, E2, E5, E14, E15, E16
E17, E19, E21, E22, E25, E26:
TMP Excavations

CONTOURS: METERS
ABOVE SEA LEVEL

SCALE

0   50 100   200   300   400

METERS

North

Figure 6.2. Plan of Teotihuacan's civic-ceremonial core.
After Millon (1973).

or more rooms. Unpublished excavations by Eduardo Matos in the 1990s revealed that the earlier stage included white and orange-red murals with geometric motifs, including a checkerboard pattern (personal observation). This color scheme, with motifs probably representing transverse cuts through conch shells, also appears in early murals in the Ciudadela palaces and in an early stage of the "Ward Temple" in the La Ventilla district (Cabrera and Gómez 2008). Batres incorrectly reconstructed the fore-platform at an angle to the main pyramid, about 23 degrees north of true west, but its actual orientation is the same as that of the main pyramid. Whatever additional reasons there may have been for its construction, one consequence is that it provided a place for activities easily visible from the sizable plaza in front of the pyramid. The top of the pyramid itself is so high that anything carried out at that level would have been hard to see from the plaza. At least in later times, however, the plaza itself was separated from the Avenue of the Dead by a long platform several meters high, with stairways lining both sides that gave access from the Avenue. Within the Sun Plaza are smaller pyramids and room complexes, including the "Palace of the Sun." Many fallen stone sculptures, of uncertain date, have been found in the Sun Plaza. These include felines, human skulls, and other motifs, some probably representing period-ending fire ceremonies (Fash et al. 2009). Most pertain to the fore-platform, which must have used cut stone to an extent second only to the FSP.

Stage Four enlarged the previously modest Moon Pyramid to cover about nine times its former area, which means that its volume was increased about twenty-sevenfold, probably at the very beginning of this period, not long after construction of the Sun Pyramid. Probably a little later, the great Ciudadela complex, including the FSP, was built, as were a pair of huge low platforms (the Great Compound) enclosing a large plaza that was possibly a marketplace, just across the Avenue of the Dead from the Ciudadela. Numerous other pyramid complexes were built (including the Group Five triadic group east of the Moon Pyramid and its western counterpart, Group Five-Prime). Previous pyramid groups, such as Plaza One, were enlarged. The Avenue of the Dead Complex, which I formerly thought was built somewhat later (Cowgill 1983, 2007) was probably constructed in this period, although in later times floors in its courtyards were considerably raised and other alterations were made.

The Moon Pyramid

Sugiyama (Sugiyama and López Luján 2007) argues that Stage Four of the Moon Pyramid was contemporary with the FSP, but the ceramics in its fill suggest it was somewhat earlier. Stage Four was about 89×89 m

Table 6.1. Construction stages and tombs at the Moon Pyramid

Stage	Tombs	Likely phase	Date	Comments
First		Patlachique	100–1 BCE	Before Sun Pyramid
Second		Tzacualli	1–100 CE	
Third		Tzacualli	1–100 CE	
Fourth	Two and Six	Terminal Tzacualli or Early Miccaotli	80–150 CE	After Sun Pyramid
Fifth	Three	Miccaotli	100–200 CE	Roughly coeval w/ FSP?
Sixth	Four & Five	Early Tlamimilolpa	170–250 CE	Coeval w/Altun Ha cache?
Seventh		?	ca. 400 CE	
Seven-A		Xolalpan (Early?)	350–550 CE	

at the base (Sugiyama and Cabrera 2007). Its orientation was close to the Teotihuacan standard. Construction stages of the Moon Pyramid are numbered from earliest to latest, but tombs are numbered in the order in which they were discovered, which can be confusing. Table 6.1 should help the reader keep track of which tombs were associated with which construction stage. This table represents my opinions about ceramic phases and absolute dates, based on tabulations of ceramics in the construction fill by Pedro Baños and Zeferino Ortega, my observations on tomb contents and many sherd lots in construction fill, and study of the obsidian by William Parry and Shigeru Kabata (2004). They differ somewhat from those of Sugiyama and López Luján (2006).

Stage Four was covered by plaster-coated concrete. It made the Moon Pyramid the second largest pyramid in Teotihuacan, although the Ciudadela has a greater total volume of construction material. A chamber (Tomb 2) at ground level within Stage Four was completely filled with earth and rocks (as were all the burials at the Moon Pyramid and the FSP). It contained remains of one bound human victim, two pumas, one wolf, nine eagles, three rattlesnakes, and incomplete remains of other animals. The only ceramics were eight Storm God jars. They are in an early style, very similar to the Tzacualli examples found in Plaza One (Figure 5.7). Other offerings included a tableau with an upright greenstone female statuette 31 cm high (Figure 6.3a), unusual for Teotihuacan in showing breasts and genitalia. She stands on a rosette of large bipointed, bifacial obsidian knives. Nearby, a slightly smaller recumbent greenstone figure, lacking sexual attributes, but probably representing a male, lies on another rosette (Figure 6.3b). Teotihuacan

Figure 6.3. Greenstone statuettes from the Moon Pyramid, Stage 4, Tomb 2. (a) standing female, (b) recumbent male.
Courtesy of Saburo Sugiyama.

imagery rarely shows or suggests genitalia, even in nude figures. This recumbent figure may have been deposited standing and may have fallen over subsequently, but the fact that its hands are cupped so that they could have served as containers only if the figure was horizontal, a feature found on some other Teotihuacan stone statuettes (López Luján et al. 2006), suggests that it was intentionally laid flat. The tableau was perhaps a dominant female figure standing over a male, whose subordination is indicated by his recumbent position and smaller size. Another possibility, less likely, is that he is her child. The identities of these figures are mysterious. The female shares none of the attributes of the proposed "Great Goddess" of Teotihuacan, and I cannot relate either figure to any other entities in Teotihuacan imagery except some of the stone statuettes illustrated by López Luján et al. (2006). The tableau indicates a high status in early Teotihuacan thought for some female entities.

Tomb 6 is a large pit about half way to the top of Stage Four, apparently created very soon after Tomb 2, which it resembles in many ways (Figure 6.4). It contained 12 human victims. Ten were without

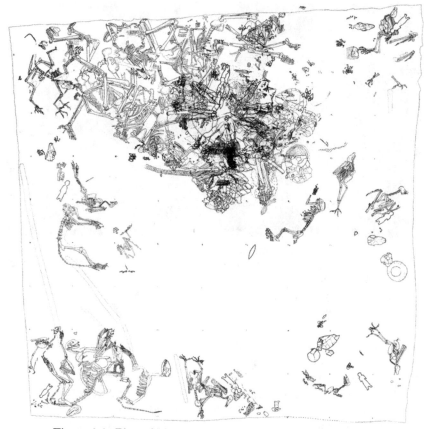

Figure 6.4. Plan of Moon Pyramid, Stage 4, Tomb 6.
Courtesy of Saburo Sugiyama.

ornaments or offerings and had been bound and decapitated. Their skulls and first cervical vertebrae were lacking. Apparently they had been killed on the spot, then tossed haphazardly into the north side of the pit. Two other humans were also bound, but not decapitated. They were richly attired and one had a collar of imitation human maxillae (upper jawbones) made of worked marine shells (also found in Tomb 2), much like those worn by a number of the victims at the FSP in the Ciudadela. Other offerings in Tomb 6 included a unique greenstone mosaic figure and nine pairs of very large obsidian objects, 34 to 53 cm in length. Nine is a number of wide significance in Mesoamerica. One member of each pair is a feathered serpent (Figure 6.5a). The other is

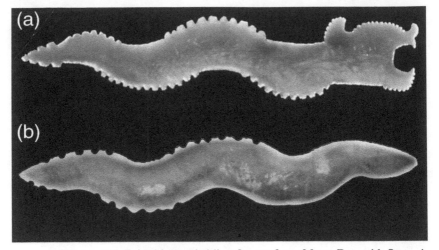

Figure 6.5. Paired large obsidian figures from Moon Pyramid, Stage 4, Tomb 6. (a) Feathered Serpent, (b) possible lightning bolt. Each about 40–50 cm long.

Courtesy of Saburo Sugiyama.

bipointed and undulating (Figure 6.5b). It is probably the lightning staff carried by the Storm God in many murals, and in some later Storm God jars. It is tempting to conjecture that the Storm God (who would be difficult to represent in obsidian except by some associated attribute such as his lightning staff) and the Feathered Serpent are represented here as joint heads of the Teotihuacan pantheon. Sacrificed animals in Tomb 6 include eagles, felids, and canids. Ceramics were scarce except for seven Storm God jars, very similar to those in Tomb 2. All are quite different from Storm God jars of the type found in Burial 14 at the FSP (Figure 6.6). This difference suggests a time difference.

Nearly 20 percent of the ceramics in the fill of Stage Five of the Moon Pyramid were identified as Miccaotli; only a handful may be Early Tlamimilolpa (Sugiyama and Cabrera 2007). This suggests to me that Stage Five was probably built at about the same time as the FSP. The analysis of obsidian by Parry and Kabata (2004) also suggests this. The east-west dimensions of the Moon Pyramid were unchanged, but the north (rear) face was extended so the pyramid now measured more than 104 m north-south. The front face was cut back so as to provide a large projecting fore-platform, atop the earlier pyramids of Stages One to Three, analogous to the smaller fore-platform at the Sun Pyramid. Both the Moon and Sun Pyramids face sizable plazas. All this implies

0   5   10 cm

Figure 6.6. A Storm God jar of the type found in Grave 14 of the FSP.
Photo by author.

an interest in producing spectacles that could readily be viewed by large
audiences, in addition to whatever more esoteric rites may have been
carried out atop the pyramids.

Tomb 3 is associated with Stage Five. It is a large pit at ground level
under the rear face of Stage Five. It contained four sacrificed men, as
well as rich offerings that included heads of 18 animals and two small
greenstone figurines seated in cross-legged "tailor" style and wearing
tau-shaped headdresses similar to those found on some standing greenstone figurines in offerings at the FSP (Figure 6.7). The simplicity of the
headdresses and absence of anything like them in Teotihuacan paintings
suggests they were only tenons for headdresses of perishable materials.

Stage Six also substantially enlarged the Moon Pyramid and brought
it close to its present size. East-west and north-south archaeological
tunnels atop Stage Five found a well-preserved concrete floor, but no
sign of any masonry structures atop it. A pit dug into the center of this
upper floor, never resealed and apparently made as the initial step in
the construction of Stage Six, contained Tomb 5. Tomb 5 contained
the remains of three high-status individuals seated in cross-legged tailor position. This position has not been observed in other Teotihuacan

Figure 6.7. Small greenstone figures from Moon Pyramid, Stage 5, Tomb 3.
Courtesy of Saburo Sugiyama.

burials but is known from elsewhere in Mesoamerica, notably among sacrificial victims in some of the burials in Teotihuacan-style Pyramids A and B at Kaminaljuyú in Guatemala (Figure 1.2/25, Kidder et al. 1946). The posture is also seen in a greenstone figure in Tomb 5 and in the two small greenstone figures in Tomb 3 of Stage Five. Objects indicating a Maya connection in Tomb 5 include two greenstone or jade pectorals in Maya style. Ceramics in the fill of Stage Six date it to the Early Tlamimilolpa phase. Stage Six is probably a little later than the FSP, but, according to the chronology I have adopted for this book, it is unlikely that Tomb 5 was any later than 250 CE. Parry and Kabata (2004) link the obsidian in Stage Six to that found in a cache at Altun Ha in the Maya lowlands (Figure 1.2/26). All this indicates significant interaction between the Maya and Teotihuacan long before the events recorded on stelae at Tikal (Figure 1.2/27) and elsewhere, discussed in Chapter 7.

Stage Six also includes "Tomb" 4, at ground level at its rear. It consisted of 17 human skulls, plus one bone from another individual, with no offerings. The disrespectful treatment of these victims suggests something quite different from Tombs 2, 3, 5, and 6, although it recalls the

Figure 6.8. The Moon Pyramid in its present form.
Photo by author.

ten decapitated victims in Tomb 6.[1] Stage Seven is a minor enlargement of Stage Six, resulting in the structure that was restored in the early 1960s by INAH and is presently visible (Figure 6.8). Finally, a low platform was added to the rear of Stage Seven, apparently sometime in the Xolalpan phase, perhaps around 450 CE. A wide trench excavated by Sugiyama and Cabrera on the rear slope of the pyramid included about 6 percent Aztec ceramics, indicative of some Aztec activity.

Each of the Moon Pyramid tombs differs from the others. However, except for Tomb 4 (the 17 skulls), they share a number of features, including the presence of one to twelve human sacrificial victims (37 in all); rich offerings in obsidian, greenstone, and perishable materials; sacrificed animals of fierce species often associated with military orders (pumas, jaguars, wolves, eagles, rattlesnakes); scarcity of ceramics (except Storm God jars in Tombs 2 and 6); and the absence of any individual likely to have been a Teotihuacan ruler.

Structure 6:N5W1, just west of the Moon Pyramid and attached to Stages 6 and 7 Figure 6.2/2), consists of rooms, porticoes, patios, corridors, and low platforms, built on a three-meter-high platform that covered an earlier structure. Its central *talud-tablero* structure faces south. Great quantities of obsidian debris were found in its nucleus, and under the floor of a patio on its north side (Carballo 2007). Radiocarbon dates suggest that the last major construction stage was in the 400s, although it may have continued in use later. Higher layers included some Epiclassic ceramics of the Coyotlatelco complex. This small Epiclassic occupation immediately adjacent to the Moon Pyramid is an exception to the tendency of Epiclassic people to reside somewhat outside the old civic-ceremonial core of the city. An east-west, free-standing wall at the north edge of the 6:N5W1 complex is almost 3.5 m wide at its base. The height of most free-standing walls at Teotihuacan cannot be determined because they have so thoroughly collapsed, but TMP excavation E5 traced this wall to where it joined the northwest corner of the Moon Pyramid. Its top is five m above local ground level. Millon (1973: 39) says it dates to the Tlamimilolpa phase.

The front of the Moon Pyramid faced south in all periods, and at least in its later stages it faced directly onto a large plaza, about 135 m east-west by 175 m north-south. The Moon Plaza forms the northern climax of the Avenue of the Dead. It opens onto the Avenue without any barrier, in contrast to the platforms separating the Sun Plaza and the Ciudadela Plaza from the Avenue. The Avenue of the Dead was not a thoroughfare connecting different districts of the city. Instead it is fitted for processions culminating in the Moon Plaza.[2] This plaza is flanked by eight stepped pyramids in *talud-tablero* style, with two more a little off to the sides. Two structures are located on its north-south center line. In its middle is a low square platform, about 22 m on a side, with stairways on all four sides. It is very similar to the platforms found in the plazas in front of the Sun Pyramid and the FSP, and much like the smaller platforms or altars found in the central courtyards of many residential compounds. North of this platform, just in front of the fore-platform of the Moon Pyramid, is a unique structure, the Building of the Altars (36:N5E1), a walled room, inside of which are masonry features set at 45-degree angles to the canonical Teotihuacan orientation. They recall the "intercardinal" 45-degree motifs seen in cosmograms in sixteenth century codices, and those painted on the walls of enigmatic Structure 1B-prime:N1E1 in the Ciudadela Plaza. Tombs 2 and 6 in Stage 4 of the Moon Pyramid also feature offerings set at the intercardinal points as well as at the center and the four cardinal points. This structure in the Moon Plaza must also have been a cosmogram.

Sugiyama and Cabrera (2007) tunneled into one of the pyramids just off the Moon Plaza (TMP structure 1:N5W1). They found at least six construction stages, showing that the Moon Plaza has a long history of complicated modification. A compound adjoining the southwest corner of the Moon Plaza, the Quetzalpapalotl "Palace," also shows a

Figure 6.9. The *"Diosa de Agua"* (Water Goddess). Height 3.19 m.
© Fine Arts Museums of San Francisco (1988).

long history of rebuilding (Acosta 1964b). The earliest stage probably
dates to 100–250 CE. It is residential architecture of exceptionally high
quality, including a low platform with polychrome murals and square
stone pillars with huge carved reliefs of conch shells, on the east side of
a courtyard. Its principal occupants must have been of very high status.

What deity or deities were associated with the Moon Pyramid? The
obsidian rattlesnake figures and Storm God vessels in Tombs 2 and 6
suggest association with the Feathered Serpent and the Storm God.
However, there are additional possibilities. The second largest stone
sculpture associated with Teotihuacan is a monolith some 3.19 m high
and weighing nearly 24 tons (Figure 6.9). It was found in the late 1700s,
face down, to the rear of a pyramid on the west side of the Moon Plaza
(3:N4W1), in a magnificent state of preservation (López Luján n.d.).
It may have originally been associated with that pyramid, or it may
have stood on the Moon Pyramid and at some time been carefully low-
ered from that spot. Who might have moved it, when, and why, remain
mysteries. At least by the time of the Spanish Conquest, it must have

been hidden by rubble. Otherwise it would have been destroyed as a heathen idol. Its flat and slightly recessed upper surface suggests to me that it was a monumental pillar to support a crossbeam, perhaps of wood, likely a lintel for a large entryway, although López Luján (personal communication, 2013) questions this. A large stone survives within the Moon Plaza, battered into shapelessness. Yet (as pointed out to me by Annabeth Headrick) just enough remains to indicate that it was a counterpart of the "Diosa de Agua." Evidently it was not hidden and therefore was demolished, although we cannot say when or by whom.

The chronology of sculptural styles at Teotihuacan is unknown, and these monoliths may actually date to the next period, discussed in Chapter 7. Their close spatial association with the Moon Pyramid strongly suggests a symbolic connection. The attire of the well-preserved one is unmistakably womanly. Some have proposed that it represents a supposedly pervasive "Great Goddess." However, there is no good evidence for such a deity at Teotihuacan (Paulinyi 2006). Paulinyi (2013) suggests it may be a maize goddess. The Aztecs did not fully understand Teotihuacan symbolism, yet they may not have been mistaken in labeling the nearby pyramid the "Moon" Pyramid. Could this figure represent a moon goddess? None of the finds in the Moon Pyramid burials has any obvious lunar significance, yet it is tempting to wonder if the Moon Pyramid, the Sun Pyramid, and the FSP represented the astronomical triad of Moon, Sun, and Venus.

Whatever the validity of these speculations, a high-status priesthood was surely associated with the Moon Pyramid. It was probably powerful enough to be largely independent of civic units associated with other major structures such as the Sun Pyramid and the Ciudadela.

The Ciudadela Complex

The Sun and Moon Pyramids were much larger than most other Mesoamerican pyramids, but they were variants of a widely shared, basic kind of structure and idea: a solid multi-bodied high platform that represented a sacred mountain, often with a temple atop, used primarily for religious ceremonies, although these religious events might have considerable political significance. Few people, if any, actually lived on Mesoamerican pyramids, although residences for priests and others associated with the pyramid were often located in the immediate vicinity. The Ciudadela complex is very different (Figure 6.10). It is enclosed by great outer platforms, about 400 m long. To some extent these platforms resemble the large, low platforms around the Sun Precinct, but those platforms are separated from the pyramid by distances of 30 to 40 m,

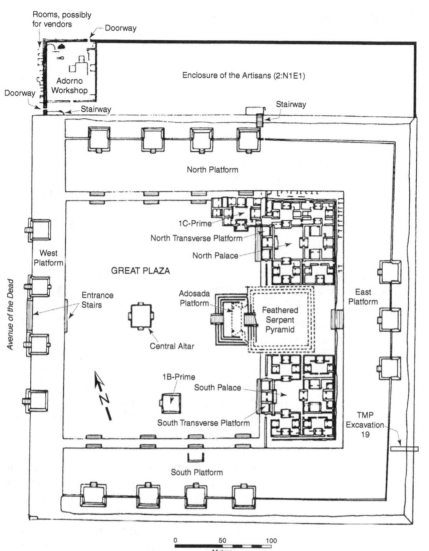

Figure 6.10. Plan of the Ciudadela complex.
By S. Vaughn, after Cabrera et al. (1982a).

only enclose it on its sides and rear, and are overshadowed by the pyramid itself, while those at the Ciudadela are an integral and highly visible part of the complex. No evidence for any such enclosing platforms exists at the Moon Pyramid. Pre-Ciudadela structures were thoroughly razed and a wholly new complex was built. This suggests a sharp break with what went before. Architecturally, the Ciudadela complex was without precedent, and it was never copied except at Teotihuacan outposts, such as Chingú, in the Tula region (Díaz 1980). Probably, this architectural innovation somehow reflects new religious and political ideas and practices. Just what these were is a tantalizing problem.

The Feathered Serpent Pyramid

The Feathered Serpent Pyramid measures about 65 by 65 m at its base and was originally about 20 m high, making it the third largest pyramid at Teotihuacan. Sugiyama's (2005) careful reconstruction indicates that there were originally seven superposed bodies, rather than the six thought by Marquina (1951). Their façades are in *talud-tablero* form, but, unlike those on all other Teotihuacan pyramids, they are composed of huge cut stone blocks carefully fitted together, each weighing several hundred kilograms. The andesitic raw materials probably were obtained from various sources in the Teotihuacan Valley, and/or a few kilometers farther away, in the vicinity of Texcoco. Undulating relief profiles of the Feathered Serpent amid seashells cover the sloping *taludes*. The vertical *tableros* are covered with serpent reliefs from which three-dimensional heads project (Figure 1.5). Quarrying, transporting, and then carving all these stone blocks, using only other stones as tools, must have required a huge amount of labor. A thin grayish sandy layer below the surface surrounding the pyramid (personal observation) suggests that the blocks were roughly shaped at quarry sites and then finished and fitted together when set in place at the pyramid. Postholes observed by Martin Dudek in the 1988 INAH-Brandeis field season may be from scaffolding used during the construction process. Sugiyama estimates that in spite of its much smaller size, the total labor involved in constructing the FSP may have been comparable to that at the Sun Pyramid. This is in addition to the immense labor represented by the outer platforms of the Ciudadela.

One member of each pair of three-dimensional figures on the *tableros* is the Feathered Serpent, a rattlesnake whose body and rattles are shown in low relief. The other image is often identified as the Storm God, but it has few attributes of the Storm God, and its prominent rings are some distance from its eyes, rather than encircling them. Armillas (1945: 58, 1947) identified the feathered serpent with Tlaloc and argued that the pyramid was dedicated to the rain god. He saw the feathered serpent heads as representations of lightning or thunder clouds. Drucker (1974) suggested that the other image belongs to Cipactli, the crocodilian creature that marked the first day in the 260-day cycle for the

Aztecs. The squares on its face may be alligator-like skin. Alfonso Caso and Ignacio Bernal (1952: 113–16) argued that this image is equivalent to the Oaxacan "*dios con el moño en el tocado*," probably identical to the Aztec Xiuhcoatl or fire serpent, which also means year serpent or turquoise serpent. Alfredo López Austin et al. (1991) argue that this image is the headdress of Cipactli, carried on the body of the Feathered Serpent, who is seen at the moment of the creation of time. They see the pyramid as dedicated to the origin of time and the calendar, especially the 260-day and 365-day cycles. The Feathered Serpent is also closely identified with Venus. These are only some of the interpretations proposed for these stone figures. The Storm God was already prominent at Teotihuacan, as seen in the Storm God jars in the Sun and Moon Pyramid burials, but emphasis on the Feathered Serpent appears stronger at the FSP. Most likely it was a place for worship and ritual connected with both the Storm God and the Feathered Serpent.

Because the upper parts of the pyramid are destroyed, the total number of heads on its façades is unclear. Sugiyamá (2005: 55–65) estimates it was between 361 and 404, and none of the likely numbers are of calendrical significance. Why are there so many? Perhaps it was simply the Teotihuacano love of multiple repetitions of figural elements, seen so often in their murals. Also, larger stone figures with the desired projecting geometry that were not architecturally unstable may have been beyond Teotihuacano technology. If smaller figures were to be made impressive, it could be done by having a great many of them.

The project directed by Cabrera in 1980–82 (Cabrera et al. 1982a, 1982b, 1991) was the first large-scale work in the Ciudadela since that of Gamio and Marquina in 1917–1922. It included more clearing of the north and south "palaces," excavations in the walled enclosure attached to the north side of the Ciudadela (the Enclosure of the Artisans), further work at the FSP, and elsewhere along the Avenue of the Dead. Excavations along the south edge of the FSP detected an elongated east-west burial pit with the remains of eighteen individuals, as well as isolated pits with single individuals at either end (S. Sugiyama 1989). This find prompted another project at the pyramid by Cabrera, Sugiyama, and Cowgill in 1988–89. Further excavations were carried out in 1992–94, under the direction of Cabrera. Remains of 119 individuals were found in the 1988–89 operations, bringing the total to 137, mostly sacrificial victims arranged in a highly structured pattern of mass graves (Figure 6.11). More victims were found in the 1992–94 operations. Cabrera et al. (1991) is a preliminary report. A full report is in preparation. Sugiyama (2005) provides extensive data and his interpretations, and numerous articles report on specific topics.

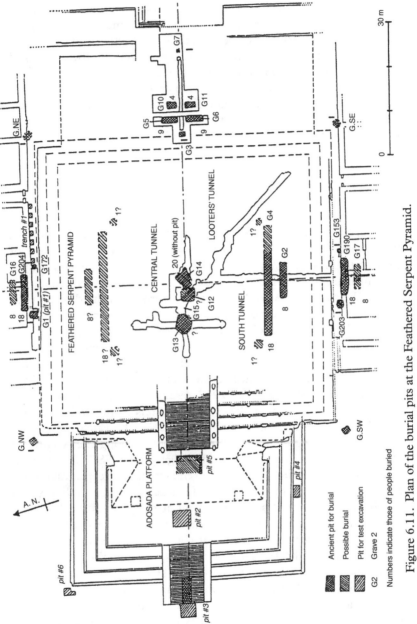

Figure 6.11. Plan of the burial pits at the Feathered Serpent Pyramid.
© Cambridge University Press and Saburo Sugiyama (2005).

Not the entire pyramid was explored, but symmetry considerations imply that a total of around 200 victims had been buried at ground level during construction of the pyramid. Marquina (1979[1922]: 158–161) reports disturbed remains of several individuals were found atop the pyramid in the project directed by Gamio, together with offerings that included marine shells, beads, earspools, figurine heads of greenstone and jade, a Storm God jar, and at least two "serpent" nose pendants. Given what we now know of burial pits at upper levels in the Moon Pyramid, it is likely that something similar existed at the top of the FSP, but by 1918 they were already badly disturbed by erosion. In the 1920s, Pedro Dozal (1925) found four more individuals buried in deep pits at the four corners of the pyramid.

The pyramid was built in a single episode, probably shortly after construction of the enclosing platforms of the Ciudadela. Its fill consists of cells of unworked stones set in mud mortar, into which were packed other stones, earth, and some debris, including fragments of worn *metates* (milling stones), potsherds useful for chronology, and forty-six of the large conical stone objects that I believe were derived from an earlier civic-ceremonial structure, discussed in Chapter 5.

Sugiyama (2005) describes the graves, the victims, and associated grave goods in detail. Most or all had their hands tied behind their backs, and many seem also to have been bound at the ankles. They were in good physical condition at the time of their deaths and it is possible they were buried alive. All were well dressed, some considerably more so than others. Stable isotope analyses of the bones and teeth of some victims (White et al. 2002) suggest that many had not lived for long in the Teotihuacan region. It might seem they were captured enemies. I doubt this, for several reasons. One is that, in Mesoamerica, captives were often stripped. Another is the uniformity of the attire of various sets of victims. If they had been soldiers of foreign powers, it seems their dress would have been more varied. It has also been suggested that the victims may have been low-status Teotihuacanos dressed up as soldiers before being sacrificed. Perhaps osteobiographies can detect signatures of their occupations – whether as soldiers, artisans, or laborers. Meagan Rubel (2009) has taken a first step in this direction.

I suspect that the victims in military attire were members of an elite guard attached to the household of whoever was at the apex of the Ciudadela hierarchy. There are good reasons for using foreigners as guardsmen – they have no local family ties to provide conflicting loyalties and they are highly dependent on the well-being of their patron. There are numerous examples of this elsewhere, including use of Nordic "Varangian" guardsmen by Byzantine emperors, janissaries by the Ottoman Turks, and Swiss guards at the Vatican.

Box 6.1 Stable and Unstable Isotopes

Because isotopes of an element have different numbers of neutrons (see Box 1.2), they have slightly different weights, and this has a slight effect on chemical processes, which can lead to enrichment of one or another isotope. Food and water ingested by humans may contain slightly different proportions of different isotopes of an element, depending on local geology, temperatures, sources of rainfall and ground water, and biological processes in the plants and animals eaten. Methods of storing and preparing foods also affect the isotopic composition of human tissues. These differing isotopic ratios are preserved in teeth and bones. The composition of teeth is set at the age of mineralization and is little influenced by the surroundings after death. Comparing isotopic ratios in teeth that mineralize early, such as permanent incisors, with those that mineralize late, such as third molars, can preserve evidence pertaining to different stages in the early life history of an individual. Bone tends to regenerate over time, so its isotopic ratios pertain to the last few years of a person's life. Unfortunately, bone composition, and to a lesser extent tooth composition, are susceptible to influences from the surroundings after death (Lee-Thorp 2008; Knudson 2009; Bentley 2006).

Stable isotopes of carbon are especially useful for inferring ancient diets, since different kinds of plants and animals tend to accumulate somewhat different proportions of ^{13}C and ^{12}C. For inferring places where a person has resided, the elements most used are strontium and oxygen. Applications of these methods to archaeological problems are still under development, and there are some problems, especially with oxygen (Knudson 2009). Another limitation is that different places may have similar isotopic signatures for any particular element. In sourcing minerals by quite different techniques, such as neutron activation analysis (NAA), this problem is greatly reduced by using many elements, since it is unlikely that the minerals in any two small regions will have the same combination of trace amounts of all the elements measured. Using single elements, as in many stable isotope studies, rarely leads to a unique source region. Using two elements in combination can help, but it would be better if more elements could be used, and still better if additional kinds of evidence point toward the same region. Further compounding the problem is that many regions of Mesoamerica have not yet been sampled well enough to determine the local "signature": the range of isotopic ratios exhibited by individuals who beyond reasonable doubt spent nearly all their lives within the region, including residents with different diets. One may be able to distinguish locals from non-locals, but provenance of the non-locals may remain uncertain. At Teotihuacan, the "local" signature is based on a quite small sample and limited to a few locations, such as the Tlajinga 33 compound, where some of the deceased may have been migrants. It may not adequately represent the full local range. For all these reasons, I am cautious in interpreting results of stable isotope studies.

The occupants of the graves fall into well-defined status levels. Graves 10, 11, 16, and 17 have the least rich offerings and tend to be furthest from the pyramid, with sets of eight female victims in their early teens, with few surviving offerings except beads, disks, and earspool components, all of shell, together with some large and small obsidian projectile points, but no ceramics. Most of their attire would have been textiles, feathers, and other perishable materials. These are Level 1. It is interesting that a few projectile points (clearly not knives) were found with these young women.

Level 2 is represented in graves 190, 2, 4, 5, 6, and 204[3]; elongated pits at ground level, some just outside the pyramid and others inside it, containing sets of 9 or 18 males, generally in their early twenties, with abundant obsidian projectile points and slate disks worn on the lower back that were backings for pyrite mirrors similar to those shown in depictions of soldiers in Teotihuacan and later Mesoamerican imagery (called *tezcacuitlapilli* by the Aztecs). Size distribution of the obsidian points is bimodal: smaller ones are mostly 2 to 4 cm long, and the larger ones mostly 6 to 10 cm (Sugiyama 2005: 125–26) (Figure 6.12). The larger points would have been attached to spear shafts, while the smaller might more aptly be called dart points. Spears and spear-throwers, of perishable materials, are a prominent feature in Teotihuacan imagery. A study of musculoskeletal stress markers on bones of some of the better-preserved victims (Rubel 2009) found only a few with good evidence for use of atlatls or shields and, unexpectedly, slightly better evidence for use of bows, although there is no evidence for bows in Teotihuacan imagery. These preliminary results suggest that only some of the victims had much experience in actual warfare or practice with weapons, but they need further testing.

The most striking element in the attire of many level 2 victims was a collar made of shell plaques, from which were suspended imitation human upper jaws (maxillae), also worn by some individuals in Moon Pyramid Tombs 2 and 6. Most were imitation human jaws made of individual

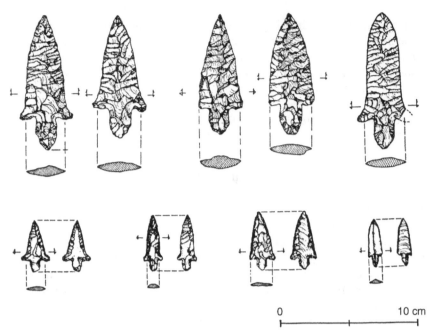

0   10 cm

Figure 6.12. Large and small obsidian points from Status Level Two
burials at the Feathered Serpent Pyramid.
© Cambridge University Press and Saburo Sugiyama (2005).

teeth carved from white marine shells and set in a perishable matrix covered with stucco. A few wore real human maxillae (Figure 6.13), and
some real and imitation maxillae of canids and felids were also present.
Persons with real maxillae do not seem to be otherwise distinguished
from those with imitation maxillae, and reasons for the difference are
unclear. Some of the real maxillae, "victims of the victims," appear to
have lived at Teotihuacan, while others were from elsewhere (Spence
et al. 2004). The predominance of imitation maxillae suggests that possibly there had not been much recent warfare to provide real victims.

I know of no examples of maxilla collars in Teotihuacan imagery. The
only known parallels come from Oaxaca. At Cerro Tilcajete, 18.5 km
south of Monte Albán, dated to Monte Albán II, a fragment of a cut
human maxilla appeared in surface survey (Duncan et al. 2009). Sue
Scott (1993) illustrates two large hollow ceramic figures from Oaxaca
that wear trophy maxillae, probably dating to Epiclassic or even later
times. This suggests that the practice lasted longer in Oaxaca than at
Teotihuacan.

Figure 6.13. Feathered Serpent Pyramid Burial 5-H, a victim wearing trophy human upper jaws.

© Cambridge University Press and Saburo Sugiyama (2005).

Except for one or two coarse open bowls, ceramics were absent in level 2 burials. Several of the multiple burials with eighteen victims were accompanied at either end by graves of single victims with richer "level 3" offerings (Graves 1, 153, 172, and 203), bringing the total to twenty. The relative uniformity of attire of the level 2 victims resembles the uniformity of dress of elaborately costumed figures in Teotihuacan processional murals and contrasts markedly with the attention to variety and individuality in Maya imagery. It is another example of the "ethos of uniformity" that was so prevalent at Teotihuacan.

A third level is best represented by "Grave" 14, at the exact center of the pyramid, where twenty individuals were laid directly on the ground (Figure 6.14; Sugiyama 2005: 30–31, Figures 10 and 11). They were mostly somewhat older than level 2 victims. They were accompanied by numerous greenstone (rarely jade) ornaments, including beads, earspools, and nose pendants in the form of terminal rattles of rattlesnakes (Figure 6.15b). Many of these objects were worn by the victims, but others were included as offerings, as was a set of small

Figure 6.14. Reconstruction of sacrificial victims in Grave 14, Feathered Serpent Pyramid.

© Cambridge University Press and Saburo Sugiyama (2005).

conical greenstone objects (possibly some kind of gaming markers) (see Figure 7.15b), huge quantities of marine shell, small stone figurines, obsidian figurines of humans and serpents, some bifacial obsidian points, and hundreds of exceptionally fine pressure-flaked obsidian prismatic blades (see Figure 7.10). These blades show no signs of use, and retro-fitting indicates that many were made from the same polyhedral cores, clearly as offerings. Spatial clusters of diverse kinds of objects associated with traces of organic materials suggest that bags with rather standard-ized combinations of objects were strewn over the bodies. "Trophy" jaws were not found in Grave 14. As with burials of levels 1 and 2, there were no ceramic figurines, and pottery was absent, except for fragments of two well-made polished black Storm God jars of a type quite different from those in Tombs 2 and 6 of the Moon Pyramid (Figure 6.6), and a few coarse ware open bowls. Except for a moderate number of obsid-ian points, military attributes are not obvious. Other graves that fit this level 3 category are some of those containing single individuals found just outside the pyramid: Graves 203, 153, 1, and 172. The disturbed

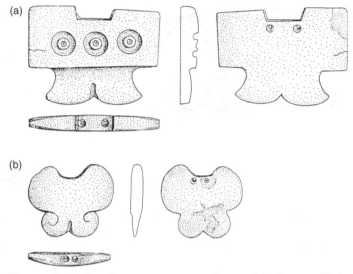

Figure 6.15. Teotihuacan nose pendants. (a) Storm God type, (b) Serpent type.

Courtesy of Oralia Cabrera.

remains reported by Marquina (1979[1922]) atop the pyramid probably also belong to this category. Grave 14 seems roughly comparable in richness to the tombs at the Moon Pyramid.

A fourth status level is probably represented by Grave 13, a large pit about 4.2 by 3.3 m dug into the *tepetate* subsoil on the east-west center line of the FSP, west of Grave 14 (G13 in Figure 6.11). It was almost totally emptied by ancient looters who tunneled into the pyramid from its southeast corner (Sugiyama 2005: 28, Figure 8). This had been another multiple burial, but only disturbed fragments of one individual remained, plus one complete undisturbed person at the western margin of the pit. He was an unusually robust male who had exceptionally large greenstone earspools and a "Storm God" nose pendant consisting of a rectangular crossbar on which three circles are incised and from which a split tongue hangs down (Figure 6.15a). A second very similar nose pendant of this type was found in the disturbed fill of this grave. Other examples of "Storm God" pendants variably show a split tongue or three or five fangs. This type comprises signs 150 and 153 in James Langley's (1986: 275–78) catalog of standardized Teotihuacan signs. I call attention to its being worn by a robust male in Grave 13 because this evidence fits poorly with Pasztory's (1973: 155) claim that

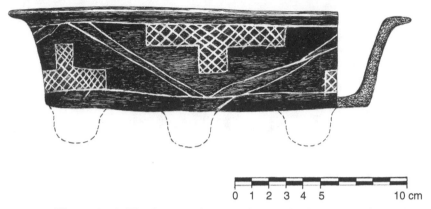

Figure 6.16. Flat-bottomed outslanting bowl with incised decoration, in ancient looter backdirt from Feathered Serpent Pyramid burial 13. By Verónica Moreno.

sign 150 is a diagnostic of a supposed Teotihuacan Great Goddess. Its connection with "Spider Woman" (Taube 1983) is also dubious. Other occurrences of this type of nose pendant are in the so-called Jade Tlaloc figures in murals at the Tetitla residential compound, in stone reliefs in the West Plaza Group in the Avenue of the Dead Complex (Morelos García 1993) (see Figure 7.4), and in the mouths of the headdresses carried by feathered serpents on the façades of the FSP. It also appears on a pyrite-encrusted disk found at Kaminaljuyú (Kidder et al. 1946, Figure 175) (see Figure 8.19) and on Stela 11 at Yaxha in the Maya lowlands (Berrin 1988: 128). Both these figures at Maya sites wear the Teotihuacan tassel headdress, interpreted by Clara Millon (1973) as a marker of high Teotihuacan authority, and the Yaxha figure carries weapons. As I discuss in Chapter 8, this type of nose pendant is probably an insignia of very high status.

In contrast to the scarcity of ceramics other than Storm God jars in the unlooted burials at the FSP and the Moon Pyramid, the debris left by looters at Grave 13 includes fragments of several fairly nice serving vessels, including a White-on-red vase and an unusual variant of a flat-bottomed outslanting bowl, with incised "tau" motifs filled with cross-hatching (Figure 6.16). Another notable find was a wooden staff, carved the form of a feathered serpent (Figure 6.17).

A possible fifth status level is perhaps represented by whoever else the looted Grave 13 contained, as well as by a large completely looted pit dug into *tepetate* just beyond the foot of the stairway of the FSP (pit

0   10   20 cm

Figure 6.17. Wooden serpent staff in ancient looter backdirt from Feathered Serpent Pyramid burial 13.

© Cambridge University Press and Saburo Sugiyama (2005).

#5 in Figure 6.11). Grave 13 and this other pit may have held heads of the state.

These finds tell us that hierarchy was already publicly symbolized at Teotihuacan by marked differences in costume, at least among the military and other office holders. Early Teotihuacan was not egalitarian, even in theory. In openly recognizing status differences, it resembled other early states in Mesoamerica and elsewhere. What was unusual about Teotihuacan was the de-emphasis on individuality, at least at intermediate status levels.

Numbers that occur repeatedly in the FSP sacrificial burials are 8, 9, and 18 (twice 9), and perhaps 20. These patterns were surely intentional. However, I have reservations about the degree of calendrical significance proposed by Sugiyama (2005) and others. The number 9 also appears in the nine pairs of huge obsidian figures in Burial 6 at the Moon Pyramid. Its associations with the underworld make it a logical number in burial contexts.

The "Plataforma Adosada"

In the 1988 season, the interior of the fore-platform that later hid much of the front of the FSP was partially explored. There are hints that it may have been preceded by a much lower platform, coeval with the FSP, but a little in front of it and free-standing, perhaps similar to the earliest fore-platform at the Sun Pyramid and the low platforms in front of Mounds A and B at Kaminaljuyú (Kidder et al. 1946). It included fragments of clay motifs that apparently came from a destroyed structure that once stood atop the FSP, discussed in chapter 7 (Figure 6.18).

The Ciudadela Platforms and the Great Plaza

The outer platforms on the north, east, and south sides of the Ciudadela are about 7 to 8 m high and 80 m wide. Their solid fill of adobe

Figure 6.18. Fragment of modeled earth friezes originally atop the FSP, found in the fill of the later fore-platform.

© Cambridge University Press and Saburo Sugiyama (2005).

bricks was constructed in the Miccaotli phase, probably early in that phase. A series of concrete floors atop these platforms span the Early Tlamimilolpa through Late Xolalpan or Metepec phases and added about a meter to their height (TMP Excavation 19, a trench across the eastern platform, Figure 6.10). Four stepped pyramids now sit atop the north platform and another four are on the south platform, while three are on the east platform. The stairways of all these pyramids face toward the interior of the Ciudadela complex and lead to the floors atop the outer platforms. More stairways on the north and south platforms lead down to the great plaza of the Ciudadela. On the east platform, there is only a stairway aligned with the central pyramid. It leads to a floor at the rear of the FSP, between the north and south residential complexes. Perhaps this early, walls connected the pyramids on the platforms. They were about 1.4 m thick and variously reported as 2.5 m (Martínez and

Jarquín 1982) or 5 m (Jarquín and Martínez 1982) high. They were painted red (TMP field notes). It doesn't seem they would have added much defensive value – the steep outer slopes of the platforms already made them hard to scale – but they would have made the interior of the Ciudadela less visible. Together, the north, east, and south platforms constitute a U-shaped design. Box-like cists along the inner benches of the east platform and the eastern parts of the north and south platforms contained offerings, still not fully analyzed.

The impression that all four sides of the Ciudadela complex are much the same is misleading. The west side is quite different. Here, the enclosing platform is only 3 to 4 m high and only about 35 m wide. Four stepped pyramids project above it, with stairways that face outward, toward the Avenue of the Dead, in contrast to the inward orientations of the pyramids on the other outer platforms. There is no sign of a wall between the pyramids on the western platform. Between the middle two pyramids there is a broad stairway, 32 m wide, that grants easy access from the Avenue to the great plaza. Drucker (1974: 272–78) argued that the western platform may have originally been much lower. Excavations in 1980–82 confirmed an earlier lower stage (Cabrera 1991), which means the Ciudadela was originally quite open on the west. But even the higher stage does little to impede access to the great plaza, which is about 250 m north-south by 200 m east-west. Allowing for structures within it, its effective area is about 4.4 hectares, enough to hold up to a hundred thousand people without much crowding. The volume of all four of the surrounding platforms, not counting their associated pyramids, is about 627,000 cubic meters, greater than the volume of the Moon Pyramid and nearly two-thirds the volume of the Sun Pyramid.

A concrete floor, probably coeval with the FSP, covers the entire plaza. It was renewed twice. Near the plaza's center is a large, low, square platform, 20 m on a side, with stairways on all sides. It looks like a larger analog of the altars in the courtyards of residential compounds known from the next Teotihuacan period, or the platform in the Moon Plaza. In the southern part of the great plaza, 1B-prime:N1E1 is an enigmatic structure that violates usual Teotihuacan symmetry by having no counterpart in the north. Fragments of what appear to be pre-Ciudadela structures were found in its lowest layers (Cabrera 1991). A mural on a later but still early floor contains interlocking scrolls similar to those in the early stage of the structure called "Edificios Superpuestos," probably derived stylistically from the Gulf lowlands (Cabrera 1991). Walls of a still later stage, belonging to the next period, bear mural motifs probably representing cosmograms (Figure 6.19). It seems 1B-prime was a pre-Ciudadela structure that was not razed, but rebuilt in the same spot

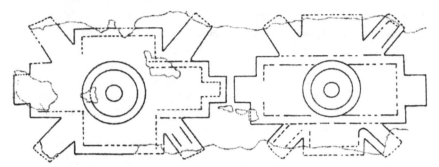

Figure 6.19. Probable cosmograms in mural in structure 1B-prime:-N1E1 in the Ciudadela plaza.
After R. Cabrera (1995).

throughout Teotihuacan's history. Perhaps it was considered the exact center of the universe, too important to be moved even when most of the pre-Ciudadela was razed. That might explain its odd location.

On the eastern margin of the great plaza, north-south transverse platforms separate the plaza from all but the front part of the FSP and from the room complexes on either side of this pyramid. TMP excavation 25S in the south transverse platform revealed early stages dating to Early Tlamimilolpa or earlier, then a long hiatus before renewed building in the Metepec phase. The front of the FSP originally faced directly onto the great plaza but was later covered by a large stepped platform.

Several authors have suggested that the great plaza of the Ciudadela was periodically flooded, creating a reflecting body of water, a fitting materialization of its aquatic associations. There are examples elsewhere of temples in the midst of waters, notably at Angkor Wat (Higham 2000) and the Golden Temple of Amritsar. But these temples are connected to dry land by causeways or bridges, and there is no sign of any such connection at the Ciudadela. I am skeptical of flooding at the Ciudadela.

Ciudadela Room Complexes: Palaces?

East-west corridors separate the north and south sides of the FSP from two large room complexes, each about 80 m north-south by 60 m east-west, giving each an area of about 4,800 square meters (Figure 6.10). This is well above the median area of residential compounds elsewhere in the city, although a few appear to have been even larger (Techinantitla, in sector N5E2, partially excavated, may have exceeded 7,000 square meters). Previously, I estimated that these two complexes might together have housed 160 to 270 persons (Cowgill 1983). This seems too high. Cabrera's 1980–82 project confirmed that each complex consists of five apartments arranged around a large central courtyard in a far more orderly fashion than in most other Teotihuacan residential compounds. The courtyards lack altars and are not surrounded by platforms. Presumably, the FSP made ritual structures within the complexes superfluous. Assuming ten occupants per apartment, that would be no more than 100 people in the two complexes together. More telling is the apparent absence of special-purpose rooms, for storage or anything else. These room complexes look very ill-suited for the activities of rulers, other than receiving brief visits. Perhaps, as Sugiyama (2005) suggests, the Ciudadela never was intended for rulers at all, and these structures merely housed priests and others in the service of the FSP. But, if so, why is the Ciudadela so different from everything else at Teotihuacan? I continue to suspect it was built and first occupied by persons who held unprecedented kinds of political office, however important the associated religious practices were.

Evidence for the existence of an early stage of these residential complexes was discovered by the TMP in the South Palace (excavations 25N and 25S, Drucker 1974) and considerably expanded by excavations in the North Palace directed by Cabrera in 1992–94. The limited areas uncovered provide little information about overall layouts, but they were clearly very different from those of the later stages now visible. This construction stage appears to be earlier than the FSP but later than the pre-Ciudadela structures described in the previous chapter. Particularly notable are murals consisting of large orange-red motifs on white backgrounds (Cabrera Castro 1995: 13) (Figure 6.20), reminiscent of the color of murals at an early stage of the fore-platform of the Sun Pyramid (personal observation) and in both color and motif (the "cut conch shell") to some of the early murals in the "Ward Temple" compound in the La Ventilla district (Cabrera and Gómez 2008). This motif has a remarkably long history in Mesoamerica, appearing in almost the same form in stone reliefs at Epiclassic Xochicalco (Figure 1.4/20) and at Early Postclassic Tula. The pit excavated by the TMP on the south transverse platform, at the western margin of the South Palace, found bits of orange and white painted plaster in an early layer (Drucker 1974: 321) and adobes painted in various colors, including yellow sea shells on a green background (Drucker 1974: 297–98).

The extensively excavated later stages of the north and south room complexes were very similar to each other and probably coeval with the FSP. This suggests dual political or religious offices, but other evidence

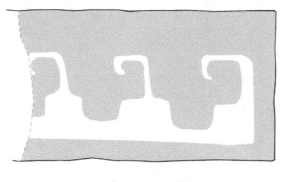

0 ——————— 25
Cms.
(Approximate)

Figure 6.20. Red on white mural motifs, early stage of the Ciudadela north palace.
By S. Vaughn after photo by author.

for such duality at Teotihuacan is elusive. Institutionalized dual office, such as the paired consuls of Republican Rome, should not be confused with the practice, well-attested in sixteenth century Mesoamerica, of leaders of two or more ethnic units co-residing in the same settlement and sharing political power. The south complex seems to have maintained its layout until collapse of the Teotihuacan state. In contrast, the northern complex was significantly modified over time. Some doorways were blocked, changing the circulation pattern and making some parts less accessible.

Enough remnants of original plaster survive in these complexes so that traces of murals should still be visible if they were ever present, but evidence for murals is curiously lacking, although they had been present in an earlier building stage. Perhaps the occupants were of high enough status to use other means, such as fine tapestries, to embellish their walls.

It was probably in this period that a room complex spilled over from the North Palace into the northeast corner of the Ciudadela plaza (1C-prime:N1E1) (Cabrera 1991). It has a broad entryway, and its interior connects with the North Palace. This addition has a certain dignity, but it breaks the symmetry of the great plaza. It suggests that activities connected with the North Palace required more space, at the expense of some loss to the visual impact of the plaza. Presumably these activities were administrative and/or commercial. It differentiates the two palaces. Perhaps the South Palace was devoted mainly to ceremonial activities.

The Meaning of the Ciudadela

Whatever was going on at the Ciudadela, it coexisted with the meanings and practices associated with the Sun and Moon Pyramid, since the major enlargement of the Moon Pyramid in Stage 4 seems to have taken place only slightly earlier than construction of the Ciudadela complex. Perhaps long-established priestly organizations, endowed with rich resources, persisted at the Sun and Moon Pyramids, while the Ciudadela complex was created to be the seat of a new line of potentates, although surely the offices associated with the Ciudadela were highly sacralized, since pyramids are so prominent there. Possibly something took place a little like the differentiation of palaces from temples in early Mesopotamia. It is unlikely that new political institutions would have had a purely secular basis for legitimacy, but the FSP, in spite of the labor and skill invested in it, is only one part of the Ciudadela complex, while the Sun and Moon Pyramids wholly overshadow associated platforms and room complexes.

Long ago, Armillas (1964: 307) suggested that the Ciudadela was the seat of the rulers of Teotihuacan. René Millon (1973: 55) was inclined to agree, as was I (Cowgill 1983). Sugiyama (2005) doubts this, and argues that the numerous sacrificial victims found at the FSP were dedicated to gods rather than to rulers. However, I continue to think that the Ciudadela was probably built as a new political center for a changing Teotihuacan state, occupied by persons whose activities intertwined the sacred and the secular.

The Enclosure of the Artisans

On the northern exterior of the Ciudadela is what I call the Enclosure of the Artisans, a great enclosure about 380 m long and 80 m wide (2:N1E1, Figure 6.10). Its east, north, and west sides were bounded by a freestanding wall, 3–4 m high,[4] buttressed by low *taludes* on both sides. The south side is bounded by the Ciudadela itself. A stairway connected it to a room atop an early stage of the Ciudadela's west platform, and another stairway to an early stage of the north platform, north of the easternmost of the four temples on this platform, not far from the north palace. Probably the only other exits are one or two narrow doorways at ground level (Rodríguez García 1982: 59). There is nothing else like this enclosure at Teotihuacan, except possibly a very large walled area with abundant evidence of obsidian working just northwest of the Moon Pyramid (Carballo 2007). The Enclosure of the Artisans seems to have been most actively used in the next period, when artisans in the western part of the enclosure used molds to make coarse censers and fine clay censer ornaments, but the two early stairways show it already existed in this interval.

The Great Compound

Facing the Ciudadela, on the west side of the Avenue of the Dead, the great, low platforms of the Great Compound (Figure 6.2) were begun in this period. In striking contrast to the high platforms of the Ciudadela, obvious to the most casual visitor, the Great Compound platforms rise only about a meter above their surroundings, and their very existence went unrecognized until 1962, when they were revealed by combined use of air photos and ground survey (Millon 1973: 18–20). The platforms are very broad, varying 164 to 190 m in width on the north and south sides, although narrower on the east and west. The overall dimensions of the Great Compound are 374 m east-west and about 530 m north-south, a total area of 20 ha. They enclose a large central plaza, about 254 m east-west by 214 m north-south, slightly over 5.4 ha. An unimpeded ground-level entrance on the west side of the plaza, 32 m wide, connects directly to West Avenue. On the east side, an open 60 m-wide entrance faces the Avenue of the Dead. Surface survey of the relatively undisturbed north platform revealed about fourteen structures, whose sizes are comparable to Teotihuacan residential compounds. None have yet been excavated, but it is unlikely that they are ordinary residences. Sload (1987) proposes that different structures may have represented interests of different city districts, responsible to the state but somewhat independent. The southern platform has been much more disturbed by recent construction, but it was probably similar to the northern platform.

There are no signs that there were ever any pyramids at the Great Compound. Nor is there any evidence of substantial structures anywhere in its central plaza. Some structures along the east outer face of the Great Compound, along the Avenue of the Dead, have been excavated in INAH projects. The fullest excavation data come from TMP Excavation 17, carried out by Matthew Wallrath (Millon 1992: 378–80; Rattray 2001:450–52, and Tables of Frequencies of Ceramic Wares). This was a trench 14 m long that began in the northern part of the plaza and extended several meters into the north platform. It was carried to sterile subsoil along much of its length. Ceramics date the earliest layers (earth floors) to Miccaotli. This is followed by Early Tlamimilolpa earth floors of a low platform (Millon 1992: 379), so it seems likely that the Great Compound existed when the FSP was built, or soon thereafter. The first concrete floors date to Late Tlamimilolpa, and the Great Compound saw its heyday in the next period.

R. Millon (1973: 20, 37) suggests that, together with the Ciudadela, the Great Compound may have been the city's bureaucratic, religious, and commercial center. The city's principal marketplace may have been in the central plaza of the Great Compound. At least one posthole in the plaza and concentrations of food-serving vessels found in TMP Excavation 17 offer some support for this hypothesis. Vendors may have set up temporary stands to offer goods and food to customers. In other parts of the world a central marketplace is often located adjacent to a central palace. Good examples occur in cities of Imperial China.

The Avenue of the Dead Complex

Some structures now recognized as parts of the Avenue of the Dead Complex, such as the *Edificios Superpuestos* (Superposed Structures) (1:N2W1) and the Viking Group apartment compound (3:N3E1, Figure 6.2/11), had been excavated earlier, but Bruce Drewitt and Matthew Wallrath (R. Millon 1973: 35; Wallrath 1967), in the course of the TMP, were the first to recognize a distinctive "macrocomplex" of pyramids, platforms, plazas, and other architectural features, covering 12–13 ha and mostly enclosed within an outer wall (Figure 6.2/13). It straddles the Avenue of the Dead, halfway between the Sun Pyramid and the Ciudadela (Figure 6.21). It is bisected by the Avenue of the Dead, but access from the Avenue is limited. Even in its first stage, it was separated from the Avenue by north-south platforms with up and down stairs that had to be traversed in order to enter the main courtyards. Its spatial center consists of a triadic group on the west (the West Plaza Group) and a larger triadic group mirroring it on the east side of the Avenue (18:N2E1, where there have been no modern excavations). There are various other pyramids, platforms, and room groups within the complex, including another notable triadic group in the part east of the Avenue (52:N2E1), and the *Edificios Superpuestos* complex west of the Avenue. The structures within the walls of the Avenue of the Dead Complex offer facilities for religious and other ceremonies, fine residences, and possibly administrative activities, although there seems to be no evidence for storage. It could have housed a sizable number of people. Burials appear to be absent, but this may mean little if bodies

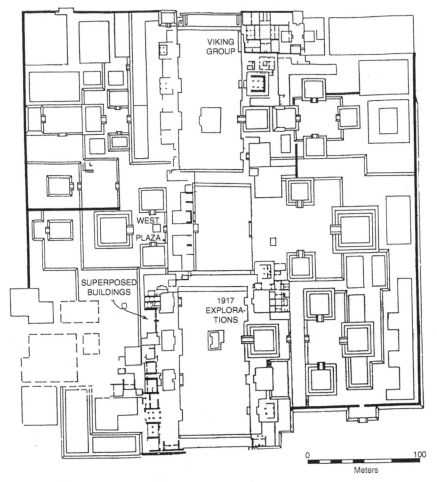

Figure 6.21. Plan of the Avenue of the Dead Complex.
By S. Vaughn, after R. Millon et al. (1973).

of deceased elites were wrapped in mortuary bundles, rather than being buried, as suggested by Headrick (1999, 2007).

In 1980–82, much of the western half of the Avenue of the Dead Complex was excavated by a team headed by Cabrera (Cabrera et al. 1982a, 1982b, 1991). Noel Morelos (1993) reports on the West Plaza Group, the central part of the western half. He distinguishes two major architectural stages but provides no ceramic evidence to date them. The

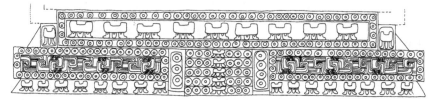

Figure 6.22. Interlocking scrolls and Storm God symbols in mural on an early structure at Edificios Superpuestos.
By S. Vaughn, after R. Cabrera (1995).

layout of the West Plaza Group was established in Stage 1 and was little changed in Stage 2 except that the courtyard and plaza floors were raised by about a meter (Morelos 1993).

Perhaps the *Edificios Superpuestos* were not yet within the walled area of the Avenue of the Dead Complex. In the absence of radiocarbon dates or ceramic data, except for limited information at the Viking Group (Armillas 1944), the age of Stage 1 of the Avenue of the Dead Complex is unclear, but several lines of evidence suggest it was probably built as early as the FSP, or not long after. Ceramics at the Viking Group probably belong to the Early Tlamimilolpa phase. Faded remnants of a mural in the West Plaza Group look stylistically early. So do those in the early stage at *Edificios Superpuestos*, which are geometric, featuring interlocking scroll motifs likely derived from Gulf lowland antecedents, as well as motifs that resemble Storm God nose pendants (Figure 6.22). The foundation underlying the earliest floor in the West Plaza Group courtyard consists of cells built of rock walls with the spaces between filled more loosely with rubble, a technique also used in the FSP, different from later building practices at Teotihuacan.

I have suggested (Cowgill 1983, 2007) that the Avenue of the Dead Complex represented a major shift in Teotihuacan political practices, following desecration of the FSP; probably a shift from more autocratic rule to a system in which a larger number of the elites had a significant voice – some kind of oligarchy. However, if Stage 1 was as early as I now suspect, its occupants already played a significant role in the Teotihuacan state during the time when the FSP flourished. If so, their roles must have been somehow complementary to those of people in the Ciudadela and those associated with the Sun and Moon Pyramids. Perhaps it housed middle-level bureaucrats. But possibly it housed rulers, while the Ciudadela was occupied by priests rather than heads of state.

The Xalla Complex

This architectural group covers about four hectares (Figure 6.2/7). Its combination of small temples, rooms, and walled courtyards is unlike anything else at Teotihuacan. It is markedly unlike triadic groups, the Ciudadela, and only a little like the Avenue of the Dead Complex. It is notable for fine sculptures, such as feline figures and a human who appears to be the victim of sacrifice by spears (López Luján et al. 2006). Its function remains enigmatic. Conceivably it was the center for a distinctive religious cult.

Civic-Ceremonial Complexes within the City's Core

The Avenue of the Dead was by now a major civic axis 50–60 m wide and over 5 km long, more a ceremonial way than a thoroughfare, lined with many large and a few immense structures (Figure 6.2). Platforms continuously lined both sides of the Avenue and a number of pyramids sit atop these platforms. Larger pyramid groups along the Avenue sometimes occur in facing pairs, the one on the east (facing west) often a little larger than its western counterpart. The northernmost set consists of Group Five on the east (6:N5E1) and Group Five-Prime on the west (5:N5W1). Each is a triadic group. They face each side of the Moon Pyramid but each is separated from it by about a hundred meters. They should probably be considered outlying elements of a macrocomplex that includes the Moon Pyramid itself, structures immediately adjoining the Moon Pyramid, such as 6:N5W1 (Carballo 2007), the Moon Plaza and its pyramids, and the Quetzalpapalotl Palace (Acosta 1964b). Group Five-Prime is surrounded by walls that form an enclosure about 200 m east-west by 135 m north-south. It was partially excavated in a project directed by Eduardo Matos in the 1990s. Reconstructed parts can be seen next to the Teotihuacan Mural Museum. Group Five is known only from surface exploration. The two groups do not align perfectly. The center line of Five-Prime is about 20 m south of the Group Five center line, relative to the canonical Teotihuacan orientation. That is, the line connecting them is less than 15.5 degrees south of true east. The reason for this "glitch" in Teotihuacan planning is unclear.

Just south of the Moon Plaza, the "Temple of Agriculture," on the west side of the Avenue of the Dead, is the eastern element of an apparent triadic group (5:N4W1), highly unusual in that its central pyramid faces north. East of the Moon Plaza, tracts 10 and 11:N4E1 comprise a triadic group that faces west, a short distance behind pyramids that front on the Moon Plaza. Southeast of this and about 400 m east of the

Avenue, but still part of the civic-ceremonial core, is the Xalla Complex, discussed previously. Fronting the west side of the Avenue, south of Xalla but north of the Sun Pyramid, is the Plazuela de las Columnas (25:N4W1), the largest of all triadic groups in the city, whose largest pyramid is the fourth largest in the city. To judge by its size, it must have been associated with some particularly powerful social entity. On the east side of the Avenue, 73:N4E1 is a counterpart to the Plazuela de las Columnas. The TMP excavated here in 1977 (Excavation 26), finding abundant evidence of its fiery destruction. Its main pyramid is smaller than those in the Plazuela, and it is doubtful whether it is part of a triadic group.

South of the Plazuela de las Columnas on the west side of the Avenue is the Patio of the Four Small Temples (1:N3W1), which (in spite of its name) is a relatively small triadic group. It faces the Palace of the Sun on the east side of the Avenue. The next major group to the south is the Sun Pyramid complex. On the west side of the Avenue, facing the Sun Pyramid, there is a gap. Perhaps this is because anything comparable to the Sun Pyramid would have destroyed its uniqueness and also blocked its westward view, while anything much smaller would have been dwarfed by it. A tempting speculation is that a ceremonial way once led up to the Sun Pyramid from the west. In fact, the early 20th century highway, still in active use, in sector N3W2, nearly follows the canonical Teotihuacan orientation and points toward the Sun Pyramid, before it connects to the modern cobbled ring road, cut through the ruins in 1964, that encircles the civic-ceremonial core. But otherwise, there is no evidence that there was ever at any time an east-west processional way leading to the Sun Pyramid. If such a thing ever existed, it must have been later obliterated.

Still farther south, there are platforms and some small pyramids, but nothing major until one reaches the Avenue of the Dead Complex. South of that complex, platforms and a few more temples line the short stretch that remains before the Río San Juan crosses the Avenue. South of that stream, the only major structures are the Ciudadela and the Great Compound.

Considering the northern part of the Avenue of the Dead as a whole, its vast scale and the number of platforms and lesser temples gives a first impression of multiplicity. Actually, there are only a limited number of major complexes, and no two are much alike. From north to south, I count nine: the Moon Pyramid macrocomplex, the Temple of Agriculture group, Xalla, the Plazuela de las Columnas, the Patio of the Four Small Temples, the Sun Pyramid complex, the Avenue of the Dead Complex, the Ciudadela, and the Great Compound. Any person or group who wanted something impressively large along the Avenue of the Dead would have found space in short supply. Taking this into account, it is less surprising that some sizable civic-ceremonial structures persisted or were created outside the central core of the city.

Teotihuacan differed from other highland Mesoamerican cities, such as Monte Albán, Tula, and Tenochtitlan, in having no single compact structural complex that was a central focus. It did not have a central plaza around which all the most important buildings were arrayed. Yet Teotihuacan's arrangement is more patterned and concentrated than Maya centers.

Although the Sun Pyramid is not a jarring anomaly in the overall layout of the civic-ceremonial district, we would not have the sense of "something missing" if it were absent, and the same is true of the Ciudadela. Since the Sun Pyramid reached nearly its final size when the Moon Pyramid was still relatively modest and when pre-Ciudadela structures were much less monumental than the Ciudadela, the Sun Pyramid complex was probably the civic-ceremonial heart of the Tzacualli phase city. Accurately dating the structures along the Avenue of the Dead to see what was there in Tzacualli times is critical for testing this conjecture, since if the Avenue existed at this time it would mean that the civic-ceremonial focus already extended well beyond the Sun Pyramid. But even if the Sun Pyramid was a strong epicenter in Tzacualli times, the subsequent vast enlargement of the Moon Pyramid and construction of the Ciudadela created an elongated north-south principal axis.

The Sun Pyramid's location to one side of the Avenue permits an uninterrupted visual sweep of over two kilometers along the Avenue, and a distant view of the Moon Pyramid that is not seriously interrupted by the six low transverse platforms that cross the Avenue. Probably the layout of the civic-ceremonial core developed over time, but in such a way that new features meshed harmoniously with what was there before.

The burials at the Moon Pyramid, the Sun Pyramid, and the FSP have many points in common in addition to human sacrifice. They share emphasis on the Feathered Serpent (seen in worked obsidian as well as the stone friezes on the FSP) and on the Storm God (in Storm God jars as well as the fragments of clay friezes from the structure atop the FSP that was destroyed in the next period). Symbolism at the Sun Pyramid perhaps did not emphasize the Feathered Serpent. Surviving stone carvings from the plaza in front of the Sun Pyramid and murals in the Sun Complex emphasize jaguars, human skulls, and diving figures with macaw attributes, which likely relate to the sun. Some of the jaguars may represent the night jaguar of the Underworld, but others are entwined with vegetation and seem more related to fertility. Possibly the Sun Pyramid was dedicated to the Sun God as well as the Storm God.

How was it decided which social entities got to build something large along the Avenue of the Dead? They must have been especially powerful entities and/or the entities most closely associated with the central civic and religious hierarchies of the state. The only reasonably good dates for the earliest stages of structures within the civic-ceremonial core of the city are for the Moon and Sun Pyramids, the Xalla Complex, the Ciudadela, the Great Compound, and 1:N5W1, a pyramid in the Moon Plaza whose interior was explored by a tunnel dug by Sugiyama and Cabrera as part of the Moon Pyramid project. Of these, only the Sun Pyramid, the small early stages of the Moon Pyramid, probably 1:N5W1, and the Pre-Ciudadela structures seem to date to the Tzacualli phase. All the rest were begun or at least greatly enlarged in the Miccaotli phase. On the basis of this tenuous evidence, I suggest they represent social units or other elements of the Teotihuacan state hierarchy that had their beginnings in the Miccaotli or Early Tlamimilolpa phases, while large civic-ceremonial complexes outside the civic-ceremonial core were perhaps associated with entities already powerful in Tzacualli times, or even earlier; entities that either did not desire to be represented in the newly prominent core district, were not permitted to build within it, or both. This suggestion needs to be tested by exploring the earliest stages of more structures along the Avenue of the Dead and elsewhere.

Civic-Ceremonial Structures Outside the Core

Outside the civic-ceremonial core of Teotihuacan, a few structures interpreted by the TMP as small and/or low pyramids and platforms may prove upon excavation to be residential compounds, as was the case at Oztoyahualco 15B:N6W3 (Manzanilla 1993) (Figure 1.6/8). Among larger structures outside the civic-ceremonial core are south-facing triadic groups such as Plaza One (1:N5W2, discussed in the previous chapter), a pair in tandem in sector N6W3 (11 and 12:N6W3), 1:N4W3, and 80:N3W1, which is 290 m west of the Avenue of the Dead but may have been part of the civic-ceremonial core (Figure 6.23). Other major south-facing pyramids not closely associated with the Avenue of the Dead and probably or definitely not parts of triadic groups are 40:N7W2 (a northern outlier of the city), 31:N3W2 (possibly not a triadic group), and 46:N3W1, 150 m west of the Avenue of the Dead and clearly part of the civic-ceremonial core. See Millon et al. (1973) for these and other tracts not shown in this book. In the far west, a pyramid with associated platforms, excavated by Rodolfo Cid (1:N3W6), is quite

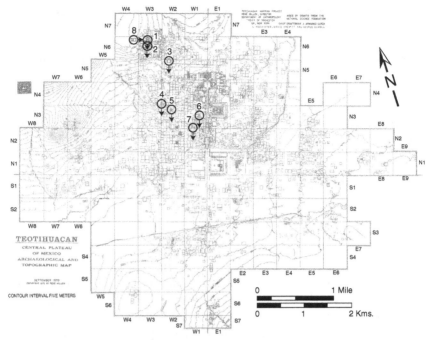

Figure 6.23. Triadic (three-pyramid) groups outside the civic-ceremonial core of Teotihuacan.

Arrows indicate the direction faced.

By S. Vaughn, after R. Millon (1973).

small but has carved stone serpent heads on balustrades. It is unusual in that it faces east, toward the core, rather than south. Also east-facing is a large unexcavated pyramid, possibly part of a triadic group, in the extreme northwest margin of the city (1:N6W4, Figure 6.23/8).

In the northeastern quadrant of the city, there are no triadic groups outside the civic-ceremonial core. 23:N3E2 (located mostly in sector N3E3) is a single pyramid that faces west. An isolated pyramid in the far east of the city, 1:N1E7, in the Hacienda Metepec area, also faces west.

West Avenue runs directly into the Great Compound. East Avenue points toward the rear of the Ciudadela but does not lead into it. Instead, it turns northward about 450 m east of it and then turns west at the Río San Juan, which it appears to parallel as far west as the Avenue of the Dead. Neither East nor West Avenue is lined by any large civic-ceremonial structure, but there is good evidence of their existence. Small platforms within East and West Avenue are significant. A low platform athwart East Avenue, 11:N1E6, 2,750 m east of the Avenue of the Dead, contained an exceptional cache that included a number of figurines of women and children and a cylinder vase showing a serpent that stylistically dates to this period (Rodríguez and Delgado 1997; Fernández and Jiménez 1997). I discuss this cache later in this chapter. Structure 34:N1W6 appears to be an equidistant platform in West Avenue, 2,750 m west of the Avenue of the Dead. It is tempting to think that these equidistant platforms in the avenues represented sociopolitical thresholds of some sort, but so far there is no evidence of that. The city extended well beyond them, both east and west.

South of East and West Avenues, there is no good evidence for any triadic groups. There are a few scattered clusters of modest civic-ceremonial platforms and pyramids along the southern extension of the Avenue of the Dead. These include tracts 1, 2, and 12:S2E1, a group lining the west side of the Avenue in sectors S3W1 and S4W1 of the Tlajinga district (including a very doubtful example of a triadic group), a small group east of the Avenue in sectors S4E1 and S5E1, a group on a wide platform facing north in S6E1, and a west-facing group in S7E1, at the extreme southern margin of the city. Although the placement of all of them along the Avenue extension is surely meaningful, nothing south of the Ciudadela and the Great Compound can be considered part of the city's civic-ceremonial core. Signs of any civic-ceremonial structures unrelated to the Avenue of the Dead in the southern half of the city are sparse and ambiguous. There are several possible low platforms, but they may be unusually large residential compounds.

What is the significance of civic-ceremonial structures that are outside the civic-ceremonial core of the city? They are far too few and too patchy in their distribution to be plausible centers for wards (*barrios*). A better candidate for a neighborhood administrative or religious center, if such things existed, is the Yayahuala apartment compound (1:N3W2, see Figure 7.8c), as suggested by Millon (1976b: 225) on the basis of excavated architectural features, including relatively easy access to its large central courtyard and the unusually large platform on the east side of the courtyard. Cabrera and Gómez (2008) propose that one of the compounds in their La Ventilla 1992–94 excavation was a ward temple. Manzanilla (2012) argues that Teopancazco (1:S2W2, Figure 1.6/11) was a barrio center. It is unlikely that any of these structures would have been identified as anything special by surface survey alone.

It is more likely that the pyramids and pyramid groups outside the core district represent cult centers associated with social entities that were somewhat independent of the administrative system of the Teotihuacan state. Could they have been associated with deities that were lesser members of the Teotihuacan pantheon? The carvings on the small pyramid in sector N3W6 are versions of the Feathered Serpent, but this and other outlying pyramids perhaps were associated with social entities that were not prestigious enough or not well-enough integrated into the Teotihuacan state to merit or possibly even desire a place in the civic-ceremonial core. They might have been specific kin groups, sodalities that crosscut kin ties, or ethnic groups. A few, such as Plaza One, might be associated with very old groups that were prominent in Teotihuacan from its beginning, and which successfully resisted entirely losing their autonomy as the state became more centralized. Distinctive Zapotec-style temples have been found in the Oaxaca enclave, but these modest one- or two-room structures have been recognized only through excavations (Croissier 2006).

The Río San Juan and the Río San Lorenzo

The course of the Río San Juan was altered to conform to the Teotihuacan grid (Figure 6.24). This must have begun in pre-Ciudadela times. Course alteration possibly begins around sector N6E4, in the northeasternmost part of the city, since the stream's course is suspiciously straight in a southward direction for about two kilometers, into Sector N3E4. However, this stretch bisects the Enclave of the Merchants and runs a little off the canonical orientation, so it may be a recent development. It then runs in a straight line 45 degrees southwest of the canonical orientation, into sector N2E2, where it follows the canonical orientation westward for about 1,400 m, passing a little north of the Ciudadela and the Great Compound. Just west of the Great Compound, it makes a 90-degree turn and runs about 250 m south, where it again turns west and runs about 600 m along the north side of West Avenue. It then turns south again and runs another 250 m, before finally turning 45 degrees southwest and running another 500 m or so, then resuming a probably unaltered course. In total, the stream's course was altered for at least 4 km. Its original course must have run through the Ciudadela and the Great Compound, and it was altered to avoid them. The east-west segment just north of these complexes is not symmetrical with regard to the Avenue of the Dead. Instead, it extends over 800 m east of the Avenue but only about 500 m west of it. Sugiyama (2005: 47) argues that the total length of this east-west segment is about 1,638 times the standard Teotihuacan measurement unit (TMU) of about 83 cm. He points out (Sugiyama 2005: 33) that the Classic Maya had an 819 day calendrical cycle. But channel erosion has made the length somewhat uncertain, and I am not convinced that

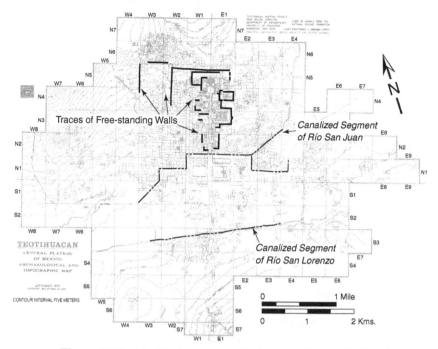

Figure 6.24. Modified courses of the San Juan and San Lorenzo streams, and traces of free-standing walls.
By S. Vaughn, after R. Millon (1973).

the 819-day cycle was important at Teotihuacan. It does not explain why the east-west segment is not symmetrical with respect to the Avenue of the Dead. Perhaps it reaches farther to the east than to the west simply because it must, in order to connect with the 45 degree segment farther east.

The Río San Lorenzo is another small stream that traverses the southern part of the city (Figure 6.24). In sectors S2E5 and S2E6 its course is sinuous and looks natural. Between sector S2E4 and sector S3W3, there is a stretch of 3.5 km that is unnaturally straight, running about eight degrees north of true west. This deviation is just one half the canonical deviation. It is unlikely that it is accidental, but the reason for it remains a puzzle. The Tlajinga district, whose residents probably already included some specialists in working lapidary materials (Widmer 1991), is just south of the Río San Lorenzo. This and other districts south of the Río San Lorenzo seem somewhat isolated from the main city. Possibly the Río San Lorenzo marked a socially significant boundary.

Commoners

I defer discussion of craft activities to the next chapter. Early in this period, the Sun and Moon Pyramids were faced with concrete, and concrete was used for the Ciudadela and its residential structures, but most people probably still lived in adobe structures until late in this period. By then, many were living in multi-apartment residential compounds. We know much less about their layouts than we do about those of the next period, because most of what we know is based on limited excavations into the lower layers of compounds whose later stages were more fully excavated. However, earlier stages of concrete compounds were built of the same materials and by the same methods that were used later. Many floors were of Teotihuacan concrete 6–10 cm thick laid over somewhat thicker crushed *tepetate* substrates and covered with a thin layer of plaster. Other floors were of small rounded river cobbles, and some were earthen. Abundant sherds of earlier periods often attest to earlier occupations, but traces of earlier structures were thoroughly removed in laying the *tepetate* foundations. In a few cases, traces of earlier fields with small irrigation channels underlie the earliest concrete floors (Nichols et al. 1991; Gazzola and Gómez 2009). Wall heartings were of rubble composed of uncut stones, *tepetate* chunks, and sometimes adobes, surfaced on each side with a 5–10 cm layer of concrete, which was in turn covered by a thin layer of white plaster, often with a *talud* about a meter high added on one or both sides (Figure 6.25). A few residences had wall murals. At Tlajinga 33 (33:S3W1, Figure 1.6/7, and see Figure 7.8d) the outer limits of the earliest surviving structure were different than in later stages. Although good evidence is scarce, I suspect that most residential compounds at this time were not as large or as integrated as they became later.

It has been proposed that these concrete-faced residential compounds replaced less substantial structures rather rapidly, in something like an "urban renewal" process, perhaps orchestrated by the state, and reflecting a state concern with the bulk of the population – a concern unusual in Mesoamerican societies. That may well be. But possibly the effect that Douglas Massey (1999: 37) calls "relative deprivation" was at work. As long as all one's neighbors lived in adobe structures, few would have felt dissatisfied with their housing. But if some people of moderate status began to live in more substantial structures, their neighbors may have felt deprived until they could emulate them. The absolute quality of their housing hadn't changed, but they began to feel it was substandard *relative* to those who had houses with concrete-faced and plastered floors and walls. This bottom-up process, as well as improved access to

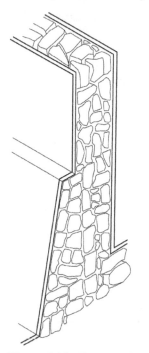

Figure 6.25. Cross section of a typical wall in a Teotihuacan residential structure.
By S. Vaughn.

lime through political expansion, may explain the apparent rapidity with which new building materials were adopted throughout the city. State intervention was perhaps less important than we have thought.

Even the earliest stages of these compounds follow the canonical 15.5 degrees east of true north that was already well-established in the civic-ceremonial core. Yet perhaps this reflects no more state intervention than enforcement of straight streets. At least in later times, in more densely occupied parts of the city, outer walls of adjacent residential compounds were sometimes separated by no more than two or three meters. That may seem narrow to us, but for a society without wheeled vehicles or beasts of burden, it would have been ample. In outlying districts of the city, residential compounds were more widely spaced, which would have allowed for "green" spaces that could have been used for intensive agriculture. Even here, however, buildings such as Tlajinga 33 approximately followed the canonical orientation. Today, a north-south country road in sectors S1W5 to S4W5 follows the orientation exactly for about 1.5 km, from just east of the parish church of San Juan Teotihuacán to the small town of San Lorenzo (Millon 1973: Map 3). The TMP found no evidence of archaeological remains in this area. Evidently, the canonical orientation extended some distance beyond the city, into the countryside. Much of this road is 2,265 to 2,270 m above sea level, at or slightly beyond the highest altitude possible for spring-fed canal irrigation. Perhaps it marked the eastern boundary of the irrigated lands in the lower valley.

The new kind of housing suggests better access to regions with the limestone from which lime was produced. The area around Tula was very likely by now under the control of the Teotihuacan state, as perhaps was the state of Tlaxcala and adjoining parts of Puebla.

The most interesting evidence about the city's spatial organization at this time comes from statistical analyses of TMP ceramic collections carried out by Ian Robertson (1999, 2001, 2005). Using proportions of several categories of plain and serving ware ceramics as indicators of socioeconomic status, Robertson derived composite indices interpretable as high, intermediate (with two sub-groups) and low status. There is no reason to think that these were distinct social strata recognized in Teotihuacan society. They are, instead, the best we can do with current information in dealing with what was probably a continuum of socioeconomic levels. There may have been a socially recognized distinction between the highest elites and everyone else, but Robertson's "high" category surely includes mainly intermediate and lesser elites. When he did this for Miccaotli phase ceramics, the four categories formed clear spatial patterns (Figure 6.26). Tracts in the "high" status group are most abundant in and near the civic-ceremonial core, but quite a few occur some distance from this core. Tracts in the "low" status group are most abundant near the edges of the city, but some occur near or even within the core. Tracts in the two "intermediate" groups tend to be spatially intermediate.

Robertson's study indicates that already, in the early part of this period, there was a very roughly concentric pattern, with higher status households more often residing near the center and lower status households more often toward the edges of the city. But the exceptions to this generalization are notable, and the pattern is far from neat. Any single district had a mix of high and low status households. Millon (1976b) long ago observed this mixing for some districts, on the basis of differences in quality of architecture in residential compounds that were not far from one another. Robertson's work corroborates this mixing and extends Millon's observation to the entire city.

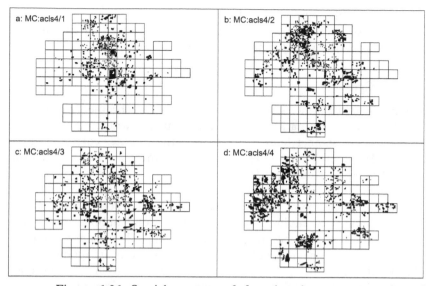

Figure 6.26. Spatial pattern of four broad status categories of Teotihuacan residential compounds in the Miccaotli phase.
Courtesy of Ian Robertson.

Robertson went beyond consideration of individual tracts, to consider whole neighborhoods. He characterized neighborhoods by their *mixes* of compounds of varying statuses. One neighborhood might consist mostly of high-status households, with a scattering of those of intermediate and low status, while another neighborhood might have mostly low status households but a few of high status. His map of types of neighborhoods for the Miccaotli phase is broadly similar to his map of types of tracts, but patterns are more clear-cut, although there are still many exceptions to a purely concentric model.

If the Teotihuacan state had imposed neighborhoods segregated according to socioeconomic status, the spatial patterns would have been much more distinct. The patterns obtained by Robertson are likely the result of choices by individual households or slightly larger kin groups – that is, bottom-up rather than top-down phenomena. I see no evidence of active resistance to top-down control in Teotihuacan, but plenty of evidence that top-down control was limited and left room for bottom-up expression of local group and individual interests.

A few foreign sherds derived from Oaxaca were found in the construction fill of the FSP, and Oaxaca-style sherds are sparsely scattered elsewhere in the city. By the latter part of this period, people from Oaxaca had established a small enclave in the western part of the city. I discuss this enclave in Chapter 7.

Ceramics

Ceramics at this time were predominantly monochrome. Serving vessels tended to have dark brown or black surfaces, ranging to medium brown. These somber hues contrast with the brighter colors of earlier phases. However, White-on-red persists and there are red and red-on-natural slips on some vessels, typically a deeper red than before and sometimes with glistening particles of specular hematite (Cowgill 1998; Cowgill and O. Cabrera 1991). Polychrome resist decoration was scarce. Flat-bottomed outcurving bowls with small solid nubbin tripod supports (Figure 6.27a) became very common and remained common throughout the remainder of the Teotihuacan Period, although over time they tend to become lighter in color and more outcurving and the small nubbins become vestigial or disappear. Some have incised decoration. A "cloud" motif of ascending arcs was especially popular. Also common were monochrome and polychrome flat-bottomed cylindrical vases with outcurving lips and solid nubbin supports. Some cylindrical vases of this early form had White-on-red incised decoration (Figure 6.27b). Direct-rim tripod cylinder vases with slab or hollow round supports, often considered a Teotihuacan hallmark, were absent or very rare. Other serving ware forms include a variety of convex bowls and, early in this period, small, nearly flat saucer-shaped objects only about 10–15 cm in diameter (Figure 6.27c). Polished serving ware jars had outflaring necks that joined the vessel body in a sharp angle and often had nubbin supports and decorated bodies (Figure 6.27d). They were quite distinct from utilitarian ollas, which tended to be much larger, were burnished rather than polished, and were rarely decorated. Storm God jars much like those in Burial 14 of the FSP occurred in some burials in residential compounds outside the civic-ceremonial core. The special vessel form called "*florero*" continued, but their tubular necks became longer and thinner and their rims more widely everted (Figure 6.27e). Thin Orange Ware vessels, mostly simple hemispherical bowls with ring bases (Figure 6.27f), were imported from southern Puebla in considerable quantities.

Plainware ollas had moderately tall necks and lips that made an angular junction with the neck (Figure 6.27g). Other utilitarian forms include craters (Figure 6.27h) and cazuelas. Granular Ware amphoras

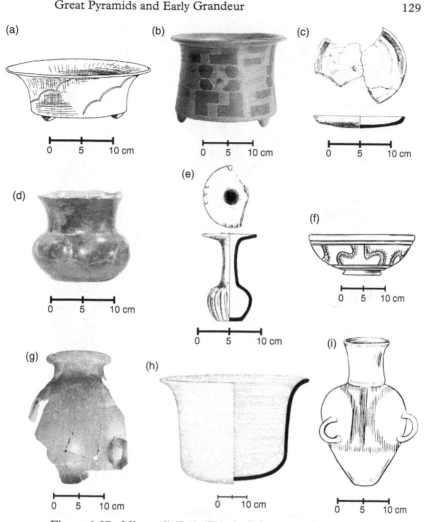

Figure 6.27. Miccaotli–Early Tlamimilolpa ceramics.
(a) polished black outcurving flat-bottomed bowl with incised "cloud"
motif, (b) out-curving-lip cylindrical vase with White-on-red decoration, (c) small polished black saucer, (d) serving ware jar, rim broken
off, (e) *florero*, (f) imported Thin Orange hemispherical bowl with ring
base, (g) plainware olla, (h) tan crater, (i) imported Granular Ware
amphora. Scale approximate. (a), (f), and (i) after Séjourné (1966a),
(b)–(e), (g)–(h) after Rattray (2001).

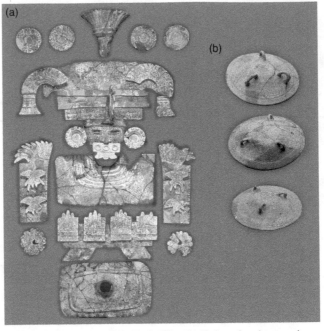

Figure 6.28. Miccaotli–Early Tlamimilolpa ritual ceramics.
(a) composite censer with handmade ornaments, (b) "handled covers".
(a) after Berrin and Pasztory (1993), (b) after Rattray (2001).

with a distinctive fabric from outside the Basin of Mexico, almost certainly made in Guerrero (Reyna and Schmidt 2004), were imported
in such quantity that they can be considered a normal household ware
(Figure 6.27i). Possibly their porous fabric made them good water cool-
ers. *Comals*, large flat ceramic griddles, were present but scarce, implying that tortillas, a staple of later central Mexican cuisine, were not yet a
large part of the diet, although abundant fragments of stone *metates* and
manos indicate that ground maize was important. Most likely it was consumed in the form of mush, gruel, or tamales.

Ritual ceramics consisted mainly of large "composite" ("theater")
censers, probably used in rituals that involved all the occupants of a
multi-apartment compound, often in commemoration of key ancestors
and in communication with them. At this time, the ceramic ornaments
("*adornos*") attached to these censers were handmade (Figure 6.28a).
Shallow matte bowls called "handled covers," or *tapaplatos*, were probably used for burning incense (Figure 6.28b). They are often sooted on
their concave upper surface. Many have three small loops that served

Figure 6.29. Miccaotli–Early Tlamimilolpa ceramics from a cache in a platform on East Avenue (TMP tract 11:N1E6).

(a) cylinder vase with serpent, (b) figurine of infant in cradle with original colors, (c) women with "wide band" headdresses, original colors.

After *Teotihuacan: Cite des Dieux*. Musée du Quai Branly, Paris, 2009.

as supports. This is indicated by wear facets on the loops, showing they had been set on a hard, flat surface. If *tapaplatos* were turned over, they could serve as lids, possibly secured by cords passed through the loops. *Candeleros*, small incense burners probably used in personal rituals, abundant in the latter part of the next period, were absent. Ceramic figurines were still largely handmade.

Especially striking is a cache in 11:N1E6, a low platform athwart East Avenue near the eastern edge of the city. It included numerous ceramic figurines of elaborately-dressed women and infants, together with an early style incised polychrome vase with a representation of a serpent, probably a featherless variant of the Feathered Serpent (Figure 6.29) (Rodríguez Sánchez and Delgado Rubio 1997; Fernández Mendiola and Jiménez Hernández 1997). This find is notable for the excellent preservation of the fugitive postfiring painting on the figurines (usually only traces remain on specimens found in fill), for the information it provides about costume, and especially as a deposit clearly representing women's interests, associating them with the Feathered Serpent.

The Sociopolitical System of Teotihuacan in Its Early Flowering

By 250 CE, all the major monumental features of Teotihuacan were in place, and it is time to take stock of this configuration and consider what it may mean about Teotihuacan society, politics, and religion. Different architectural complexes within the civic-ceremonial core may have served different ritual and/or bureaucratic functions for the state, but perhaps some were headquarters for kin-based interest groups or for sodalities that crosscut kin affiliations, as suggested by Headrick (2007). Contrary to earlier beliefs that military symbolism was late at Teotihuacan, it was already prominent in this period. Military themes are well represented in the sacrificial burials at the Moon Pyramid and the FSP. Perhaps military sodalities existed. Some argue that these themes were largely symbolic, but more likely warfare was very real, and associated with expansion of the Teotihuacan state.

Teotihuacan's civic-ceremonial zone is compact relative to the immense spread of its residential districts, but it covers about 150 ha, and the distance from the Moon Pyramid to the Ciudadela is over two kilometers. The Sun and Moon Pyramids are basically similar to one another and differ mainly in their size, but the Ciudadela is quite different from both. This difference suggests that it was the constructed material setting for institutions and practices quite different from those at the Sun and Moon Pyramids. The challenge is to go beyond this: *just how* were they different, and what do these differences mean about Teotihuacan society as a whole? It is too simple to suppose that the Ciudadela was the setting for secular, kingly, and military power, while the Sun and Moon Pyramids were the places for priestly authority, because there is far too much religious symbolism at the Ciudadela and not enough that is clearly palatial. Yet it may not be wholly wide of the mark, for surely all political authority and power at Teotihuacan was legitimized and reinforced by sacred aspects. I am wary of the term "heterarchical," because it has been used to mean several different things (Brumfiel 1995). However, authority and power at Teotihuacan may have been divided among two or more hierarchies. Perhaps one, centered on the Sun Pyramid, retained much of its previous authority and power but now had to share with other social entities associated with the Moon Pyramid and the Ciudadela. It is unlikely that these entities duplicated one another. Probably there was some division of labor among them, with religious activities dominant at the two pyramids and a stronger (but not exclusive) emphasis on politics at the Ciudadela.

Another issue is that of bureaucracies. There is a large body of literature on this topic for imperial China and other documented societies, but it seems curiously neglected in thought about prehistoric polities, beyond the simplistic assumption that "states" will require administrative hierarchies with more levels than do "chiefdoms," and that administrative levels can be inferred by discerning gaps in rank-ordering of regional site sizes. One of the most important aspects in the creation and management of larger polities is the extent to which administrative offices become more sharply defined and administrative practices become technically more skilled – an important aspect of what I mean by statecraft. Newly created large polities, pristine states in the language of some scholars, were managed by people with vaguely defined roles, many of whose practices were ad hoc. Over time, roles became more differentiated and more sharply defined, and growing bodies of lore and precedent were drawn on as resources for practices (for early China, see Falkenhausen 2006).

There is more to it than that, however. An important feature of bureaucracies is their tendency to take on lives of their own, inexorably proliferating and to a significant extent serving aims of their own rather than those of either rulers or subjects. C. Northcote Parkinson (1957) brilliantly explored these phenomena. There is also a tendency for established practices to become more rigid – less flexible and less able to react creatively to new circumstances. During the Tzacualli phase, Teotihuacan bureaucracies may have been weakly developed and flexible. In the period discussed in this chapter they were probably proliferating and becoming more differentiated and formalized. The polycentric-built environment within the civic-ceremonial center probably reflects multiple religious hierarchies, and perhaps by this time, a distinct military hierarchy, rather than any great degree of bureaucratic proliferation. It is easy to imagine that proliferation and rigidity increased more in later periods.

The audacity and scale of construction in early Teotihuacan suggests a degree of initiative and ambition unlikely to have been the work of committees. It suggests very powerful individual leaders in the early stages of Teotihuacan's growth. Perhaps a series of domineering rulers arose in the Tzacualli phase, who operated within a nominally "corporate" system but subverted it to their own ends in order to seize a high degree of de facto power, at the same time that a few other sociopolitical groups survived at pyramids outside the core precinct. This may have still been the case for a while after 250 CE. Archaeological evidence discussed in Chapter 7 may reflect reassertion of a more collective system among the highest elites, as well as growing bureaucracies.

Elsewhere in the Basin of Mexico

The spatial extent of the Teotihuacan state and the nature of its political integration is unclear, but by this time it was at least a regional state that dominated the Basin of Mexico and some distance beyond. Regrettably, at the time of their surveys, Sanders et al. (1979: 108) could not distinguish the ceramics of this period from those of the next period. Many sites, of varying sizes and characteristics, existed in the Basin. Probably there was substantial recovery from the population decline of the Tzacualli phase. Sanders et al. (1979: 114) estimate that something like 40 to 50 percent of the Basin population now resided outside the city. Given my estimate of probably as few as 80,000 residents for Teotihuacan, maybe nearly 60 percent resided elsewhere in the Basin.

Teotihuacan continued to be by far the largest single settlement in the Basin and surrounding valleys, but within the Basin there were now some sizable "second tier" centers. Among them was Azcapotzalco, on the western side of Lake Texcoco. Esther Pasztory (1997: 43) illustrates an extraordinary collection of obsidian objects, said to be from Cuauhtitlán, farther north in the western part of the Basin. They strongly resemble many of the objects found in the largest pyramids, and nowhere else at Teotihuacan. If they really came from near Cuauhtitlán, it implies a burial of very high status in that area. Perhaps they came from the nearby site called Axotlán, recently partially excavated by Raúl García (García Chávez et al. 2005). None of his finds are comparable to those illustrated by Pasztory. The grave lots described by Sarah Clayton (2009, 2013) suggest persons of intermediate status, but Axotlán may turn out to qualify as a second administrative rank center of the Teotihuacan polity.

The southeastern Basin had presumably by now recovered from the ash fall from Popocatépetl described by Siebe (2000), but population in this region remained sparse. Restudy of the ceramics excavated at Cerro Portezuelo (Figure 1.4/13) by George Brainerd in the 1950s shows that this period is well represented there (Clayton 2013). Jeffrey Parsons (1971: 196) estimated its area as about 60 ha. The ceramics, mostly locally made, with minor differences in technological and decorative style from those at Teotihuacan, are not generally of exceptionally high quality. Perhaps Cerro Portezuelo was only a "third tier" settlement.

Richard Blanton (1972: 79) estimated the area of a site at Cerro de la Estrella, on the western tip of the Ixtapalapa peninsula, as 76 ha, with 380–760 occupants. However, Teotihuacan sherd cover may have been underestimated because of the heavy Epiclassic occupation, and Cerro de la Estrella may have been a second-level center. For the entire Basin of Mexico, including the northern slope of Cerro Gordo, Sanders et al. (1979: 108) count ten provincial centers, seventeen large villages, seventy-seven small villages, 199 hamlets, two large ceremonial precincts, fifteen other special-purpose sites, and several isolated salt-making stations.

Teotihuacan's Interactions Outside the Basin of Mexico

Teotihuacan interacted with a wide diversity of other societies and cultures within Mesoamerica. Kenneth Hirth (1978) defines an "inner hinterland" for Teotihuacan, consisting of the Basin of Mexico and perhaps immediately adjoining parts of the states of Tlaxcala and Hidalgo that are closely connected topographically to the Basin. Teotihuacan would have consolidated its power in this inner hinterland in the previous period, before 100 CE, and then expanded into a more distant "outer hinterland" between 100 and 250 CE.

Most of Morelos, along with portions of the Toluca Valley and parts of the states of Puebla, Tlaxcala, Hidalgo, and Guerrero belong to this outer hinterland. In Tlaxcala and Puebla, the parts closest to Teotihuacan, within 50 km or so, were culturally quite similar to Teotihuacan. Cholula, 96 km from Teotihuacan, by now may have covered as much as 400 ha (Geoffrey McCafferty, personal communication 2007), about a fifth the area of Teotihuacan. Its ceramics are rather similar to those of Teotihuacan, but it may have been the capital of an independent polity. Farther east in Puebla, most sites were culturally quite different and probably not closely controlled by Teotihuacan.

Teotihuacan-like materials occur in the Valley of Toluca, just west of the Basin. Hirth and Angulo (1981) say that in eastern Morelos the population more than doubled, and ceramics and architectural features (including *talud-tablero* structures) they consider diagnostic of Teotihuacan appear at many sites, some rather large. They believe that San Ignacio, a large ceremonial center, probably the capital of an independent chiefdom in the previous period, now controlled the Amatzinac Valley, as an outpost of the Teotihuacan state. There are problems with their analysis, notably their treating trade wares, Thin Orange and Granular, as evidence of a Teotihuacan connection, as pointed out by Enrique Nalda (1997). Eastern Morelos is considerably closer to the southern Puebla source of Thin Orange Ware than is Teotihuacan, and people in Morelos may have obtained it directly from the source. This is even more the case for Granular Ware, probably produced in Guerrero. Other categories they consider diagnostic of Teotihuacan are not described. Nevertheless, it is likely that by this time there was a strong Teotihuacan presence in eastern Morelos. Hirth and Angulo (1981) thought Teotihuacan influence was not so strong in western Morelos, but this does not seem supported by their evidence, since forms such as "cylindrical vases" appear to be present at a higher proportion of sites in western Morelos than in the east. They postulate that Teotihuacan politically controlled eastern Morelos as a source of subsistence goods, while in western Morelos the Teotihuacan state deliberately reduced the previous level of political complexity. It is questionable whether their interpretation of the situation in eastern Morelos will be supported by further studies. As providers of basic foodstuffs for the city, closer sources with lower transport costs seem sufficient. More important would have been crops that could not be grown in the Basin of Mexico: cotton and avocados and some other fruits. This, alone, could have motivated political control of parts of Morelos. Other reasons include the suppression of potential rival polities, and perhaps the need to control a buffer area against more distant possible competitors.

The situation in the Yautepec region of central Morelos (Figure 1.4/21) is clearer, because I have inspected some Teotihuacan-like ceramics found there (courtesy of Lisa Montiel). Few, if any, seem to be imports from Teotihuacan, but there are a number of locally made close parallels. Some, including large olla rims, incised red-on-natural sherds, flat-bottomed outcurving bowls with solid nubbin supports, and types of rim flanges on Matte Ware censers, stylistically suggest this period (100–250 CE). They point to similarities in ritual practices, serving wares, and utilitarian forms. Other Teotihuacan-related ceramics from the Yautepec area, such as twin-chambered *candeleros*, are later. San Martín Orange, a plainware made in later times by specialists at Teotihuacan, is absent. This is not surprising, since it is absent even at Cerro Portezuelo, much closer to Teotihuacan. San Martín Orange was made for local consumption within the city and its immediate vicinity. Montiel (2010) says many other ceramics of this time in the Yautepec Valley are a continuation of local traditions. It is unlikely that there was any massive immigration of Teotihuacanos into central Morelos. Yet Teotihuacan influence was strong. Teotihuacan likely dominated eastern and central Morelos politically. The situation in western Morelos is less clear.

Thus, within the Basin of Mexico and a little beyond, most ceramics were locally made but stylistically so close to those made at Teotihuacan that, whatever the ethnic identity of their makers, they imply a high degree of shared culture, and probably political subjugation by the Teotihuacan state. Fear of Teotihuacan armies and receptivity to Teotihuacan traders likely spread much farther.

Signs of a Teotihuacan presence in the Gulf Lowlands are spotty. Matacapan (Figure 1.2/15) had strong Teotihuacan ties in the next period, but apparently none this early (Arnold and Santley 2008: 293). Influences running from the Gulf to Teotihuacan seem stronger, including interlocking scroll motifs and imports of fine ceramics in a group of wares called "Lustrous," not to be confused with "*Lustrosa*," which is possibly related but different. The sources of Lustrous Ware are unknown, but are likely scattered in central and northern Veracruz, perhaps not far from the later site of El Tajín (Figure 1.2/12). Lustrous Ware imports include direct-rim tripod cylinder vases, which began to be made at Teotihuacan in local fabrics at the very end of this period or the beginning of the next. This distinctive type of cylinder vase became popular at Teotihuacan and largely replaced the everted-lip vases with small nubbin supports that are typical of this period. None of these influences or presences has clear-cut political implications.

Filini and Cárdenas (2007) report some Teotihuacan connections in the Lake Cuitzeo basin in Michoacán (about 145 km west of the city, not far west of Ucareo), including Thin Orange Ware, green obsidian from the Sierra de las Navajas source, and a slate disk incised with the image of a raptorial bird in Teotihuacan style. Some of these objects may be later, but an everted-lip cylinder vase is in the early style diagnostic of this period at Teotihuacan. It may be an import from the city. These Teotihuacan-related objects appear in elite contexts. The slate disk suggests a military connection, although this need not mean conquest or the presence of a Teotihuacan garrison. This Michoacán connection is also manifested at 19:N1W5 (Figure 1.6/15), just east of the Oaxaca Enclave, where Sergio Gómez found evidence of migrants from Michoacán (Gómez 2002; Gómez and Gazzola 2007). The Cuitzeo Basin connection may have waned later. Farther to the west and north, signs of a Teotihuacan presence are faint, and there were several independent traditions, such as Teuchitlan in Jalisco.

Teotihuacan's foreign involvements seem to have extended much farther to the south and east than to the west. In the Valley of Oaxaca, Monte Albán had become the capital of a state. It was in contact with Teotihuacan but probably maintained its political independence, interacting through two-way diplomatic and trade relations (Marcus and Flannery 1996; Blanton et al. 1999). Monte Albán seems to have set up a frontier-defense outpost in the Cuicatlán Cañada that may have been a response to Teotihuacan military expansion. Within Teotihuacan, an enclave of people from Oaxaca was established.

There was a strong Teotihuacan presence in Pacific Guatemala at Balberta (Figure 1.2/22) and other sites (Bove and Medrano Busto 2003). At least 144 objects of Central Mexican green obsidian have been found, including ten projectile points in Teotihuacan style. A few Thin Orange sherds have been found, and more numerous fine paste imitations, probably from lowland Veracruz, according to NAA analyses. It is likely that Teotihuacan traders or emissaries were offering these goods to elites in local polities, in exchange for cacao, feathers of quetzal birds, and other materials foreign to the Central Highlands. It is interesting that the Aztecs extended their empire to include coastal Chiapas and coastal Guatemala, important to them for cacao. Cacao, the source of chocolate and other tasty beverages, grows well in many parts of Mesoamerica, but some of the very best came from this area. Teotihuacan people may have used coastal Guatemala as a base for later movements into highland Guatemala (especially at Kaminaljuyú) and then to lowland sites such as Tikal and Copán (Figure 1.2/31).

Zachary Hruby (personal communication, 2008) reports large obsidian serpents, very similar to those in Tomb 6 of the Moon Pyramid, of unknown provenance, in a Guatemala City museum. In an NAA and stylistic analysis of 121 Lowland Maya sherds found at Teotihuacan, Clayton (2005) found that seventy-three were stylistically Early Classic. It is likely that some belong to this period. A Teotihuacan-related cache atop a tomb at Altun Ha in Belize has ceramics stylistically very similar to Teotihuacan ceramics of this period but not made at Teotihuacan. The tomb appears to be Protoclassic in the Maya sequence (Pendergast 1990, 2003). At Caracol (Figure 1.2/30) Arlen Chase (personal communication, 2010) has found in a high-status burial green obsidian spear points and a bifacial knife much like those in the FSP.

Teotihuacan presences on the way toward coastal Guatemala that may begin this early include Mirador in central Chiapas (Figure 1.2/20) (Agrinier 1970, 1975) and Los Horcones on the Pacific coast of Chiapas, in the Tonalá region just northwest of coastal Guatemala (Taube 2000b; García-Des Lauriers 2007). Los Horcones is on the slopes of Cerro Bernal (Figure 1.2/21), a prominent granitic rock outcropping ideal for a "gateway" site linking Central Mexico to Pacific Guatemala. There is no local source of the obsidian or chert needed for cutting tools. Analyses of obsidian from Los Horcones by García-Des Lauriers (2008) found obsidian from at least six sources. By far the best represented source (in a total collection of 717 objects) is the Sierra de las Navajas near Teotihuacan (41 percent), followed by 34 percent from El Chayal in Guatemala, 15 percent from San Martín Jilotepeque (also in Guatemala), and less than 4 percent each from other sources in Central Mexico, including Otumba.

In sum, by this time people from Teotihuacan, perhaps mostly merchants, probably often accompanied by soldiers, were moving as far west as the Cuitzeo Basin of Michoacán, east into the Gulf Lowlands, and southeastward as far as Belize and Pacific Guatemala. Possibly they were largely independent of the Teotihuacan state. They may have depended more on ties with local trade partners.

Between about 250 and 550 CE, an interval spanning several ceramic phases, Teotihuacan was at its height. Changes in spatial patterns of occupation within the city were not dramatic. Sherd densities tend to increase in areas somewhat removed from the Avenue of the Dead, especially in a broad eastern and southern region and in the far northwest (the northwesternmost part of the large Oztoyahualco district). Most notable was further increase in the far northwest, increase in the Tlajinga district in the south (where by now there were some workshops of specialized potters), and decline along most of the Avenue of the Dead. Figure 7.1 shows the spatial distribution for the Xolalpan phase, the latter part of this period.

Population and Housing

Before dealing with other aspects of Teotihuacan during this interval, it is necessary to come to grips with the task of estimating population. This is the first period for which there is enough evidence about residential architecture to make the attempt feasible. My estimates for earlier periods are based on TMP sherd counts, the assumption that sherds produced per person per year did not vary much over time, and assumptions about the durations of ceramic phases. They are all very rough estimates. It is natural to suppose that ceramics of early periods would be underrepresented in surface collections. But if that was the case at Teotihuacan, populations of earlier periods must have been far larger than those later than 250 CE, which is highly improbable. Excavations in tracts that had large enough surface collections to make sampling vagaries small have not found abundant sherds of earlier phases that were not well represented in the surface collections. Probably this is because deposits are usually not deep and because earlier material was often recycled for use in the fill of later structures.

It has been hard to dispel the belief that the population of the city continued to grow and reached a peak sometime in the 400s or 500s.

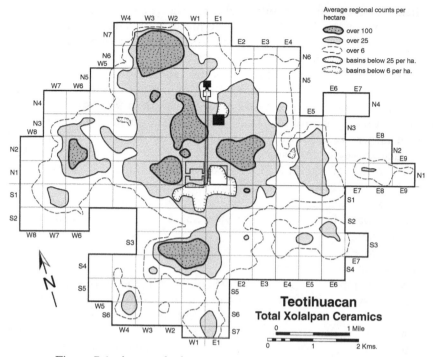

Figure 7.1. A smoothed contour map of Xolalpan phase sherd densities per hectare collected by the TMP.

By S. Vaughn, after original by author & W. Powell.

In fact, there seems to have been little further growth within the city after about 200 CE. Between 300 and 500 CE, the population may have increased by another 10–20 percent, but estimates of sherds per century suggest that after 200 CE there was a long population plateau without any pronounced peak. The spatial bounds of the city scarcely changed. Millon (1976b: 212) estimated a peak population around 100,000–200,000, but estimates of prehistoric populations are notoriously difficult, and I have made new estimates.

There is good evidence from the TMP survey that about 2,300 residential compounds were occupied during this period, although probably they were not always fully occupied. Most compounds are rectangular, often nearly square, although some have irregular outer limits, with elbows or jogs. Sizes vary widely. Some are roughly 60 m on a side. Many are considerably smaller than that and a few are much larger. Few compounds have been excavated fully enough to determine their exact dimensions, but sizes of most could be estimated fairly accurately by the TMP from surface indications. The median of these estimates is about 1,830 square meters (equivalent to a square about 43×43 m). The midspread (the range within which the middle half lie) is from 900 (about 30×30 m) to 3,160 (about 56×56 m). More than three-quarters are smaller than 60×60 m; a number often believed to be typical. Some are estimated to cover less than 900 square meters, while others range up to 8,000 (nearly 90×90 m) and a very few are even larger. Techinantitla was interpreted on the basis of the TMP surface survey as four separate compounds plus an open area (TMP tracts 2, 9, 11, 12, and 13 of sector N5E2), but subsequent partial excavation suggests it was a single exceptionally large compound running about 95 m north-south by 75 m east-west; a total area of about 7,125 square meters (Millon 1988b: 86). Techinantitla is also notable for the quantity and quality of its murals (many of them looted and now in foreign collections) (Berrin 1988) and for above-average percentages of fine ceramics.

Most compounds have outer walls about a meter thick, and they usually have one main entrance and one or two smaller ones. I suspect many began as two or more smaller compounds that were eventually amalgamated into larger units, as proposed by Jorge Angulo Villaseñor (1987) for Tetitla (see Figure 7.8a). Plans of final stages of excavated compounds suggest that few had more than four to six separate apartments, each of which was presumably occupied by one household or domestic unit. A compound with six apartments and an average of six persons per apartment would have had a total of thirty-six residents. Even an average of ten persons per apartment would not have brought the total to more than sixty. Thus, estimates of 60 to 100 seem high, and an estimate of 30 to 60 looks more realistic.

The fact that many of the city's residential structures are smaller than most of those excavated suggests that some may have housed only three or fewer households. If we assume that the mean number of households per compound was somewhere between three and five, then there would have been somewhere between 6,900 and 11,500 households in the city. Allowing another hundred compounds possibly missed by survey in heavily silted parts of the city would bring the upper estimate to 12,000 households. It is likely that most apartments in most compounds were occupied most of the time, but allowing for the possibility that any one apartment may have been empty as much as 25 percent of the time widens the estimated range to 5,175 to 12,000 households. If households averaged as few as five people, the total population of the city might have been as low as 26,000. On the other hand, if all apartments were occupied all the time, if there was an average of five apartments per compound, and if the average size of a household was 10 persons, we get a maximum of 2,400×5×10, or 120,000 people. Adding a few thousand people living in small room groups or in insubstantial structures would bring these minimum and maximum estimates up to around 30,000 to 140,000. This is a very wide range, but it realistically reflects the difficulty of estimating prehistoric populations. For what it's worth, the midpoint of this range is 85,000.

Millon (1973: 44–45) estimated population by different methods. He assumed about 30 sleeping rooms in a 60×60 m compound and 1–3 persons per sleeping room, to get 60–100 occupants. But if a compound of that size had six apartments, this would mean ten to seventeen persons per apartment, larger than most households in other societies. The numbers per household would have been even greater if there were fewer apartments. Millon also estimated thirty to fifty occupants of a 40×40 m compound and twelve to twenty in a 25×25 m compound. He arrived at a minimum population of 75,000, with 125,000 more probable and perhaps more than 200,000, if his assumptions were too conservative. I think his assumptions were too generous.

Yet another way to estimate Teotihuacan's population is to consider the quantity of Aztec sherds collected by the TMP within Teotihuacan's urban zone. The vast majority of these sherds are Late Aztec (1300 CE to after 1520, running somewhat into the Colonial period). Even if we assume that most pertain to the 125 years between 1425 and 1550, it turns out that Aztec sherds per year are about 80 percent of Teotihuacan sherds per year in the 150 to 550 CE interval. If there was little difference between sherds per person per year in Teotihuacan times and in Aztec times, this implies a fifteenth-century Aztec population within the TMP survey area of 24,000 to 120,000, far above estimates based on sixteenth-century documents. In Aztec times, households may well have had much larger ceramic inventories and generated far more sherds per person per year than in Teotihuacan times, but that is an untested speculation. Also, Aztec sherds may have been less subject to fragmentation into pieces too small to have been collected. However, some TMP field crews under-collected Aztec sherds because of their abundance, and a substantial part of the Aztec Teotihuacan Valley population lived outside the TMP survey area. In spite of all these ambiguities, a comparison of Aztec and Teotihuacan sherds per year suggests previous estimates of the Teotihuacan population may have been too high.

These separate lines of evidence, rethinking likely numbers and sizes of households at Teotihuacan and the implications of Aztec sherd abundances, lead me to suggest that Teotihuacan's population during the 200–550 CE "plateau" may have been somewhere around 85,000. A maximum of 125,000 seems possible, but so are estimates much lower than 80,000. All my population estimates for earlier and later periods, for which we have far less data on residential structures, are even more tenuous.

Population estimates are of interest not only for giving us an idea of the number of people who interacted with one another within the city, and the labor force available for building and for warfare, but also because they have a bearing on the size of the sustaining area required to provision the city with food, firewood, and other needs. Perhaps city size stabilized at a level where it could be provisioned over a long term without doing irreparable environmental damage.

If the high infant mortality inferred by Rebecca Storey (1992) at Tlajinga 33 (33:S3W1, Figure 1.6/7), a compound occupied by low-status potters, was typical, and if public health conditions in historically known premodern cities are any guide, Teotihuacan death rates were probably high enough to exceed birth rates, and a constant trickle of in-migration would have been needed just to avoid population decline.

The Ciudadela, the Feathered Serpent Pyramid, Its New Fore-Platform, and the Enclosure of the Artisans

At the Ciudadela, the FSP suffered desecratory damage and a stepped platform was built that covered most of its front (Figure 7.2). This new platform is often called the Plataforma Adosada. Sometimes it is called the New Temple of Quetzalcóatl, but this is misleading, because we have no evidence about the deities associated with it. I prefer to call it a fore-platform. Before the Gamio and Marquina project, the ruins of these conjoined structures formed a single irregular mound (Gamio 1979[1922]). They only restored the western façade and stairway of the FSP, and only made tests in the rest of it. But they found enough surviving traces of the added platform to accurately reconstruct its earlier size and shape. They also made a deep transverse cut between the old and new structures, revealing the amazing stone façade that once covered all four sides of the FSP. Most of the carved serpent heads were still in place on the front (west) side, but they had been damaged by a fire so hot that it blackened and cracked many of the stones.

Further major excavations were carried out under the direction of Cabrera in 1980–82 and by Cabrera, Sugiyama, and Cowgill in

Figure 7.2. The large fore-platform of the Feathered Serpent Pyramid. Photo by author.

1988–89. The new platform that covered much of the front of the FSP differs significantly from the earlier fore-platforms attached to the Sun and Moon Pyramids. Those platforms do not overshadow the main pyramids and do not push them into the background in the way that the new platform does to the FSP. Unlike the Sun and Moon Pyramids, the FSP was not so large that activities on its top would have been difficult to see from the ground.

The new fore-platform was much larger than the postulated original one (Chapter 6). In spite of its size, it was not built simply to hide the FSP, for it did not entirely cover its front, and the other three sides of the older pyramid were left exposed. Building the new platform was very different from the common Mesoamerican practice of completely covering an earlier structure with a later one, as in the sequence at the Moon Pyramid. Enlarging an earlier structure, often after its reverential termination (Mock 1998), suggests that the meaning of the structure and the rites to be carried out there were much the same as before, but on a grander scale. The extent of damage to the FSP looks too intense for reverential termination. There was a fire so hot that potsherds and obsidian fragments melted into glassy froth, and large slabs of modeled clay ornamentation from a structure that once stood atop it were incorporated in the fill of the new platform (Figure 6.18). Sugiyama (2005: 76–84) believes some of these fragments relate to the Storm God. It looks like desecration, marking rejection of what the FSP had stood for and the initiation of new practices (Cowgill 1983: 338; Millon 1992: 396–98).

Unlike the solid stone façades of the FSP, the new stepped platform used the standard Teotihuacan technique of *talud-tablero* construction. Ceramics in its fill include a few sherds of the Late Tlamimilolpa phase and suggest a date in the mid-300s. A small pit excavated just inside the *tablero* of the first level contained a few sherds of the Xolalpan phase in upper layers. Probably the architecturally somewhat unstable *talud-tablero* outer parts of this stepped platform had to be rebuilt some time after its initial construction. Traces of polychrome murals survive in patches of the plaster covering its concrete facing, but they are too faded to make out much. They must date to the final renovation of the platform, perhaps as late as the Metepec phase. Armillas (1945:58) noted a *flor colgante* motif that he associated with the Storm God, in blue on a red background, on the *tablero* of the first body, north of the stairway. Millon (1992: 397) reports "symbols associated with the Great Goddess" but, as I discuss in Chapter 8, this interpretation is improbable. In my own inspection I've seen no sign of Goddess or Feathered Serpent imagery.

Far less labor went into construction of this new platform than had gone into the FSP. The diagram in Gamio (1979[1922], Vol II, p. 151, Figure 35) is a conflation of data from the FSP and the new platform. The compact cellular fill shown in this figure pertains only to the FSP itself, while the manner of constructing the *tableros* pertains only to the new platform. The interior of the FSP consists of rough but very compact and solid walls of stones set in mud mortar, which formed cells within which looser fill was added. The interior composition of the new platform contrasts markedly. A framework of large wooden poles was left embedded in the platform (Gamio 1979[1922]; Millon 1973, Figure 33), but there was no cellular structure. The fill of the new platform was remarkably loose and unstructured, and there were large hollow spaces between irregular stones. In the highest layers this can be explained by a looter trench and other disturbance in post-Teotihuacan times, but the loose character of the fill continues to the lowest depth reached by our 1988 excavations, in undisturbed fill. Either the builders of the new platform did not control the resources to build it as solidly as the FSP, or they chose to use those resources in other ways.

Nevertheless, the new platform was large enough to have provided considerable space for activities on its upper surface. Performances atop it would have been visible to a large audience in the great plaza of the Ciudadela.[1] They would have been very public, far from being esoteric, unlike rites in small enclosed rooms, as was often the case in the temples atop Maya pyramids. The large altar in the center of the great plaza (Figure 6.10) also provides a broad stage for ceremonies. Recalling that the plaza is accessible from the Avenue of the Dead by a wide stairway, this implies an effort to engage many people in whatever ideology was enacted by performances visible in the plaza. One thinks of the large crowds amassed on occasions by rulers of modern states, both authoritarian and more democratic (Kertzer 1988).

The exterior of the Ciudadela was colorful, not the drab surfaces seen today. Martínez and Jarquín (1982) report fragments of painted stucco, in red, yellow, green, black, and white in the debris on its eastern face. Still, the Ciudadela as a whole was probably a little less open now than it had been before. It was probably in this period that the west enclosing platform was raised, although it remained much lower than the platforms on the other three sides. It seems a step toward making the Ciudadela less welcoming. Additionally, at all times the north and south transverse platforms within the Ciudadela separated the room complexes on the east from the great plaza on the west.

Not all important activities at Teotihuacan were visible to large audiences. The Avenue of the Dead Complex is mostly surrounded by a wall and contains no really large plazas. Its layout suggests that no parts were readily accessible to large numbers of people, and some parts of it were less accessible than were other parts.

While the FSP was apparently left in visibly desecrated condition during this period, the adjoining North and South "palaces" were probably still in use. However, the South Palace was perhaps not rebuilt during this long interval. At least, its layout was not drastically altered. In the North Palace, some doors were blocked, significantly altering circulation patterns.

The Enclosure of the Artisans, surrounded by a high wall and with only narrow exterior doorways, probably already existed, but saw its greatest use in this period. The two earlier stairways connecting it to the Ciudadela were rebuilt (Cabrera 1991). Most of the Enclosure remains unexcavated. However, INAH excavations toward its western end in 1980–82 revealed abundant evidence for the manufacture of mold-made ornaments (*adornos*) for Coarse Matte Ware composite censers, and evidence for manufacture of the censers themselves and for certain types of mold-made ceramic figurines (Múnera

1985; Múnera and Sugiyama 1993; Sullivan 2007). Artisans whose movements were restricted and who were in some way closely connected with the occupants of the North Palace of the Ciudadela produced these ceremonial objects. The plan of the structure within the enclosure where these remains were found looks much like other Teotihuacan apartments, suggesting the artisans may have been permanent residents.

Small rooms are attached to the exterior of the Enclosure of the Artisans, facing the Avenue of the Dead. They may be shops for selling items produced within the enclosure to customers in the Avenue. The artisans probably worked under state supervision, but some of their products may have been distributed by sales to individuals.

Nothing like this enclosure ever existed on other sides of the Ciudadela. Aside from the FSP, there is evidence of rebuilding episodes at the Ciudadela but no sign of destruction before the collapse of the Teotihuacan state. New structures, such as the platform attached to the FSP, show that the Ciudadela continued in use but suggest that its uses changed. Just what those changes were remains controversial. Activity in the Enclosure of the Artisans suggests an increased elite interest in craft production. The Ciudadela Complex may have been originally built as a new locus for the heads of the Teotihuacan state. Desecration of the FSP, combined with continued use of the rest of the Ciudadela, might reflect a major change in Teotihuacan's political system. But perhaps the targeted desecration is more the reflection of some change in the religious system. Could it have been an attack on the Feathered Serpent? Could sixteenth-century accounts of the conflict between Quetzalcóatl and Tezcatlipoca be a faint reflection of real factional struggles at Teotihuacan? Even if so, the Feathered Serpent was not wholly vanquished, since representations of it continue in later Teotihuacan imagery, although perhaps not so prominently as before.

The Avenue of the Dead Complex and Elsewhere in the Civic-Ceremonial Core

After construction of the FSP, no new structures on a grand scale were started at Teotihuacan. This does not mean a decline in building activity. All along the Avenue of the Dead, and elsewhere, existing structures were considerably enlarged. The base of the Sun Pyramid was enlarged, possibly to deal with slumping. In the Quetzalpapalotl Palace, at the southwest corner of the Moon Plaza, the latest construction stage is

(a)   (b)

Figure 7.3. Stone figures on the balustrades of the stairs of the principal pyramid in the West Plaza Group, Avenue of the Dead Complex. (a) Serpent and feline features mingle in the first stage. (b) Feline features predominate in the second stage.

Photographs by author.

several meters above an earlier stage (Acosta 1964b). The final stage of *Edificios Superpuestos* (1:N2W1), part of the Avenue of the Dead Complex, was several meters higher than before and had a drastically different layout. Pyramids in the West Plaza Group that had three *talud-tablero* bodies in Stage 1 had only two bodies in Stage 2 (Morelos 1993). Since the heights of the pyramids were not increased, their stairways were rebuilt with less steep slopes. The levels of courtyard and patio floors were often raised when Teotihuacan apartment compounds were rebuilt, with little or no increase in the levels of platforms facing these courtyards. Ordinarily, this meant that the short stairways (as well as *taludes*) leading up to the platforms became shorter, rather than less steep. But the change in slopes of stairways in the West Plaza Group is clear, especially in the stairway on the east side of that group's major pyramid (40A:N2W1). Here the balustrades of the Stage 1 stairway carry large heads with predominantly snake-like attributes, while heads on the balustrades of the Stage 2 stairway have more jaguar-like attributes (Figure 7.3). It has been suggested that these reflect a decline in the importance of the Feathered Serpent and increased power of a competing faction identified with the jaguar. Whether or not that is so, the shift in symbolism was probably somehow meaningful, and it could possibly be linked to desecration of the FSP.

The *tablero* of the platforms that bounded the courtyard of the West Plaza Group had a low relief stone frieze, a feature otherwise rare at Teotihuacan. The frieze probably dates to Stage 2. It consists of multiple

Figure 7.4. Stone wall frieze from the West Plaza Group courtyard, Avenue of the Dead Complex – a major dignitary? Width
2.2 m. Rectangles are individual stone blocks. A photo (Berrin
1988: 70) shows there are small errors in this drawing.
After Morelos García (1993, figure F.2).

representations of a frontal figure wearing an elaborate headdress that
includes frontal birds and profile serpents. The figure's widespread
hands hold budding shoots and flaming bundle torches (Figure 7.4).
I will say more about flaming bundle torches in Chapter 8. They are a
recurrent Teotihuacan symbol, both at home and abroad, and probably
part of the symbolism of the Teotihuacan state. The figure in the West
Plaza Group has been claimed as a representation of a supposed "Great
Goddess," which has discouraged other interpretations. However, Zoltán
Paulinyi (2006) has convincingly discredited the "Great Goddess" concept, and this requires consideration of alternative possibilities. The figure in the frieze wears the "Storm God" nose pendant. Representations
of this pendant type appear in a number of contexts, in Teotihuacan and
abroad. Two pendants of this type were found in looted Grave 13 of
the FSP – the grave that possibly once held the remains of a head of
the Teotihuacan state (Figure 6.15a). The frieze in the Avenue of the
Dead Complex probably relates to Teotihuacan rulership, or at least
high political office.

Besides one nearly complete example of this stone relief figure, fragments of another were found (Morelos García 1993), which implies that originally there was a series of them. They are probably not specific individuals. But the fact that they are in carved stone indicates an investment beyond that represented in mural paintings. The individual blocks are much smaller than those on the façades of the FSP, and the carvings are in low rather than high relief. The labor involved was far less than at the FSP. This could mean that by this time rulership was a less exalted position than it had been before, or possibly the frieze represents some office or personage of slightly lower rank.

Box 7.1 The Problem of Ball Courts

Ballcourts bounded by parallel platforms, usually with a stone ring projecting from each side, are widespread in Mesoamerica. The games played in them were of great religious and political significance (Scarborough and Wilcox 1991). No architectural evidence for ball courts of this kind has been found at Teotihuacan, in spite of a diligent search by the TMP. However, a fragmentary mural in the Tepantitla compound (1:N4E2) shows in profile what may possibly be ball court (Figure 7.5, at bottom), while a nearby scene shows players of a different kind of ball game, using bats, on a field that lacks enclosing platforms but is demarcated at each end by a composite stela of the kind found in the La Ventilla A compound (5:S1W2, (Figure 7.6) (Aveleyra 1963a, 1963b; Millon 1973: 33.). This is a little south of the La Ventilla compounds excavated by Cabrera and his group since 1992 (Cabrera and Gómez 2008). Elements of another such composite stela are in the Teotihuacan site museum, and another was found in the "Mundo Perdido" district of Tikal, a striking example of Teotihuacan influence in the Maya area. The significance of this Teotihuacan type of ballgame is unclear. Barbara Stark (2012) points out that in many Mesoamerican ball courts only a few persons could have had a good view of the game, which implies that commoners had little access to it. The Teotihuacan game may have been played on an open field and visible to large crowds of commoners. However, the quality of the stone markers indicates that it was not a casual "sandlot" sport.

(continued)

Box 7.1 (*continued*)

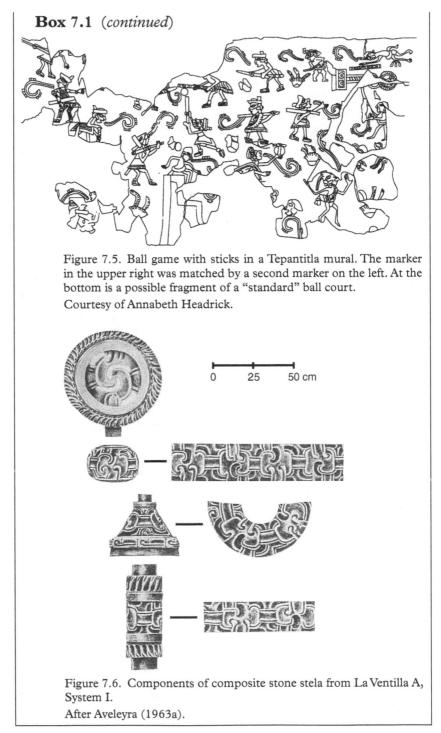

Figure 7.5. Ball game with sticks in a Tepantitla mural. The marker in the upper right was matched by a second marker on the left. At the bottom is a possible fragment of a "standard" ball court.

Courtesy of Annabeth Headrick.

Figure 7.6. Components of composite stone stela from La Ventilla A, System I.

After Aveleyra (1963a).

Multi-Apartment Residential Compounds

Architecturally substantial multi-apartment residential compounds were now pervasive throughout the city. They housed most of the city's population. Complementing the dramatic finds of pyramids and palaces, they tell us about the lives of lesser elites and ordinary people. About 2,300 were found in the TMP survey. Only a few have been even partially excavated. The majority were identified by the TMP on the basis of low mounds (rarely more than a meter high) with Teotihuacan Period sherds and other artifact fragments on their surfaces, and the characteristic fine gravel of volcanic scoria (*cascajo*) that is a reliable indicator of disintegrated Teotihuacan concrete. Architectural remains almost never project much above the present ground surface, but, in 932 cases, traces of walls with rubble cores and concrete facing were detected. Wherever long enough wall stretches were visible, compass readings showed that walls were almost always within a degree or two of the canonical Teotihuacan orientation. In 942 cases, some of which also showed wall traces, there was evidence of concrete-and-plaster surfaced floors in place. Millon (1973: 27) says that traces of such walls and/or floors were detected in over 1,200 tracts. All too often recent disturbances, including looter pits and modern road cuts, show a kind of crude surgery, exposing superposed concrete floors, walls, and other features, indicating up to four or five stages of construction.

No two residential compounds have identical plans, but there is a "vocabulary" of modular elements that were assembled in various ways. Mary Hopkins (1987a, 1987b) used network analysis to characterize variations in layouts. There was a strong preference for bilateral or fourfold symmetry. Wood was used sparingly (and often reused) for columns, lintels, and flat roofs. In the finer compounds, cut stone blocks (ashlar) were used for stair steps and balustrades. There is no evidence for second stories anywhere. These architecturally substantial compounds had walls whose cores were composed of varying combinations of stone rubble, roughly shaped chunks of *tepetate*, and mud bricks (adobes), set in mud mortar (Figure 6.25). Most were faced on both sides with several centimeters of Teotihuacan concrete, covered with a thin layer of white plaster. In finer compounds, some plastered walls were adorned with polychrome fresco paintings. In less elaborate compounds, borders or steps had simple red outlines, or no decoration at all. A disproportionate number of excavated compounds have been selected for excavation because of evidence that they had mural paintings. In the TMP survey, fragments of murals were found on the surfaces of a few unexcavated tracts, but there must be some decorated compounds with no surface evidence of murals. The proportion of residential compounds with mural paintings is unclear.

Throughout Teotihuacan, residential compounds often had a nearly square main courtyard, usually with a small altar or shrine in the center. Sometimes there are one or more additional courtyards. The more elaborate courtyards were surrounded by platforms a meter or so high on the north, east, and south sides, and often there is also a platform on the west side. The east platform is usually somewhat larger and higher than the others. Atop each platform there is generally a single room, with a pillared portico in front. These platforms with room and portico have often been called temples. There is some justification for that, because they do not connect directly to the residential apartments within the compound, and because they somewhat resemble structures identified as temples in highland Oaxaca (Marcus and Flannery 1996). But it is hard to believe that so many Teotihuacan residences had a large part of their total area reserved for ritual alone, and I am sure that many mundane activities were also carried out on these platforms and rooms. Possibly they were reserved for only some occupants of the compounds, perhaps only relatively high-status adults. However, activities on the platforms and rooms connected to a courtyard must have pertained to occupants of all apartments connected to the courtyard. It is unclear if occupants of apartments attached to the exterior of a compound were involved in courtyard activities. Mundane activities must also have been carried out in the courtyards themselves, as well as rituals focused on the courtyard altar.

The total area of all TMP collection tracts is 1,811 ha (18.11 km^2), not including areas that could not be surveyed and areas where no evidence of Teotihuacan occupation was found. The roughly 2,300 residential compounds cover a cumulative area of about five square kilometers. This is only a fourth of the total area of the city because parts of it are taken up by civic-ceremonial structures, streets, plazas, insubstantial structures, and other open spaces between compounds. Open spaces are often broad in the outer parts of the city.

Overall dimensions of compounds vary greatly and they differ considerably in construction quality, ranging from elegant to shoddy. Average room sizes also differ among compounds. Even within a single compound, different apartments may vary in construction quality and room sizes. Figure 7.7 shows average dimensions of apartment compounds within each arbitrary TMP 500-meter sector. Each number is derived from the mean of the areas of compounds within that sector. However, what is shown is the square root of the mean area, i.e., the length of one side that a square compound with that area would have had. In the

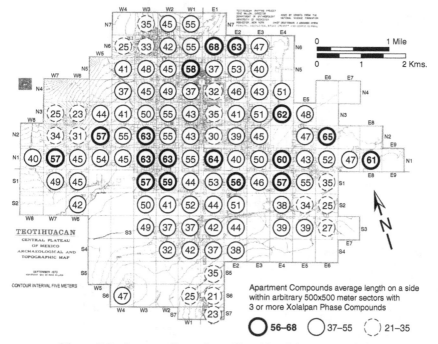

Figure 7.7. Average dimensions of residential compounds in 500×500 meter sectors of Teotihuacan.

By S. Vaughn.

densely built-up area running 0.5 to 1.5 km west of the Avenue of the Dead, from about as far north as the Moon Pyramid to 500 m south of the Great Compound, sector averages range from 45 m to as high as 63 m. That is, many residential compounds in this part of the city have dimensions not too far from 60×60 m. This is also true in a few other sectors, including a few on the periphery of the city, such as N1E8, N3E4, N1W7, N7W1, N6E1, and N6E2. But many sectors have means in the twenties and thirties. In N6W3, noted during the survey as an area of unusually small compounds, the mean is only 33×33 m. Within 500 m of the Avenue of the Dead, most sector means north of the Ciudadela range from 32×32 m to 43×43 m. Many survey tracts in this part of the city consist of relatively small structures associated with pyramids. In the Ciudadela itself the mean is elevated because the North and South "palaces" are unusually large.

Smaller compounds imply fewer occupants. Possibly this correlates with lower status, since wealthier "houses" tend to have more members

Figure 7.8 Some Teotihuacan residential structures with clear outer limits. (a) Tetitla, (b) Zacuala "palace," (c) Yayahuala, (d) Tlajinga 33. (a)–(c): After Séjourné (1966b). (d) After Storey (1992).

in many societies. However, this possibility has yet to be tested for Teotihuacan.

Few residential structures have been excavated to well-preserved outer limits. Examples include Tetitla (1:N2W2, Figure 7.8a), Zacuala "Palace" (3:N2W2, Figure 7.8b), Yayahuala (1:N3W2, Figure 7.8c), Tlajinga 33 (33:S3W1, Figure 7.8d), and La Ventilla 92–94 Fronts 1, 2, and much of Front 3. Other compounds, such as Xolalpan (2:N4E2), Tepantitla (1:N4E2), Atetelco (1:N2W3), Teopancazco (1:S2E2), 19:N1W5 (with West Mesoamerican connections), and several tracts in the Oaxaca Enclave and elsewhere have been excavated extensively enough to show that they include apartments, courtyards, and platforms topped by rooms. But it is unclear how many others fit the pattern of a nearly square compound surrounded by a thick outer wall. The outer wall of Tlajinga 33, occupied by low-status residents, is not very thick, and the platforms around its courtyards are low. This is also the case at Oztoyahualco 15B (15B:N6W3) (Manzanilla 1993), which is the only adequately excavated residential structure in the district that Millon (1973) labeled the "Old City," in part because, in surface survey, the residential structures there appeared to be smaller than those in most of the city. The Tlamimilolpa residential area excavated by Linné (2003b[1942]) (1:N4E4) is also very different architecturally from most others so far excavated at Teotihuacan. It seems to be a large warren of small room groups, narrow passageways, and courtyards associated with low platforms. At Tetitla, the apartments on the north side are tacked on, outside the thick outer wall of the compound, and some do not even connect with the compound's interior.

The standardized orientations of the compounds imply some degree of top-down control by a powerful authority, together with considerable room for improvisation and adjustment to local interests within their outer walls. The government required streets to have the canonical orientation and to be relatively straight and unblocked, but such rules were not always well enforced. For example, the spacious entryway to Zacuala "palace" jogs far out into the street.

To what extent did the state override local interests by imposing the streets on what had been a less rigid layout? Were the streets already there when housing was still mostly of perishable materials?

Residential units composed of related households are common throughout the world, but the number of households inside the larger Teotihuacan compounds is exceptional, as is the prevalence of platforms facing courtyards but unconnected to apartments. Occupants of a compound probably consisted of a core of people who considered themselves close relatives, perhaps regarded as descended from a common ancestor, most likely male. At any rate, some biological evidence from a few compounds suggests somewhat closer biological relationships among males than among female occupants (Spence 1974). Probably the concept of "house" (Joyce and Gillespie 2000) applies, in which membership is not defined on a strictly genealogical basis. Some occupants of a compound would have belonged to a relatively stable core, while others were less closely attached. These may have included servants and more distant relatives. Likely some individuals or whole families changed residence because of marriages, internal frictions, or better opportunities in other compounds. Yet most or all occupants of the same compound probably had a sense of shared identity and participated in compound-wide rituals celebrating compound identity and life crises such as childbirth, coming of age, marriage, and death. Communion with deceased occupants was important. Healing and some other ceremonies were more likely focused on individual households. From the point of view of the state, compounds were probably important administrative units, but what went on inside them does not seem to have been closely monitored, to judge from the variety of mortuary practices identified by Clayton (2009, 2011).

There may have been still larger kin groups that included occupants of multiple compounds, such as groups regarded as descended from a common ancestor, which can loosely be called "clans" (Headrick 2007). If any such groups existed, they may have had internal ranking, with high-status families that claimed descent through a line of senior siblings (e.g., oldest son of oldest son), while lower-status families were descended from younger siblings. Examples are known elsewhere, as in Bronze Age and later China (Falkenhausen 2006). Such large kin groups, if they existed, may or may not have been concentrated in specific neighborhoods. Possibly head families lived in the civic-ceremonial core, while lower-ranked clan households were dispersed elsewhere. Conjectures about the existence and nature of clans might be tested through large-scale searches for distinctive mortuary and other ritual practices, along the lines suggested by Clayton (2009, 2011).

In addition to the architecturally substantial multi-apartment residential compounds, the TMP identified 76 substantial structures that seem too small to have contained multiple apartments. These were designated "room groups." Many are adjacent to pyramids and may have housed priests or served other ritual purposes, including storage of paraphernalia. Given their small numbers and small size, their residents would not have added greatly to the city's total population.

Insubstantial Structures

The TMP identified 833 tracts with more than trace amounts of Teotihuacan Period sherds on the surface, but no signs of architecture, no traces of walls or floors, and no building materials such as rocky rubble, volcanic gravel, or the tabular stones used in *talud-tablero* features. Some of these tracts were occupied by people living in insubstantial structures made of adobes or wattle and daub. Other tracts may have been used for special purposes such as craft activities. Still others may have been agricultural plots fertilized by waste removed from residences, or simply dumps (Cowgill et al. 1984). These tracts are about a quarter of all tracts interpreted as definite or possible residential loci. However, even if all of them in fact contained residences, they could not have included anything like a quarter of Teotihuacan's population. Far less than a quarter of the Teotihuacan Period ceramics collected by the TMP came from such tracts. If many of these tracts never were residences, the proportion of the total population that they represent would have been small. Robertson (2008) suggests that as much as 15 percent or more of the total urban population may have lived in insubstantial structures in some phases. His estimate may be a little high. Nevertheless, a significant minority of Teotihuacanos lived in small insubstantial structures, and this must be taken into account in imagining Teotihuacan society.

Occupants of tracts that lack evidence of substantial architecture were probably of very low status. These tracts are not clustered in neighborhoods. Some are interspersed among apartment compounds; others are scattered around the peripheries of the city. If San José 520, where there is evidence of pottery-making and where excavations by Oralia Cabrera Cortés (2006, 2011, Figure 1.6/10) revealed traces of adobe structures, had been within the limits of the TMP survey, it would have been interpreted as a tract occupied by insubstantial structures.

Neighborhoods

By "neighborhood," I mean a small area, of no more than 10–30 ha, within which occupants could have been in frequent face-to-face contact, roughly corresponding to a *barrio* in modern Mexican usage. I distinguish this from "district," which refers to larger areas, usually of about 100–200 ha, which for one reason or another look different from other parts of the city. Both neighborhoods and districts are inferred from archaeological data, and it is not clear that either were regarded by the Teotihuacan state as administrative units. There are a few pyramid complexes outside the civic-ceremonial core that have been proposed as neighborhood temples, as discussed in Chapters 5 and 6, but they are far too few and too uneven in their distribution to have served as neighborhood centers.

Distinguishable neighborhoods include enclaves with foreign connections and areas of craft specialists, but otherwise few clear neighborhoods can be identified. We can say more about spatial patterning in Teotihuacan than in most ancient cities because of the thoroughness of the TMP. Nevertheless, many more controlled excavations of high quality are needed to complement the TMP data. Over a thousand Teotihuacan burials have been excavated and reported with varying degrees of detail

(Rattray 1992; Sempowski and Spence 1994; Manzanilla and Serrano 1999; Clayton 2009, 2011). Burials offer information about mortuary practices, differences in socioeconomic status, and differences related to gender and age. Study of composite censer ornaments by Kristin Sullivan (2007) and unpublished studies of the spatial patterning of motifs on the small incense burners called *candeleros* have given hints of weak spatial clustering but show that many motifs are widespread in the city. There is a case of figurines made from the same mold that were found in widely separated parts of the city (Allen 1980).

Neighborhoods where persons with foreign connections were concentrated have often been called "*barrios*," but I call them enclaves. They have been identified through distinctive architecture, associated ceramics, and mortuary practices. NAA and stable isotope studies have added information about sources of ceramics and people.

The Oaxaca Enclave

Oaxaca-style sherds are scattered very thinly throughout Teotihuacan, but not in quantities or proportions that suggest ethnic neighborhoods (Rattray 1987). However, in a cluster of structures about 2.75 km west of the Avenue of the Dead, up to 5 percent of the ceramics are in Oaxacan styles. Connections are mostly with Monte Albán, although some are with other parts of Oaxaca. This enclave is toward the western end of the city, but not at the extreme western limits; scattered apartment compounds continue another 600–700 m farther west. It is located in the central part of TMP sector N1W6, and extends about 100 m into the southern part of sector N2W6 (Figure 1.6/13). There is no evidence of surrounding walls, although on most sides it is separated from other compounds by 100 m or more. Within the enclave, residential compounds are about as closely spaced as in the central parts of the city, separated by streets three to eight meters wide, with a few open areas as well. It covers about five hectares and includes about fifteen apartment compounds.[2] Excavations have been carried out in at least five of these compounds by a series of projects since the 1960s (Millon 1973; Paddock 1983; Spence 2002, 2005; Spence and Gamboa Cabezas 1999; Rattray 1993; Quintanilla 1982; Gibbs 2001, 2010; Urcid 2003; Croissier 2006; Palomares 2006, 2013).

Compounds are typical of Teotihuacan in layouts and methods and materials of construction and size ranges, except for a Oaxaca-style, two-room temple excavated by Michelle Croissier (2006). The construction quality within individual compounds is variable, as is usual at Teotihuacan, and is within the broad intermediate range, none especially high and none extremely low. Some stuccoed walls have red paint (Palomares 2006: 76), but no murals have been found. The TMP identified several tracts within the enclave that had surface scatters of sherds and lithic artifacts but no evidence of substantial architecture. These may have been outbuildings or agricultural plots, but it is possible that they were occupied by families of low status. The most notable Oaxacan features are related to religion; mortuary practices, Oaxaca-style temples, and ceramic urns. Burials were generally extended rather than flexed in Teotihuacan style. So far, seven Oaxaca-style tombs have been discovered, in three different compounds. The vertical stone jamb at the side of one tomb entrance has a single carved glyph in Oaxaca style, probably the day sign "motion" or "earthquake" in the ancient Zapotec calendar. Apparent construction phases of these tombs range from Early Tlamimilolpa to Xolalpan, although they continued in use for some time after their construction, probably into the final ceramic phase of the Teotihuacan state (Metepec). Six Oaxaca-style urn-type censers have been found, as well as fragments of at least two others, tentatively dated stylistically from Monte Albán II to IIIA. Most seem to fit best with the Late Monte Albán II phase, (or Niza) about 1–200 CE (Urcid 2003) (Table 1.1). NAA analyses indicate three were made in the Teotihuacan Valley, one at Atzompa (just north of Monte Albán), one in the Valley of Oaxaca, and one somewhere else in Oaxaca (Palomares 2006).

Most of the ceramics found in household refuse are standard Teotihuacan types. Only 3–5 percent are in Oaxaca styles, and these represent a limited range of types. They assert ethnic affiliation with Oaxaca but most are made of Teotihuacan Valley clays. They are not quite identical to Oaxacan types (Gibbs 2001: 49). Most common are coarse conical bowls (*apaxtles*), variously related to Monte Albán types G1, G2, or G35 (Gibbs 2001). These are six to seven times as abundant as fine grayware bowls, usually with two encircling grooves on the interior just below the rim, very similar to the G12 type of Oaxaca (Gibbs 2001: 66). *Comales* are difficult to tell from those in Teotihuacan style. Less abundant Oaxaca-style vessels include coarse ollas, jars, and plates; ladle censers, hourglass censers, and crude figurines (Gibbs 2001). Paddock (1983) identified conical *cajetes*, ollas, G12 rims, G21 bottoms, ladle censers, and cylindrical *cajetes*. Four sherds were a Black-and-White ware virtually unknown at Monte Albán and typical of the Mitla area. Croissier (2006) notes a few sherds stylistically similar to A6, A10, and G15/G16, which she says suggest an initial Oaxacan occupation earlier than Late Monte Albán II (before 100 CE?). Andrew Balkansky (personal communication 2001) identified a few sherds diagnostic of Monte Albán I-C (or Pe), thought to have ended by 50 BCE in Oaxaca. This would place them within the Patlachique phase at Teotihuacan. Such an early date is possible, but it raises questions about chronological alignments between Central Mexico and Oaxaca. Croissier adds that the Dainzú area, in the eastern Valley of Oaxaca (as is Mitla) shares more similarities with the Oaxaca Enclave than does Monte Albán.

On the basis of strontium stable isotope analyses of teeth and bones, Price et al. (2000; 2008) conclude that some occupants of the Oaxaca Enclave were locally born, but many were long-term or recent migrants to Teotihuacan. The place of origin of most migrants is unclear, although some could be from Monte Albán. Oxygen isotope studies also suggest varied origins of the occupants, including some who lived most or all their lives in the Teotihuacan area (White et al. 2004a; 2004b).

A controversial issue is the extent to which residents in the enclave continued to make Oaxacan pottery types long after they had gone out of use in Oaxaca itself. Emigrants often cling to old styles for a while after they have gone out of fashion in the homeland. However, Millon (1973) and Spence (1992) have argued that Oaxacan types continued to be made in the Oaxaca enclave several centuries after they had been superseded in Oaxaca, based on an early chronology that saw Monte Albán II ending around 250 CE. Others were skeptical and believed the occupation of the barrio did not last long (e.g., Paddock 1983). The most careful study of this issue is by Kevin Gibbs (2001, 2010), who made statistical studies of about 770 sherd lots from Spence's excavations in 6:N1W6. All lots exhibit some degree of phase mixing (Gibbs 2001: 57). Gibbs concludes that these data support continued local manufacture of Late Monte Albán II types into at least the Xolalpan phase at Teotihuacan. However, recent revisions of the Monte Albán ceramic chronology suggest that very late Monte Albán II (Tani) may have lasted until about 350 CE, which is when I estimate the Xolalpan phase began at Teotihuacan. If so, the persistence of slightly outmoded Oaxacan types in Teotihuacan is not so remarkable.

Whatever the case with ceramics, Oaxacan mortuary practices continued for a long time. This is particularly obvious in the construction of tomb chambers that were periodically reopened to add new bodies. Evidence seems good that some of these tombs were built in the Xolalpan phase and continued in use into the Metepec phase. This was not anachronistic: similar tombs continued to be used in Oaxaca until at least the end of Monte Albán III-A, (Pitao), 500 CE or later (Marcus and Flannery 1996: 234).

Why did people from Oaxaca come to Teotihuacan and why did they concentrate where they did? Peeler and Winter (1993) argue that they came to Teotihuacan in order to lay out the city according to Zapotec cosmological principles. There is an abstract coherence to their geometrical reasoning, but it is unconvincing for several reasons. The orientation of Teotihuacan was probably established before the enclave was founded, there is no reason to postulate a Oaxacan source for the cosmological ideas involved, and no reason to think the needed measurement skills could not have been developed locally. Possibly Oaxacans were brought to Teotihuacan because of their skills in masonry, especially in the use of concrete and lime plaster, and their descendants may have maintained this occupational niche. But evidence for this or any other occupational specialization in the enclave is not strong. Another possibility is that they were part of a Zapotec "trade diaspora,"[3] represented also by Oaxaca-style ceramics at Chingú and other sites in the Tula area (Spence 2005), but it is not clear what they were trading. Mica from Oaxaca was probably exported to Teotihuacan (Winter et al. 1998: 473), but not on a scale that would require a large resident colony at Teotihuacan. The number of occupants in the enclave, its modest architecture, and its distance from the civic-ceremonial center make it unlikely that they were emissaries representing the Monte Albán state.

A Oaxacan identity may have persisted long after the reasons for initial Oaxacan settlement had ceased to exist. I suspect that a major factor in this persistence was language, but language leaves no material traces. It would be interesting to know if loans from any Oaxacan languages can be found in any Central Mexican languages.

The "Enclave of the Merchants"

On the opposite side of the city, in sectors N3E4 and N4E4, on its northeastern margin, the TMP found a neighborhood with unusual proportions of foreign ceramics imported from the Gulf Lowlands and the Maya area (Figure 1.6/14). The enclave lies mainly on the western side of the Río San Juan, which today runs deeply entrenched in a ravine that may be post-Teotihuacan. Part of the enclave is on the eastern bank. It extends northward to include the Tlamimilolpa residential complex (1:N4E4) partially excavated by Linné in 1934–35. Linné illustrates some foreign sherds, including fragments of Early Classic Maya polychrome basal flange bowls (Linné 2003b[1942]: 179 and Plate 2). In the 1960s, the TMP carried out small excavations at 3:N3E4 (TMP operation 11, Xocotitla) and 8:N3E4 (TMP operation 4, Mezquititla). In the early 1980s, Rattray carried out more extensive excavations in this enclave (Rattray 1987, 1989, 1990a). Rattray (1990a) says the earliest foreign ceramics are from the Huasteca (northern Veracruz and adjoining parts of San Luís Potosí), in the Late Tlamimilolpa phase.

Wares from the Tuxtlas area of the southern Gulf are most abundant in Early Xolalpan. Ceramics include polychrome basal flange bowls and gloss ware jars from the southern Maya Lowlands. Perhaps significantly, Rattray does not attribute any ceramic imports to central Veracruz.

Rattray (1990a) discovered remains of at least ten circular structures at Xocotitla, ranging from 5 m to 9.5 m in diameter. Circular structures are scarce at Teotihuacan, although two structures interpreted as "D-shaped" in the Enclosure of the Artisans may be parts of circular structures. Circular buildings occur in West Mexico, but more significant is their occurrence in the Gulf Lowlands. At Xocotitla they stratigraphically underlie rectangular structures more typical of Teotihuacan residential architecture. The Tlamimilolpa complex has rectangular rooms oriented in the canonical Teotihuacan direction, but its layout is otherwise unlike most excavated Teotihuacan compounds. I suspect it is not a single compound, but several distinct residential units, separated by narrow alleys that often turn corners at right angles, rather than by wide straight streets. There are a number of small courtyards, but most of the platforms surrounding them are low. Architecturally, it suggests low-status occupants. Yet there are some rich offerings, including obsidian human figurines, rare outside the civic-ceremonial center (Linné 2003b[1942]: 135), and the base of a polychrome mural that is probably a human figure in frontal pose, wearing tasseled sandals (Linné 2003b[1942]: 116). Perhaps the occupants of this enclave were not such highly organized merchants as were present later in Mesoamerica, but they were certainly engaged in trade.

People from West Mexico

In 19:N1W5 (Figure 1.6/15), only about 150 m east of the Oaxaca Enclave, Sergio Gómez has found evidence that the occupants in the northern part of the compound had ties with Michoacán, in western Mexico, while those in the southern part of the compound had Oaxacan connections (Gómez 2002; Gómez and Gazzola 2007).

Districts

The civic-ceremonial core of Teotihuacan is mostly enclosed by freestanding walls that impede access from the rest of the city (Figure 6.24). Another well-defined district is the Tlajinga area, south of the Río San Lorenzo, with its own modest civic-ceremonial platforms along the southern extension of the Avenue of the Dead, notable especially for specialized production of San Martín Orange Ware in some compounds.

Yet another district is in sectors N6W3, N6W2, and the southern parts of N7W3 and N7W2, the northwestern part of the large area called Oztoyahualco. It was recognized as different in the TMP survey, especially because residential compounds are small and closely crowded. Linda Manzanilla's excavation at 15B:N6W3 found architecture somewhat different and more modest than in most compounds excavated at Teotihuacan. This area is marked "Old City" on the TMP map sheets (Millon et al. 1973) because Millon suspected that it preserved an early architectural style prior to the massive residential building in the Tlamimilolpa phase. In fact, densities of early ceramics are not very high in this area, and I think its major development was in the Xolalpan and Metepec phases, when there probably were many ceramic workshops in this district. The fact that it lies outside probable freestanding walls and includes two large triadic pyramid groups suggests that it may have been somewhat independent of the central authority, although its structures follow the canonical Teotihuacan orientation. The southeastern part of the Oztoyahualco area, in sectors N5W2 and N4W2 and including the Plaza One triadic group (Millon 1960; Millon and Bennyhoff 1961; Cook de Leonard 1957) has a better claim to be called "Old City," since densities of Patlachique and Tzacualli ceramics are high here.

The TMP detected segments of several long freestanding east-west and north-south walls in the northwestern quadrant of the city (Figure 6.24). They are about 2 m thick at their bases and one is 5 m high where it adjoins the northwest corner of the Moon Pyramid. Their full extent has not been traced, but they do not surround the entire city, and many residential areas are outside them. Gates have not been identified. It is unlikely that they were important for defense. They were more likely used to regulate movements within the city, which suggests that they might have defined administrative districts, but so far there is no evidence of any close correlation with status markers or differences in material culture, except that walls just northwest of the Moon Pyramid enclose a large area where obsidian working was prevalent (Carballo 2007). No walls around known ethnic enclaves have been detected. The walls running south and east from Plaza One in sector N5W2 both deviate about two degrees from the canonical Teotihuacan orientation. They are not well dated and perhaps are late in this period. These freestanding walls are another Teotihuacan enigma.

Crafts: Materials, Production, Distribution, and Consumption

At Teotihuacan, some households or other social units provided some goods and services intended for consumption by other households or units. That is, some kind of distribution or exchange was involved. Crafting for exchange was often carried out within households, but some was carried out in nonresidential precincts. Some, such as masonry, were necessarily performed at the location of the consumer, while others, such as maintaining order and upkeep of infrastructure, were public goods carried out throughout the city. Still others were conducted outside the city, such as mining raw materials, agriculture (except for house gardens), warfare, and foreign trade. As Hirth (2009) emphasizes, production of all these goods and services was part of the range of activities and strategies pursued by the producing units for their own well-being and survival, including goods and services for their own consumption.

Traces of services and perishable goods are often elusive, and only goods and services whose remains are long-lasting are easily studied by archaeologists. At Teotihuacan, studies of crafting have concentrated on ceramics and various kinds of lithic artifacts. Textiles, which last well in some hyper-arid environments, such as parts of the Andes and Egypt, rarely survive at Teotihuacan, and studies of textile crafting rely on durable tools used in their making and embellishment, and on depictions of clothing in murals and ceramics. Masonry and other building skills are evidenced in the buildings themselves, although there are difficulties with insubstantial structures and structures razed in the construction of later buildings. Important services that are difficult to study include child rearing and socialization (probably shared by men and women), many kinds of ritual performances, entertainment, information exchange, medical services, and many others (Dobres 2010).

The crafts involved in agriculture are often not thought of as crafts at all, but they were vital for many households. A key distinction is between owning or having control over land and water, which are critical resources for agriculture, as noted long ago by Sanders (1956), and the actual work of agriculture. That is, there can be officials or landlords who do little or no work on the land, and laborers who may or may not control the land they work. In early times, subsistence agriculture intended mainly for household consumption was often preferable to poorly rewarded nonagricultural pursuits, and poorly rewarded crafting might only be adopted by households whose access to land and water resources was limited. But rewards for exceptionally skilled artisans were likely high enough to encourage them even when land resources were abundant. That explains why fine crafting already appeared in Mesoamerica in Early Preclassic times or even earlier. Prosperous crafters often invest in landholding, but I doubt if many opt for the practice of agriculture – more likely they have others to do the work.

There are more data than in earlier periods on production, exchange, and consumption of craft goods at Teotihuacan. In a society as large and complex as Teotihuacan, these practices were, well, *complex*. Dichotomies such as full time vs. part time (what Hirth [2009] calls "intermittent," emphasizing that it may occur in discrete episodes of intensive work scheduled between other activities); attached vs. independent; wealth or prestige objects vs. utilitarian; and elite vs. commoner consumers are useful but too simple. Quality and purposes of objects varied on continuums along several axes: from easily made to those requiring great skill and talent, inexpensive to costly, and mundane objects with modest meanings to those fraught with meanings that made them symbolic resources for those who possessed them. The status of artisans varied along a continuum from extremely low status to highly esteemed, depending to some extent on the raw materials used but especially on the skill of the artisan. There may have been a conceptual divide at Teotihuacan between elite and commoners, but there was a fine gradation in the purchasing power of consumers, from topmost elite to the most impoverished.

Distribution could take many forms: simple exchanges among neighbors, sale in a marketplace, distribution by merchants engaged in short-range commerce or in long-distance trade, large consignments to the state or other large-scale consumers, objects paid as tax to the state, or labor owed to the state. Individual artisans or households probably often used a mix of these distribution mechanisms. Much production was carried out within residences or in adjacent work areas. In other cases, artisans who resided elsewhere carried out at least some of their work in nonresidential areas adjoining major civic-ceremonial structures – what Michael Spence (1987) calls "precinct" workshops.

Most materials consumed in any quantity at Teotihuacan could be obtained within 40–50 km of the city. These include maize and other basic food staples (including limited amounts of meat), water for crops, most building stone, most obsidian, clay for ceramics, salt from Lake Texcoco, maguey fibers for netting and coarse textiles, and much of the fuel for cooking and heating. There are no good nearby sources of fine-grained materials such as flint or chert for sharp tools, but this was not a problem for Teotihuacanos, because of the local abundance of obsidian. Fine-grained basalt was sometimes used for scrapers when great toughness was more important than a truly sharp edge. A few materials needed in large amounts must have come from a little farther away: lime for building, much of the somewhat coarse-grained basalt for grinding maize and pigments, and cotton for finer textiles from Morelos and Veracruz. Except for Veracruz, these source areas were probably controlled early on by the Teotihuacan state, which would have made access to them easier for Teotihuacanos, whether or not the state had any direct role in obtaining or distributing them.

Smaller amounts of materials were obtained from places up to a thousand kilometers away, including greenstone and other semiprecious rocks, jadeite, cinnabar, marine shells from both coasts, mica, some obsidian, slate, hematite, pyrites, feathers of exotic birds, and presumably other perishable materials such as animal skins. These distant items were probably exchanged mostly among elites, as "preciosities," rather than through merchants. Cacao was likely seen as a preciosity, but sufficiently in demand that it may have led to political control of cacao-growing areas by Teotihuacanos, including Pacific coastal Chiapas and Guatemala.

Obsidian

Figures 6.12, 7.9, and 7.10 show major Teotihuacan obsidian forms. Much of Teotihuacan's obsidian came from slightly east of Otumba, and small amounts of Otumba obsidian have been found at sites distant from Teotihuacan. However, Otumba obsidian was not markedly more in demand in Mesoamerica than obsidian from many other sources. Obsidian occurs in a limited number of volcanic deposits. People in regions without nearby obsidian deposits tended to get their obsidian from many sources, and it is not surprising that Otumba was among them.

Some obsidian came to Teotihuacan from other sources, including Ucareo in west Mexico, but obsidian from the Sierra de Las Navajas, near Pachuca, about 55 km northeast of Teotihuacan, was far more abundant. Navajas obsidian is relatively free of imperfections and is especially good for making prismatic blades – long narrow and thin flakes whose nearly parallel edges are more than razor-sharp (Figure 7.10). They were removed by pressure applied to specially prepared cores, called "polyhedral" because, seen in cross section, these cores have many slightly concave facets, created by removal of the blades. One end of a polyhedral core is a flat surface, called a striking platform, on which pressure was applied with a blunt-pointed tool such as an antler tine, in order to remove each blade. In post-Teotihuacan times, this surface was usually ground somewhat, in order to make a rough surface that would give the pressure tool better purchase. In Teotihuacan times, this extra step was not used, and the end of the blade where pressure was applied is smooth. This technological distinction has proven to be a good chronological diagnostic.

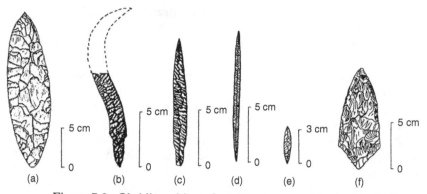

Figure 7.9. Obsidian objects from Teotihuacan. (a) bipointed bifacial knife, (b) curved knife, (c), (d) lancets, (e) small bipoint, (f) knife.
© Cambridge University Press and Saburo Sugiyama (2005).

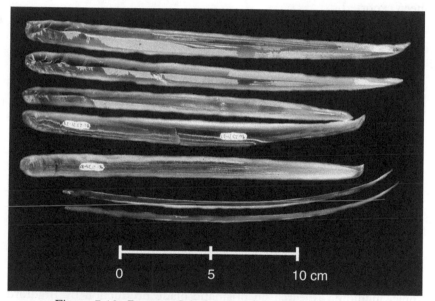

Figure 7.10. Pressure-flaked prismatic blades from burial 14 in the Feathered Serpent Pyramid.
Courtesy of Saburo Sugiyama.

A thin piece of Pachuca obsidian is translucent, with a greenish cast. It cannot be identified unambiguously by visual inspection (Gazzola 2008), as was once thought, but its NAA signature seems unmistakable. Throughout pre-Hispanic times, it was the most widely exported obsidian in Mesoamerica. It was already present in a high proportion in some of the pre-Ciudadela contexts at Teotihuacan, and probably Teotihuacanos already controlled the Navajas source. In other sites dating to the Teotihuacan Period, it is a good marker of some kind of Teotihuacan connection, direct or indirect. Alejandro Pastrana (2009) describes small Teotihuacan settlements near the Pachuca source. Most of the ceramics, some apparently dating as early as the Patlachique phase but mostly of Tlamimilolpa and Xolalpan types, were locally made, but some were apparently imported from Teotihuacan. Besides mining the obsidian, craftsmen made partially finished objects, to be exported for completion by their recipients in Teotihuacan or elsewhere, and also made a large number of finished objects of all kinds. Some of these finished objects at the mines show signs of extensive use, apparently in working wood and the fibers from various local plants, probably including *magueyes*. These perishable worked products may also have been exported.

Nevertheless, the scale and significance of Teotihuacan's obsidian export should not be overrated. Robert Santley (1983) argued for a Teotihuacan monopoly of the Mesoamerican obsidian trade, and saw it as a major factor in the rise of the Teotihuacan state. However, many obsidian source regions apparently remained politically independent of Teotihuacan, including the Oyameles/Zaragosa source near Cantona, about 165 km to the east (Figure 1.2/10) (Stark et al. 1992).

Spence (1987) assumed that in every residential compound identified as producing obsidian beyond its own needs, every household had a member involved in this production. But probably only one or two compound residents working at any one time could have produced the observed amounts of obsidian debris, so his estimates of the numbers of individuals and households engaged in obsidian crafting seem too high. In an influential article, John Clark (1986) attempted to cut the image of a Teotihuacan trade empire down to size. He went too far, having an unintended demoralizing effect on Teotihuacan obsidian research. Happily, there has been a revival of interest in the topic, including research on prismatic blade production by Bradford Andrews (1999, 2002, 2006) and mostly biface production near the Moon Pyramid by David Carballo (2005, 2007, 2011; Carballo et al. 2007).[4] The scale of obsidian production at Teotihuacan was much greater than Clark thought, and a significant amount was exported to many places in Mesoamerica. Nevertheless, it is unlikely that obsidian export played a major commercial role for the Teotihuacan state, and it is unlikely that Teotihuacan ever monopolized obsidian trade throughout Mesoamerica.

The role of the Teotihuacan state in procuring obsidian and its subsequent working remains uncertain. Spence (1981, 1984, 1987) posited three kinds of workshops: "precinct," "regional," and "local." The evidence for "precinct" workshops is strong. These are in areas close to major civic-ceremonial structures, usually with no evidence for residential occupation. Carballo (2007) describes finely screened and carefully analyzed deposits of obsidian waste (debitage) in the structure immediately west of the Moon Pyramid (6:N5W1) and in a large walled enclosure just to the north, interpreted by the TMP as possibly as much as 400 m east-west and varying 114 to 144 m north-south. Here there is a strong case for involvement by the state, in production of dart points on a large scale for its armies and small scale production of symbolic obsidian objects expressing the state's militaristic ideology. Associated ceramics suggest the deposits date to the Xolalpan phase, later than the symbolic obsidian objects in sacrificial burials at the Moon Pyramid and the FSP. This indicates a long time span for these activities.

Spence (1981) argued that the Teotihuacan state administered procurement of Pachuca green obsidian and its distribution to workshops. He based this on the fact that there is little variation in the percent of green obsidian, relative to other kinds of obsidian, in debris from all kinds of putative workshops – it is rarely less than 90 percent. However, this need not mean anything except that all blade makers strongly preferred Navajas obsidian to any other kind. Possibly the Teotihuacan state administered distribution of green obsidian to craftsmen throughout the city, but at present the evidence is ambiguous. It is, however, unlikely that the state allowed such a valuable material to be freely accessible to anyone willing to make the effort to obtain it from its source, as was probably the case with clay sources and the Otumba source of gray obsidian. I suspect that the Teotihuacan state, or some powerful group within the state, controlled access to the Pachuca source and probably also supervised its mining. They may then have sold it directly to crafting households in the city, or perhaps they sold it in bulk to middlemen who then sold smaller amounts to artisans.

At Teotihuacan, most obsidian blades are of Pachuca green obsidian, although some are of obsidian from Otumba or other sources. Bifaces, used especially for large spearpoints, smaller dart points, and knives, are usually – but not always – from Otumba obsidian. Other obsidian objects include "maguey scrapers" that may have been used in getting the sap for *pulque*, and long, narrow, pointed bifaces probably used for drawing blood in self-sacrifice rituals. Much rarer are "eccentrics": obsidian objects worked in the form of humans, serpents, other animals, or abstract symbols (Figure 7.11). Many of these are small;

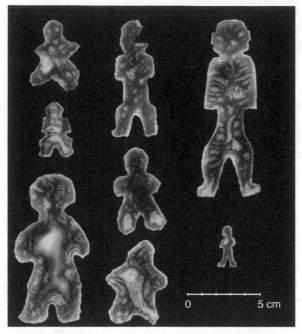

Figure 7.11. Small obsidian human figures from Teotihuacan.
© Cambridge University Press and Saburo Sugiyama (2005).

others are enormous and dazzling examples of technical virtuosity, as in some of the offerings in the Moon Pyramid (Figure 6.5) and the FSP. Even green obsidian prismatic blades can be masterworks, as in Burial 14 of the FSP, where hundreds of blades up to 23 cm long and barely a centimeter wide were deposited (Figure 7.10). Many of these blades were derived from a single polyhedral core, and absence of signs of use shows they were made specifically as precious offerings.

Ceramic Production and Consumption

Learning about the production of pottery and ceramic figurines at Teotihuacan is still in an early stage. We have good evidence from only a few localities and for only a few wares. Paula Krotser (1987) excavated probable evidence of ceramic production in the Teopancazco apartment compound (1:S2E2) and examined many TMP surface collections in search of evidence of ceramic workshops. Her ideas of what counts as a defective sherd (a "waster") were overgenerous, and she overestimated the number of Teotihuacan workshops. Nevertheless, her lists of proposed workshops are a good starting point for further research.

Mary Hopkins (1995) made extensive laboratory analyses of Teotihuacan area clays and of two major utilitarian forms: ollas made of Burnished Ware and open cazuelas/craters made of Burnished Ware in early periods and of San Martín Orange Ware, which probably began in late Late Tlamimilolpa and flourished in the Xolalpan and Metepec phases. She found vessel forms were quite variable in early phases, while later production was larger scale, with simplified preparation of materials and reduced care in finishing. San Martín Orange potters made vessels that were standardized in some respects but extremely variable in others, while olla makers, less expert and working at a smaller scale, made more uniform vessels, contrary to some authors' expectation that larger-scale producers can be expected to make more uniform products.

The TMP survey found exceptionally high proportions of San Martín Orange Ware in a district of about 50–70 ha, just south of the Río San Lorenzo, today called Tlajinga. It is somewhat isolated from most of the city, in sectors S3W1, S3W2, S4W1, and S4W2. The ware is comprised mostly of large, deep, open basin-like vessels with roughened bases, suitable for boiling or stewing, called "craters" in the Teotihuacan literature (Figure 7.12a). Narrow-necked jars, usually with loop handles and suitable for carrying liquids, called "amphoras," are less common (Figure 7.12b), and other forms are rare. San Martín Orange should not be confused with any of the categories designated "San Martín" by Tolstoy (1958) (his terminology is no longer used).

Manufacture of San Martín Orange was concentrated in the Tlajinga district. In 1980 a Penn State team excavated a compound where it was made, which they dubbed Tlajinga 33 (33:S3W1, Figure 7.8) (Storey 1991, 1992; Widmer 1987; Widmer and Storey 1993; Sheehy 1988, 1992, 1998). Subsequently, Kristin Sullivan (2006) made statistical studies of TMP surface collections from the district, identifying places most likely to have been production loci and concluding that the potters were likely working independently of the state, on a household or local level of organization. Evidence for production of San Martín Orange Ware elsewhere is equivocal and not yet confirmed.

Multivariate statistical analyses by Cowgill (2006) suggest that high percentages of San Martín Orange tend to correlate with high percentages of *candeleros*. This is partly because both were especially abundant in the Xolalpan phase, but it also suggests an association with commoner households. Cowgill et al. (1984: 166–68) suggest that San Martín Orange may have formed a higher proportion of the ceramic inventories of intermediate status households than of those of lower status, who

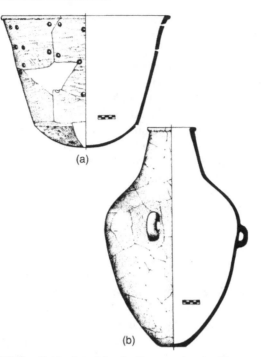

(a)

(b)

Figure 7.12. San Martín Orange vessels. (a) crater, (b) amphora. After Rattray (2001).

probably relied more on less specialized potters making other wares for utilitarian vessels.

Starting in the Late Tlamimilolpa phase and becoming well developed in the Xolalpan phase, a market niche had opened for specialized producers concentrating on a particular utilitarian ware, in contrast to earlier times at Teotihuacan when it looks as if individual potters tended to produce a wider range of types. The fact that San Martín Orange did not survive the collapse of the Teotihuacan state is probably not because of any ideological aversion to it but because market conditions would no longer support this degree of specialization.

Also in the southern outskirts of the city, about 2 km east of the Tlajinga district and in an even more spatially marginal position, is San José 520 (Figure 1.6/10). Structures here were made of adobes and other insubstantial materials. Excavation by Oralia Cabrera (2006, 2011) found many "lunates." These are small unslipped, solid, banana-shaped clay objects, 6–10 cm long, often with abrasions indicating they had been used as scrapers, apparently in shaping pots. They are most abundant in tracts where there is other evidence of pottery manufacture. Other evidence of ceramic production at San José 520 includes misfired sherds and objects probably used as supports in shaping vessels. The main product was outcurving bowls, during the Tlamimilolpa and Xolalpan phases. Outcurving bowls were the most abundant form of Teotihuacan serving vessels (Figure 6.27a), ranging in quality from finely to poorly polished. The potters at San José 520 may have made other forms, including Storm God jars, which are usually finely polished and with carefully modeled elements added, requiring a certain degree of skill and care. There is no evidence that occupants of San José 520 engaged in farming, and scarcity of *manos* and *metates* suggests that possibly they were obtaining partially prepared food from other sources. They were probably people of very low status, relying on ceramic production in the absence of better means of support.

Yet another locus of ceramic production, especially of figurines and the clay ornaments attached to composite ("theater") censers is called Cosotlán 23, a tract in the northwestern part of the city (23:N5W3, Figure 1.6/9). Quantities of objects suggestive of a workshop were noted in the field by Baños and confirmed by Barbour, who called attention to its importance. Intensive surface collections by Sullivan (2007) found defective figurine fragments and molds for figurines and ornaments, giving clear evidence of manufacture here. Sullivan compares the products of this probably independent workshop with those in the Enclosure of the Artisans.

Except for better grades of direct-rim tripod cylinder vases, often with fine post-firing polychrome stucco decoration, which were likely preciosities sent as gifts to foreign elites, it is unlikely that the Teotihuacan elite had much interest in production or distribution of pottery. Thin Orange Ware was imported in quantity from southern Puebla. Perhaps the state was involved in its importation or distribution within Teotihuacan, but there is no compelling evidence for this. Looking at the city as a whole, the ware seems ubiquitous, but, at least in grave offerings, individual compounds differed greatly in its abundance (Clayton 2009, 2011).

Utilitarian Ground Stone

About 6,455 fragments of *metates* were collected by the TMP, although some are probably earlier than the Teotihuacan Period and many are probably later. They have never been wholly supplanted by other technology and continue in use today. They are stone slabs, usually of somewhat vesicular basalt, primarily used for grinding maize, although sometimes

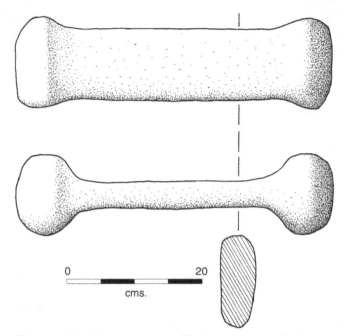

Figure 7.13. A large, very worn Teotihuacan *mano*. Scale approximate. By S. Vaughn.

for other materials, including pigments. Some pre-Teotihuacan *metates* were trough-shaped, but those of the Teotihuacan Period have an upper surface that is flat from side to side and slightly concave front to back, with three low supports. Some 6,545 fragments of *manos*, the stones that were pushed back and forth atop the metates to produce the grinding action, were collected by the TMP. Again, not all belong to the Teotihuacan Period. Teotihuacan *manos* are longer than *metates* are wide, and often have a bulbous overhang on each end that becomes more pronounced as the central section is worn down by use, producing a "dog-bone" appearance (Figure 7.13). They were intended for two-handed use, which is more efficient but more demanding than the much shorter *manos* often used with trough *metates* in other times and places, notably in Preclassic Mesoamerica and in the southwestern United States. In any household that did not acquire food prepared elsewhere, many hours a day would have been spent grinding the required amount of maize flour, an effort that considerably exceeded all the work on pyramids. Today this is overwhelmingly a task for women, and no doubt this was so at Teotihuacan.

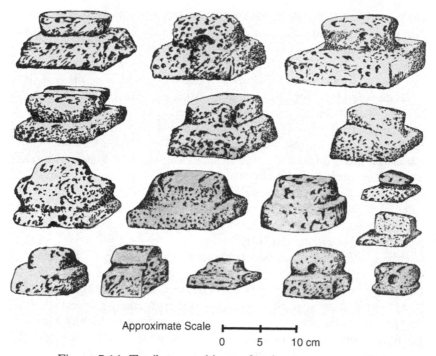

Approximate Scale

0   5   10 cm

Figure 7.14. Teotihuacan objects of unknown use, so-called plaster smoothers.

After Séjourné (1966b).

Stone mortars and pestles also occur at Teotihuacan but are considerably less abundant than are *manos* or *metates*; only 1,194 mortar fragments and 214 pestles were collected by the TMP. They were probably used for grinding condiments and perhaps pigments and other materials.

A distinctive type of stone implement common at Teotihuacan (4,240 were collected by the TMP) is the so-called "plaster smoother." These come in a variety of shapes and sizes, but always have a body with a flat face and generally a knob or loop handle on the opposite side (Figure 7.14). Most are not made of dense basalt, as are *manos* and *metates*, but of much lighter and more porous volcanic scoria, locally called *tezontle*. They probably were somehow used by masons, but even the briefest attempt to smooth moist plaster with them shows they are spectacularly unsuited for that purpose. They are also unsuited for polishing surfaces to a high luster. Perhaps they were used for abrading, possibly to roughen concrete so that plaster would adhere better. There is an open field here for experimental archaeology. A few objects also called plaster smoothers are somewhat similar in shape but made of dense basalt, and probably served some quite different purpose.

A peculiar Teotihuacan lithic form is the "chopper," a broken slab of the tabular stone used abundantly in the construction of *tableros* (Box 5.2), unworked except that one edge has been crudely flaked to make it somewhat sharp. These must have been used for heavy cutting or chopping. The TMP collected 691 of them. Curiously, finely polished stone ax or adz blades, often called "celts," common in many other Mesoamerican cultures, are almost nonexistent at Teotihuacan. They are also rare in south-central Veracruz (Barbara Stark, personal communication, 2009). Conceivably, these crude sharpened slabs took the place of celts for utilitarian purposes, although it is hard to see how they could have been hafted, and they could scarcely have been used for any purpose calling for aesthetic quality.

Other utilitarian objects of basaltic or andesitic rock found at Teotihuacan include roughly spherical stones pocked from use in pounding (including some 3,067 "hammer stones" collected by the TMP), and far smaller numbers of stones with smooth facets used for fine polishing, flattish stones that served as anvils on which things were pounded, stone drains and drain covers, and unidentifiable objects.

Stones with loops occur and are occasionally found still set in door-jambs. There is no evidence that Teotihuacan buildings ever had actual doors – solid panels with hinges. Doorways could be closed with textile hangings tied to these stone loops, important during storms or in cold seasons. This raises a question about security. It seems that Teotihuacanos did not have locks of any kind. Presumably unwanted intruders were guarded against by surveillance of entrances. Barking dogs (a very noticeable feature in twenty-first century San Juan Teotihuacán) may have helped. Possibly supernatural sanctions played a role.

Stone, generally andesitic, was also used for sculptures and friezes, discussed in Chapter 8, and for cut building blocks in parts of more finely constructed buildings, especially stairways and their bordering panels (*alfardas* in Spanish, often but somewhat inaccurately called "balustrades" in English).

Lapidary Crafts

Numerous materials, mostly imported from a distance, were crafted into fine objects of various kinds. "Greenstone" (usually fuchsite or serpentine) was used for small human figurines and occasionally larger objects,

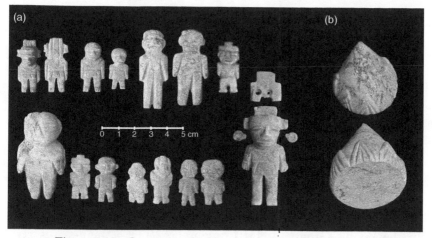

Figure 7.15. Greenstone lapidary objects from the FSP, Teotihuacan. (a) human figures, one farthest right has removable headdress and ear spools, (b) small greenstone cones from Burial 14.

After Sugiyama (2005).

as exemplified by some of the finds at the FSP (Figure 7.15). Many of these probably came from the Mezcala district in the state of Guerrero. More rarely, jadeite, probably from sources along the Motagua River in Guatemala, was used. Shells from both the Pacific and Gulf coasts were worked. Mica probably came from Oaxaca. Other materials listed by Margaret Turner (1992: 92) include travertine (also called alabaster, *tecali*, and onyx), slate, iron pyrites, freshwater shell, quartz, chert, chalcedony, malachite, cinnabar, and hematite.

Tecopac is a small neighborhood of workers in greenstone and shell, in sector N3E5, on the northeastern outskirts of the city. Turner (1987, 1992), describes workshop debris collected by the TMP from this area, and from TMP Excavation 18, in tract 8:N3E5, directed by Paula Krotser. Randolph Widmer (1991) discusses lapidary production at Tlajinga 33. Judging from their distances from any major civic-ceremonial structure, workers in these localities were probably working independently. Cabrera and Gómez (2008) discuss the industry in the La Ventilla district, where workers were likely in the service of local elites. Oralia Cabrera (1995, 2002) describes finished objects found at the FSP. At TC-8, a cluster of apartment compounds covering 8–10 ha, about 1.5 km west of the western margin of the city (Figure 2.3/1), discussed as a rural settlement by Sanders (1967), Charles Kolb (1987: 81–84) describes a plain room lacking floors, from which over 3800 whole and fragmentary spondylus shells from the Pacific were found, along with ceramics of the Xolalpan phase. No evidence of crafting was found at TC-8, and Kolb suggests that the room may have been a warehouse from which the shells were distributed to crafters within the city. However, only a small part of TC-8 was excavated, fine debris apparently was not saved, and it seems possible that shell-working was carried out there, as well as within the city. An unfinished fragment of worked shell at the FSP suggests that some of the shell platelets worn by sacrificial victims there were made at the site (personal observation).

Mica occurs in thin, shiny, almost transparent sheets. Small bits were often attached to objects such as composite ceramic censers to provide glistening spots, especially in the eyes of figures. Otherwise mica is scarce at Teotihuacan except for two remarkable deposits. In the Viking Group (3:N3E1, Figure 6.2/11), a high-status residential compound that is part of the Avenue of the Dead Complex, Pedro Armillas (1944) found a thick layer of unworked mica under a floor. Linda Manzanilla (personal communication 2011) says the mica found there weighs 35 kilograms, and adds that, in the Xalla Complex, 27 kilos of mica was found.

Textiles and Other Perishable Materials

A few wooden objects have been found at Teotihuacan, but only a few small, very degraded fragments of textiles have survived. Feathers and skins appear in imagery but I know of no survivals. Other materials such as paper probably existed. Spindle whorls are very scarce or absent in the Teotihuacan Period city. Cotton does not grow in the Basin of Mexico and it was probably imported in the form of yarn or woven textiles. However, maguey grows in abundance, and in later times its fibers were spun into yarns for bags, ropes, and coarse textiles, using larger whorls than those used for cotton (Mary Parsons 1972). It is difficult to imagine that Teotihuacanos did not also spin maguey fibers, so the virtual absence of ceramic spindle whorls is puzzling. Possibly whorls were made of some perishable material, but this does not seem to have been the case elsewhere in Mesoamerica. Weaving implements are usually of perishable materials, so their absence in the archaeological record at Teotihuacan is inconclusive. However, concentrations of bone needles and awls are known (O. Cabrera 2001; Manzanilla 2012). Apparently Teotihuacan crafters used embroidery and other techniques to add value to already woven textiles.

Construction

Abundant remains of civic-ceremonial and residential structures attest the existence of building craft workers–architects, masons, mural painters, and less skilled laborers. Tatsuya Murakami (2010) discusses materials used, changing scales of civic-ceremonial and residential building over time, and implications for state involvement.

Services and Specialties

Musical instruments, including whistles, flutes, drums, and shell trumpets, give evidence of musicians, but we have to assume the presence of many other specialists and providers of services, in addition to household activities such as cleaning, food preparation and serving, and child care. Except for priests, soldiers, and possibly rulers, humans and their activities almost never appear in Teotihuacan imagery. They would have included teachers, healers, midwives, diviners, judges and other court officials, bureaucrats, police, food vendors, petty merchants, skilled agricultural specialists, athletes, entertainers, providers of services such as waste removal, courtesans and other sex workers, relatively unskilled and unspecialized laborers, and thieves and other criminals. Readers may think of other specialties.

Marketplaces for local exchanges were probably common in Mesoamerica by this time, but institutions and practices for long-distance exchange were probably less developed than later, partly because populations of potential consumers were smaller, but especially because commercial practices like credit, banking, insurance, and all-purpose money were probably absent or not highly developed. It is unclear whether there were anything like merchant guilds or the *pochteca* of Aztec times. It is also unclear how much Teotihuacanos could offer other regions by way of exchange, other than widely valued green obsidian. Pottery was not exported in quantity. Given the undistinguished quality of Basin of Mexico clays, that is not surprising. NAA and other studies of ceramics from other sites within the Basin of Mexico, such as Cerro Portezuelo and Azcapotzalco (Clayton 2013; Ma 2003), indicate that most of their ceramics were produced locally, and little in these sites was imported from the Teotihuacan Valley, only 30–40 km away. Teotihuacan was far more an importer than an exporter of fine ceramics. When the Teotihuacanos did create precious ceramics, which were sometimes spectacular, it was not because the fabric was especially fine but because of enhancements through skilled modeling or engraving or addition of polychrome designs in a thin layer of stucco added after the vessel was fired. I doubt if Teotihuacanos exported significant amounts of any perishable materials. Most obsidian, lime, stone for building and for grinding implements, wood, and food came from less than 60 km away, often from much closer. Except for Thin Orange ceramics, Granular Ware, cotton, and cacao, imports from farther away were probably limited to precious items in small volume.

Ceramic Wares and Forms

The 250–550 CE interval includes the latter part of the Tlamimilolpa ceramic phase and all of Xolalpan. A number of new ceramic forms separate Late Tlamimilolpa from Early Tlamimilolpa, including direct-rim tripod cylinder vases (Figure 7.16). Some of those found elsewhere are exports from Teotihuacan, but others look more like copies of copies, and were definitely not from Teotihuacan. The form itself was probably derived from somewhat earlier examples made in the Gulf Lowlands, rather than from the everted-lip vases with nubbin supports that were used in the Miccaotli and Early Tlamimilolpa phases. In Late Tlamimilolpa times everted-lip vases become scarce, being supplanted by the direct-rim vases with hollow or solid slab supports or hollow round supports. Direct-rim vases vary greatly in quality: the finest ones, with polychrome stucco decoration, must have been very valuable. At the lower end of the scale some were undecorated, with poorly finished surfaces.

"Copa Ware" appears. It was locally made, but the fabric is quite fine, probably because non-clay particles were intentionally removed. It occurs in two forms. Some are small cups with low pedestal bases and sometimes trough spouts, vertical loop handles, or both (Figure 7.17a). They are sometimes called "cream pitchers." Others are direct-rim tripod cylinder vases, usually with solid slab supports with *talud-tablero* profiles (Figure 7.17b).

In contrast to everted-lip vases, flat-bottomed outcurving bowls continued to be used in great numbers, although they tend to be lighter in color and more out-slanting in profile, and by the Xolalpan phase, nubbin supports were often vestigial or absent. Together with a variety of convex bowl forms usually lacking supports, these flat-bottomed outcurving bowls continued to be the most abundant kinds of serving vessels at Teotihuacan. They were probably part of the repertoire of every household. They are very common in burials. Most are undecorated monochrome, but even these vary considerably in the care taken to provide a nice finish. Some have incised motifs, which also vary in the care with which they were made, and a few have Red-on-natural decoration.

Figure 7.16. Direct-rim tripod cylinder vases from Teotihuacan: a range of quality, styles, and techniques. (a) resist with nubbins supports, probably early, (b) stuccoed polychrome, figure shows eye-rings, "Storm God" nose pendant, and possible variant of "tassel" headdress, (c) "stick trailed," (d) stuccoed polychrome, butterfly elements and "talud-tablero" nose pendant, (e) plano-relief incising, (f) "coffee bean" appliques ringing base and lid. After various sources.

Utilitarian ollas, used for transport, storage, and cooking, did not change dramatically from those of the previous period, except for variations in necks and lips that are minor, yet good chronological markers. Utilitarian cazuelas continued. A few comals occur. A new utilitarian ware, San Martín Orange, discussed previously, began to appear in small numbers in the Late Tlamimilolpa phase, became abundant in the Xolalpan phase, and continued into the subsequent Metepec phase. Compositional studies (Sheehy 1992; Hopkins 1995) indicate that San Martín Orange vessels were made of local materials. Although there is no evidence of the use of kilns, they were fired at a higher temperature than were other Teotihuacan wares, and under more oxidizing conditions that give them a distinctive reddish-orange or brownish surface

(a)

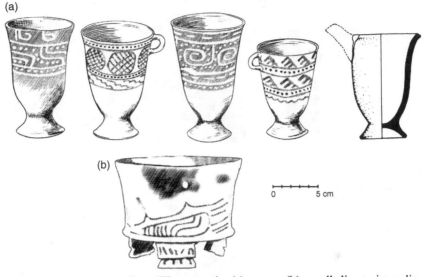

(b)

0   5 cm

Figure 7.17. Copa Ware vessels. (a) copas, (b) small direct-rim cylinder vase with *talud-tablero* supports.
After Rattray (2001).

color. Except for rare applications of thin red slips, surfaces were undecorated, but finished by a distinctive combination of striations due to scraping and widely spaced burnishing streaks. Shapes are standardized, except in the Tlajinga district, where a wider variety of forms was produced for local use. The two main forms are "craters" with intentionally roughened bases that must have been used for boiling or stewing, and "amphoras," narrow-necked vessels, often with loop handles, well-suited for transport of liquids, although they could also have been used for storage (Figure 7.12). Everything about these vessels indicates that they were turned out by potters who were skilled but uninterested in ornamentation or in deviating from the routine expectations of consumers.

Composite "theater" censers took on more elaboration and handmade censer ornaments ("*adornos*") were replaced by mold-made ones (Figure 7.18a). Variations in the flanged rims of censer bodies are good chronological markers. Other Coarse Matte Ware vessels (so-called three-prong burners) with three hollow prongs pointing upward and inward on the rim (Figure 7.18b) contained small fires used for space heating and probably some cooking. Fine Matte Ware "handled covers" ("*tapaplatos*"), probably used as incense burners (Figure 6.28/b), were more abundant than before.

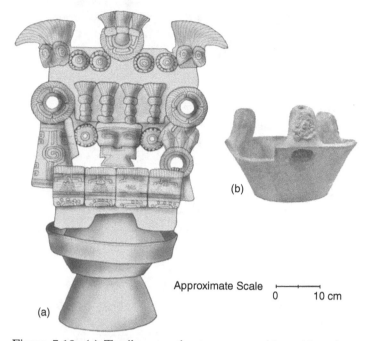

Approximate Scale

0   10 cm

(a)

(b)

Figure 7.18. (a) Teotihuacan theater censer with mold-made ornaments. (b) "Three-prong burner."
After Rattray (2001).

A new Matte Ware form is the *candelero* (Figure 7.19). These began
as small single-chambered objects but soon were often joined in pairs,
and then single objects with twin chambers became dominant. A few of
these are nicely decorated but most are quite crude, usually with finger
gouges in the soft clay. *Candeleros* were probably used as censers. They
do not seem especially associated with large temples, and statistical
analysis of TMP data shows they are associated more with San Martín
Orange than with theater censers (Cowgill 2006). This, and their abundance and simplicity, suggest they were used in frequent but small-scale
domestic events, perhaps carried out by a single individual. It is tempting to think the rituals were a very "grass-roots" thing, of little interest
to the Teotihuacan state. But several facts argue against this. They are an
innovation of this period, with no antecedents, and they do not survive
the demise of the Teotihuacan state. Post Teotihuacan bowl censers with
handles (*sahumadores*) are larger, more elaborate, fewer, and likely associated with more elaborate rituals. All this suggests that *candeleros* were
somehow connected to interests of the Teotihuacan state.

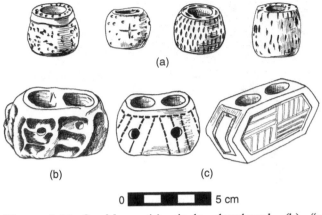

Figure 7.19. *Candeleros*. (a) single chambered, (b) "common," (c) other kinds.
After Séjourné (1966a).

Although other kinds of objects found elsewhere have been called "candeleros," the distinctive Teotihuacan type is extremely rare outside the city. A notable exception is Matacapan, in the southern Gulf Lowlands, where locally made versions occur in some numbers (Ortiz and Santley 1998). Another exception is Montana (Figure 1.2/23), in Pacific Guatemala (Bove and Medrano 2003). Isolated finds occur widely scattered elsewhere in Mesoamerica.

Ceramic Figurines

Molds were now used for many figurines and for ornaments on composite censers. Publications on Teotihuacan figurines include those by Warren Barbour (1976, 1998), Kim Goldsmith (2000), Charles Kolb (1995), and Sue Scott (2001). Molds require less skill on the part of artisans, but perhaps more important is that it makes complex motifs widely available. Different kinds of ceramic figurines likely had different uses (Figure 7.20). So-called portrait figurines, made all by hand earlier, now had mold-made heads and handmade bodies. Their identical features make them the very opposite of individual portraits. They have been interpreted as dancers because of their active poses, but, as emphasized by Barbour, it is far more likely that they represent soldiers, in the act of hurling a spear with the right hand and holding a shield in the left hand. Shield and spear would have been of perishable materials, and bald heads suggest perishable headdresses. Elsewhere in Mesoamerica,

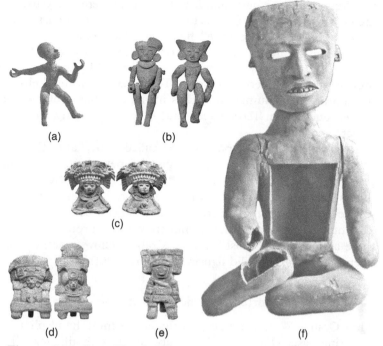

Figure 7.20. Late Tlamimilolpa and Xolalpan ceramic figurines. (a) "portrait," (b) articulated (puppet), (c) half-conical, (d) "throne," (e) "xipe," (f) "host." After various sources.

figurines with ceramic spear and shield have been found in this pose. I suspect "portrait" figurines were used in the socialization of boys as budding soldiers, in the service of the Teotihuacan state. Kristin Sullivan (personal communication) says they were produced in quantity in the Enclosure of the Artisans, next to the Ciudadela, which also suggests a connection with state interests.

Sullivan sees more emphasis on articulated figurines ("puppets") in the Cosotlan 23 workshop. Perhaps these were also gendered play-things, used in preparing girls for their roles in childcare. We must be wary of too readily projecting our own concepts of gender roles onto Teotihuacan, and more contextual data on both "portraits" and "puppets" is desirable, yet there is little doubt that most Teotihuacan soldiers were men and that most child care was by women.

Another type of ceramic figurine is the "half-conical." These are mold-made busts, lacking arms and lower body, often with elaborate headdresses. Annabeth Headrick (2007) and others have suggested that they represent mortuary bundles. If so, they were likely used in commemorative rites rather than as toys. Perhaps they were part of household shrines. Related are "throne" figurines. These may represent mortuary bundles on litters carried in processions. Presumably they refer to persons of higher status than those represented by the half-conicals. If mortuary bundles were common at Teotihuacan it would help to explain the shortage of inhumation burials in the city. Some of the dead were treated one way in Teotihuacan and others differently, but we do not understand why.

Yet another figurine type has been called "xipe," after their supposed resemblance to the Aztec "flayed god," a personage represented by a priest wearing the skin of a human victim. But Sue Scott (1993) and others have pointed out that they look more like persons wearing protective headgear. They are most likely soldiers, because players of the Teotihuacan stick ball game are not shown with protective gear. Finally, there are enigmatic "host" figures, sizable hollow ceramic effigies that open to reveal small solid figurines (Figure 7.20f).

Major Imported Ceramic Wares at Teotihuacan

Thin Orange Ware ceramics, particularly simple hemispherical bowls with ring bases (Figure 6.27) are abundant at Teotihuacan. The TMP surface collections include about 98,000 sherds of Thin Orange, as compared to about 380,000 sherds of other major wares in the Miccaotli to Metepec interval. Thin Orange is about 20 percent of the total of major wares collected. However, the Thin Orange proportion is high because plain body sherds were often collected, but only rims, supports, handles, and decorated sherds for most other wares. The actual proportion of Thin Orange vessels was probably more like 10 percent of total vessels (Rattray 1981). It once was thought that Thin Orange might have been made at Teotihuacan, and its occurrence elsewhere in Mesoamerica was taken as a sign of Teotihuacan influence. But the fabric is very different from vessels made of Basin of Mexico clays, and petrographic studies by Eduardo Sotomayor and Noemí Castillo (1963) confirmed that it was not made locally. Rattray (1990b) identified its place of manufacture near the Río Carnero, in southern Puebla, about 200 km from Teotihuacan. Nevertheless, the notion dies hard that it is diagnostic of a Teotihuacan presence wherever it is found. It is apparently supposed that some of the Thin Orange imported to Teotihuacan was re-exported by Teotihuacanos. But Rattray (1990b) found no evidence of a Teotihuacan presence in the source area. It is unlikely that Teotihuacanos could have prevented the makers of Thin Orange from exporting some of it on their own. Most likely Thin Orange is rare out-side Teotihuacan because producers who wanted to send it elsewhere could not use Teotihuacan political and commercial institutions and had to market it themselves. Consumers may have been interested in acquir-ing it partly because of the prestige of its association with Teotihuacan, but the mere presence of Thin Orange ceramics cannot be taken as a secure marker of a Teotihuacan connection.

Even within the city, in spite of its overall abundance, there are striking variations in the proportion of Thin Orange in specific places. Clayton (2009: 198–201, 2011) found that about 9 percent of the indi-viduals buried in an area of craft workers in the La Ventilla district had a Thin Orange hemispherical bowl among their grave goods, and only 1 percent had a local imitation, but at the Tlajinga 33 compound, only about 1.5 percent of those buried there had a Thin Orange bowl, and 3 percent had local imitations. In her sample of burials from Axotlán, 35 km away, 3 percent had Thin Orange bowls and 10 percent had local imitations.

Why did Teotihuacanos import Thin Orange Ware in such quantity? A few vessels are cylinder vases or other elaborate forms, but the vast majority are hemispherical bowls, which, although well formed (shaped in molds and fired in kilns) are nearly all either undecorated or embel-lished with only a few simple shallow incisions and punctations on the exterior. They are much too abundant to be preciosities. Both before and after the Teotihuacan Period, some vessels in the Teotihuacan area had crosshatched incisions in their bottom interiors, often abraded by use. These open bowls, called *molcajetes*, are used for grinding chiles and other condiments. There were no locally made vessels with crosshatched interiors in the Teotihuacan Period, but many Thin Orange bowls show considerable abrasion (but not incisions) on their basal interiors. Evidently, they took the place of incised *molcajetes* in household cuisine. Presumably their fabric had good grinding qualities that could only be obtained with local clays by making deep incisions.

If Teotihuacan had no colony in southern Puebla that could have enforced demands for Thin Orange vessels as tribute, what induced its makers to export it to the city in such quantity? If Teotihuacanos exported something in exchange for Thin Orange, what might it have been? Rattray (1990b) mentions green obsidian at source sites, but it isn't clear whether it is abundant enough to have plausibly paid for all the pottery sent to Teotihuacan. Perhaps further research in the source area will discover a Teotihuacan presence, or possibly the mere threat of a punitive raid by Teotihuacanos was enough to motivate makers to export it to Teotihuacan as a kind of "protection money."

Granular Ware was also imported to Teotihuacan in significant quantities, mainly as "amphoras," tall necked jars, often with three loop handles, that look well suited for carrying liquids, decorated with simple painted designs on unsmoothed surfaces (Figure 6.27). TMP surface collections include about 12,600 Granular Ware sherds. Its fabric is very different from local ceramics and is easily identified visually. NAA analyses put it in a tight compositional cluster, well removed from Basin of Mexico ceramics. It is more abundant in Morelos, and likely was produced in Guerrero (Padilla 2009). Granular Ware was probably imported by Teotihuacan in small quantities in Tzacualli times, and abundantly in the Miccaotli and Tlamimilolpa phases. It seems much less prevalent in the Xolalpan phase and perhaps ceased to be imported in the Metepec phase.

"Lustrous" Ware is the third most abundant ware imported to Teotihuacan. It is far less common than is Thin Orange or Granular, but forms up to 1–2 percent of the ceramics in many of the TMP excavations. Unlike Thin Orange and Granular, it is an ill-defined category. NAA analyses tend to separate it from local wares but do not put it into a tight cluster. It probably came from several sources somewhere in the Gulf Lowlands, perhaps in northern Veracruz, although it should not be confused with the ware called "Terrazas Lustrosas." Unlike Thin Orange and Granular, which were not costly enough to encourage local imitations, many Lustrous Ware vessels are fine serving vessels (especially cylinder vases) and there are imitations that are hard to distinguish visually from genuine imports (Cowgill and Neff, 2004).

Other wares were imported in much smaller quantities, from West Mexico, Oaxaca, the Gulf Lowlands, and the Maya area. Concentrations occur in ethnic enclaves, but tiny amounts of foreign ceramics are scattered throughout the city (Rattray 1987). Clayton (2005) discusses Lowland Maya sherds found at Teotihuacan.

Polity and Society in Late Teotihuacan

The nature of rulership at Teotihuacan is a thorny problem. In early Teotihuacan, the sheer size of the largest civic-ceremonial structures, the immense scale of the civic-ceremonial core, and the close adherence to a uniform spatial orientation throughout the entire city and beyond, suggest a very strong central authority. In the present period, there is less evidence for powerful individual rulers – new structures are not audacious and there is more emphasis on substantial housing for the general population. This could reflect a shift to less power for individual heads of the state, more sharing of power among high-ranking elites,

Approximate Scale   0   25   50 cm

Figure 7.21. "Big Fist" carving in the Teotihuacan Museum.
After photo by author.

and possibly also weaker controls over the general population. Yet the
evidence is less clear than we would like. There seem to be no unmistakable representations of rulers or other exalted humans in any durable
medium – stone statuary, mural painting, or decorated ceramics – either
early or late. In societies that emphasize representations of individual
rulers, such as the Classic Maya of the Southern Lowlands, celebration
of rulers may have been a strategy to bolster the authority of individuals
whose actual power was limited. Perhaps Teotihuacan's early rulers were
too powerful to need to rely on self-portraiture. Rulers of late Shang polities in Bronze Age China, whose power is attested by inscriptions and
by massive sacrificial burials, were not represented in durable media.
The apparent low profile of Teotihuacan rulers is not unambiguous evidence that their power was restricted. Also, it may be that there were
representations all along, and we haven't understood them. A gigantic
stone fist in the Teotihuacan site museum is undated and without pro-
venience (Figure 7.21). A proportional body would have been several
meters tall. There is no evidence of any such monument at Teotihuacan,
but disembodied hands are not uncommon in Teotihuacan murals. The

Figure 7.22. The Colossus of Coatlinchán.
Courtesy of Annabeth Headrick.

fist is clenched. Could it signify a strong ruler, holding his people in a firm grip? This is speculation, yet it cannot be ignored. The big fist must have meant something important.

Another speculation concerns the "colossus" found unfinished in a quarry at Coatlinchán, near Texcoco, 20–25 km south of Teotihuacan. It weighs about 180 tons and is over 7 m tall, probably the largest single carved stone in pre-Conquest Mesoamerica, perhaps in the whole New World. Using modern technology, in the 1960s it was moved, with difficulty, to its present position in front of the National Museum of Anthropology (Figure 7.22). Some think it is the Storm God, but I see no diagnostics of that deity. Others interpret it as the "Great Goddess," but the case for such a goddess is very weak. Gender of the colossus is not entirely clear, but its attire looks more masculine than feminine to me. An object of this size was surely of immense importance to Teotihuacanos. Possibly it was left unfinished because its makers realized too late that it would be too hard to move, but it is unlikely that they would have lacked the foresight to start something they couldn't finish. Could work on it have been halted because

Figure 7.23. Possible head of the Teotihuacan state. Mural in the "White Patio," Atetelco compound.

After Séjourné (1966b).

of some sociopolitical upheaval? Could it be that the colossus was planned as a self-portrait by a very powerful autocrat who overreached and provoked rebellion and a new regime of more collective rule, perhaps at the time the FSP was desecrated? Data on the ceramics near the quarry will be informative: are they primarily from the early period discussed in Chapter 6, or is there a good proportion of later pottery?

The figure in the stone frieze in the Avenue of the Dead Complex (Figure 7.4) may mark it as a place of high political office. However, it is on a far more modest scale than the enigmatic huge fist and the colossus. Even more modest is a mural figure in the Atetelco compound (1:N2W3), proposed as a ruler by Linda Schele (Annabeth Headrick, personal communication) (Figure 7.23). Both likely pertain to the period after 250 CE. Perhaps accession to rule was now by election by an elite council from among a relatively large number of elite eligibles, rather than from among only a few persons with close genealogical ties to the previous ruler. It may have worked something like the renaissance Republic of Venice (Cowgill 1997). Teotihuacan society was probably still very hierarchical, but rulers may have become more accountable to other elites, and to some extent to the public in general.

Far more effort than before went into continued construction and renovation of the multi-apartment residential compounds that had begun to appear in the previous period (Murakami 2010). All this suggests a marked change in the political system. It may have become more "corporate" in the sense proposed by Blanton et al. (1996).

Environmental Issues

If the inhabitants of Teotihuacan avoided making excessive demands on their environment, it would be an interesting contrast with many other societies, including our own, a contrast that demands explanation. It suggests a government that was well informed about environmental matters, able to enforce laws against bad environmental practices, and sufficiently free of external and internal pressures so that it could afford to take a long view. I emphasize this because there is reason to think rulers of Late and Terminal Classic Lowland Maya polities were too pressured by competition with one another to have the luxury of a long-term view. They may have felt themselves forced to adopt expedient practices even if they could see that these practices were leading to environmental damage.

Elsewhere in the Basin of Mexico

In 1962 Millon began the TMP by establishing limits of the city of Teotihuacan, using as his criterion a band of land at least 300 m wide without structural remains or other significant evidence of occupation dating to Teotihuacan times (Millon 1973: 8). As a method for determining the limits for intensive survey, this made excellent sense. However, it also encouraged the drawing of a sharp, if very sinuous, line that looks like a clear boundary of the city. But treating this as a boundary of Teotihuacan as a community is problematic. The map of architecturally substantial structures (Figure 1.6) shows a few clumps that are within 300 m of others, but still rather isolated. Maps of sherd densities show gradual declines and some isolated minor peaks around the edges. There is no evidence of outer walls or other symbolic markers of culturally meaningful borders. The Aztecs used terms such as *altepetl* to refer to the whole area of a city-state, without any political distinction between densely settled centers and rural districts. Possibly this was also the case at Teotihuacan, and perhaps it is misguided to seek any definite spatial boundary of Teotihuacan as a community.

Some residential clusters are within a kilometer of the contiguous, densely built-up area. They may or may not have been considered sociopolitically part of the city. One example is San José 520, discussed earlier as a locale of potters. Another is TC-8, about 1.5 km west of the area of contiguous settlement (Figure 2.3/1), seen by Sanders (1967) as a rural village. Other sites within the Teotihuacan Valley are clearly outside the city but within a day's walk, such as San Bartolomé el Alto (TC-83) (Figure 2.3/7) about 12 km northeast of the city center, where typical Teotihuacan residential architecture of moderate quality was found (Charlton et al. 2005; Charlton and Otis Charlton 2007). The orientation of these sites generally differs from the Teotihuacan standard. However, four small sites on the northern slope of Cerro Gordo, including TC-46 (Figure 2.3/9), align with one another and with San Bartolomé at an angle of 32 degrees south of true east (Sanders 1965: Figure 8). It may be mere coincidence that this is twice the deviation from true east of many features within the city, but it is one of several hints that rural sites were laid out in imposed geometric patterns, as well as in relation to natural resources. About 8 km due south of San Bartolomé is TC-87–89, along an extension of East Avenue that was on the trade route to the distant source of Thin Orange (Charlton 1978), which constituted 20 percent of the ceramics at this site (Charlton and Otis Charlton 2007).

In the western part of the Basin, Azcapotzalco (Tozzer 1921; García Chávez 1991, 2002) and Axotlán (Clayton 2009, 2013) continued to flourish. Some other sites, however, including Cerro Portezuelo in the southeastern Basin, may have been abandoned (Clayton 2009, 2013; Nichols et al. 2013). Because the surveys of Sanders et al. (1979) did not distinguish ceramics of this period from those of the previous period, it is impossible to say what the overall pattern was. There may have been significant changes in how Teotihuacan related to its near hinterland.

Teotihuacan's Interactions Outside the Basin of Mexico

There is more evidence than before of widespread Teotihuacan presences. The number of places and people dominated by the Teotihuacan state probably expanded, stabilized for a while, and then began to contract. This is a plausible scenario, but it will remain speculative until we learn more about Teotihuacan's impacts outside its core region. Whatever the case with political control, this was certainly the period when Teotihuacan's cultural influence was at its peak.

Relations abroad of both the Teotihuacan state and of individuals claiming Teotihuacan identity were quite different in different regions and in different periods. Stein (2005) is a valuable source of ideas on this topic. In 1988, Millon (1988a) surveyed what was then known of Teotihuacan's presences. It is now possible to add more recent data.

The Outer Core

A Teotihuacan presence occurs in the Valley of Toluca, just west of the Basin of Mexico and separated from it by a mountain range (Sugiura 2005). To the south, in Morelos, Teotihuacan presence remained strong, demonstrated by the appearance of late Teotihuacan markers such as twin-chambered *candeleros* and Teotihuacan-style composite censers in the Yautepec area (Lisa Montiel, personal communication, 1998). However, influence may have been declining in the later part of this period (Hirth 1978; Hirth and Angulo 1981).

The parts of Puebla and Tlaxcala closest to the Teotihuacan Valley, such as around Calpulalpan (Las Colinas) (Figure 1.4/18), only 40 km from the city, might be considered part of the inner core. At Cholula, the material culture was fairly similar to that of Teotihuacan, but its political status remains unclear. Farther away in Puebla-Tlaxcala there appear to have been branching corridors that linked Teotihuacan with obsidian sources (Charlton 1978) and with northern, central, and southern parts of the Gulf Lowlands and the Tehuacán Valley of southern Puebla and, beyond that, to the Monte Albán state in Oaxaca (García Cook 1981). David Carballo and Thomas Pluckhahn (2007; Carballo 2013) have used GIS methods to identify least-cost paths that relate to these corridors. Elsewhere in Puebla, Teotihuacan presence seems more limited. Cantona, about 160 km from Teotihuacan, near where the highlands drop abruptly toward the coastal plain and near the Zaragosa-Oyameles obsidian source (probably not controlled by Teotihuacan) may have gained importance before the end of this period. Cantona looks culturally quite different from Teotihuacan (García Cook 2003).

Oaxaca

The Zapotec state, centered at Monte Albán, seems to have enjoyed commercial and diplomatic relations with Teotihuacan on an equal footing (Marcus and Flannery 1996). Teotihuacanos may have bypassed the Zapotec state to trade more directly with people in the Río Verde area in the western part of Pacific coastal Oaxaca (Joyce 2003).

The Gulf Lowlands

The Gulf Lowlands, as defined by Barbara Stark and Philip Arnold (1997: 4), stretch about 1,100 km in a long narrow arc from Tamaulipas in the north through the state of Veracruz to Tabasco in the south. Teotihuacan's relations differed with different segments of this long region. In the north, El Tajín rose to prominence in the next period, but imports such as Lustrous Ware ceramics probably came from this general area.

At Tepeyacatitla, in the upland Maltrata valley (Figure 1.2/11), near the border between Puebla and Veracruz, where the land drops sharply from highlands to lowlands, on a tributary of the Río Blanco, Yamile Lira López (2004) reports large quantities of Teotihuacan-style ceramics, mostly locally made and slightly different from those found in Teotihuacan itself. It includes numerous everyday serving vessels, such as flat-bottomed outcurving bowls with nubbin supports, so it is likely that more than prestige emulation was involved. Perhaps it was a small Teotihuacan outpost to which people from the Gulf lowlands brought perishable goods for exchange. This contrasts sharply with the scarcity of Teotihuacan-related ceramics in the Mixtequilla area around Cerro de las Mesas (Figure 1.2/13) in south-central Veracruz.

In the Mixtequilla, Stark and Johns (2004) see little evidence of a Teotihuacan impact. Settlement patterns did not change much, and the only identified imports from the central highlands are small amounts of green obsidian and scarce Teotihuacan-related ceramics. Over 90 percent of the obsidian is from the Zaragoza-Oyameles source, near Cantona and probably controlled by that center. Less than 2 percent is green obsidian. Stark and Curet (1994) question whether commercial relations account for the few Teotihuacan connections they find in the Mixtequilla, and argue that exchanges were likely due to elite interactions and local emulation. They acknowledge the possibility of hegemonic Teotihuacan administration demanding tribute, but think if it occurred at all, it must have been brief.

Mary Miller (1991) identifies Stela 15 at Cerro de las Mesas (Figure 7.24) as a version of the Teotihuacan Storm God, but it has little in common with that deity except for the rings around the eyes, which appear at Teotihuacan on some images of soldiers, as well as on the Storm God. She notes the resemblance of its large feline headdress to that on Tikal Stela 4, which is associated with Teotihuacan-related newcomers there. James Borowicz (2003) argues that the Stela 4 figure represents a Teotihuacan soldier, rather than the Storm God.[5] This suggests

Figure 7.24. Stela 15, Cerro de las Mesas, south-central Veracruz.
After Stirling (1943).

a Teotihuacan military presence at Cerro de las Mesas, and possibly it
commemorates a conquest.

In southern Veracruz, Matacapan became an important Teotihuacan-
related center, notable among other things for local production of
twin-chambered *candeleros*, which are elsewhere very rare outside
Teotihuacan (Ortiz and Santley 1998). Its sphere of influence was limited (Stoner 2013), suggesting an outpost rather than control over much
territory. Other signs of Teotihuacan presence in the southern Gulf
include a stela showing "tilled field" glyphs at Piedra Labrada and a
stela with a Teotihuacanoid figure carrying flaming bundle torches said
to be from San Miguel Soyaltepec (Taube 2000b) (Figure 7.25).

West Mexico

In western Mesoamerica, Michelet and Pereira (2009) find signs
of Teotihuacan connections strongest in the states of Michoacán,
Querétaro, and Guanajuato. Evidence is especially strong in southwestern Querétaro (and adjoining parts of Guanajuato), and the Cuitzeo

Figure 7.25. Teotihuacanoid monument attributed to San Miguel Soyaltepec, in Oaxaca, in the lower Papaloapan drainage, just over the line from southern Veracruz.
Courtesy of Karl Taube (2000).

basin west of Ucareo in Michoacán. Probably independent local elites had ties with Teotihuacan. At El Rosario, 15 km from San Juan del Río (Figure 1.2/8), about 135 km northwest of Teotihuacan, in Querétaro, there are murals depicting curved obsidian knives and other objects in Teotihuacan style. It looks like a Teotihuacan settlement, probably a node in a northwestern trade route (Rodríguez 2009). Parts of Guerrero close to Morelos may have been within Teotihuacan's outer core. In coastal Guerrero, a Teotihuacan-style stela showing a soldier was found at Acatempa, near Acapulco (Figure 1.2/18) (Taube 2000b: 9). Teotihuacan obtained Mezcala style greenstone figurines from the Mezcala region, between the coast and Morelos.

Farther north and west there are fewer signs of Teotihuacan presence. In Jalisco, the Teuchitlan tradition looks independent of Teotihuacan (Weigand 2000). Anthony Aveni, Horst Hartung, and J. Charles Kelley (1982) argued for a Teotihuacan presence as far north as Alta Vista in Zacatecas (Figure 1.2/7), but their evidence is unconvincing.

Figure 7.26. The Teotihuacan Storm God stela at Los Horcones, Cerro Bernal, coastal Chiapas.
Courtesy of Karl Taube (2000).

The Maya Area

The volume edited by Geoffrey Braswell (2003) is slanted toward minimizing the impact of Teotihuacan or Teotihuacan-related people. It includes much that has been superseded by new data. In central Chiapas, Pierre Agrinier (1970, 1975) found at Mirador (Figure 1.2/20) a considerable amount of pottery that differs somewhat from that at Teotihuacan but is clearly Teotihuacan-derived. There is some evidence that users of this pottery lived at the site after an episode of violent destruction. Los Horcones at Cerro Bernal in coastal Chiapas (Figure 1.2/21) became much larger than before, with Teotihuacan-like monumental architecture (García-Des Lauriers 2007, 2008) and a stone carving of the Storm God in Teotihuacan style (Figure 7.26) (Taube 2000b).

In Pacific Guatemala, Balberta was superseded by the immense site of Montana (Bove and Medrano 2003). Pachuca obsidian and other imports from Teotihuacan are scarce. Instead, there are locally made Teotihuacan-style objects, notably variants of composite censers, direct-rim tripod cylinder vases, and "portrait" figurines in poses suggesting they held perishable shields and atlatls. Bodies of these figurines are much larger than those at Teotihuacan, but the faces may be from imported molds. The evidence suggests that Montana was a large settlement of descendants of Teotihuacan migrants, who now ruled the area, so there was no need to import preciosities for local elites (Bove and Medrano 2003). In the Guatemalan highlands, elite tombs in two mounds built in Teotihuacan style at Kaminaljuyú included offerings from many sources – a considerable number in Teotihuacan style, some imported from Central Mexico (Kidder et al. 1946).

In the southern Maya Lowlands of Belize, northern Guatemala, and bits of Honduras, rulers at Tikal, Uaxactún, Yaxha, and Copán proclaimed Teotihuacan connections in their regalia and in hieroglyphic inscriptions, and they founded new dynasties that soon returned to Maya styles (Braswell 2003). At Tikal and Yaxha, there are figures in military garb, some with spear-throwers. Analyses of stable isotopes in teeth and bones indicate that few, if any, known burials in the Maya area were of persons who lived for any significant time at Teotihuacan. There are growing numbers of finds of Central Mexican connections elsewhere in the Maya area, such as green obsidian (Moholy-Nagy 1999), ceramics, and, at La Sufricaya, Teotihuacan-like soldiers in a mural (Estrada-Belli et al. 2009). There is increasing evidence of armed interventions at a number of Lowland Maya centers by persons with a Teotihuacan identity, if not from Teotihuacan itself. Perhaps Teotihuacan settlers in Pacific Guatemala first moved into the highlands at Kaminaljuyú, and from there made forays into the Maya Lowlands. However, their descendants soon assimilated to Maya ways, and it is not clear that there ever was direct rule from Teotihuacan itself.

Maya motifs and glyphs in murals in the Tetitla compound show connections in the other direction (Taube 2003). Sherds of vessels imported from the Maya lowlands are sparsely scattered throughout Teotihuacan (Rattray 1987) but there is no spatial concentration of Maya ceramics except at the Merchants' Enclave. Of 121 Lowland Maya-style sherds from Teotihuacan studied by Clayton (2005), 73 are stylistically Early Classic, and many probably belong to this period. All but a few differ sharply from Central Mexican ceramics, and 36 exhibit strong compositional similarity to some of the Maya Lowlands specimens in the database of the Smithsonian Center for Materials Research and Education. The fact that many were not clearly assigned to specific Maya subregions does not call their Maya origin into question. The Maya database is strongly biased toward polychrome ceramics from a limited number of sites and periods, and many subregions and periods are poorly

Figure 7.27. Stuccoed Teotihuacan direct-rim cylinder tripod vase from the Margarita tomb, Copán. Spread-armed figure wears eye-rings and butterfly nose pendant.

Courtesy of Early Copán Acropolis Program, University of Pennsylvania Museum. Photo by Robert J. Sharer.

represented, as are utility wares. Ten Maya sherds from Teotihuacan are strikingly similar in composition to Tikal specimens, and another twelve are similar to multiple specimens from the central Petén region. The ceramic evidence for long-lasting relations with Tikal adds to other evidence for intense interactions between the two cities.

Copán ceramics are conspicuously absent among the compositional matches, except for three in the Hunal and Margarita tombs, which likely contain remains of Copán's dynastic founders. These three vessels are markedly similar in composition to a specimen from the Mundo Perdido district of Tikal, and probably they are imports from Tikal. These tombs include other vessels that are probably imports from Teotihuacan itself, notably the so-called "Dazzler" (Figure 7.27). Taking this ceramic evidence together with iconographic evidence and stable isotope analyses (Wright 2005), it seems likely that the Copán dynastic founder manifested symbolic ties to Teotihuacan but was actually from the central Petén, perhaps from Tikal.

Clayton found seven Maya-style sherds at Teotihuacan with strong compositional similarity to multiple specimens from the vicinity of Calakmul (Figure 1.2/29), a site with no previous evidence of any Teotihuacan connection.

Teotihuacan imagery, in wall paintings, decorated pottery, ceramic and stone figurines, stone sculpture, and architecture, demands a chapter of its own. I call it "imagery" rather than "art" because it had purposes other than art for its own sake, although aesthetic considerations were important. I focus on a few topics of special interest to me.

The first impression of anyone accustomed to European art is that Teotihuacan imagery is two-dimensional and static. Human figures appear squat, stiff, and expressionless. The flowing and naturalistic styles of the Classic Maya can be more easily appreciated. Like European art of the Middle Ages, the Teotihuacan style takes some getting used to. With more exposure to it, one sees much of it as dynamic, tension-laden, and full of depths conveyed by means other than geometric perspective. For example, in this depiction of a man-feline (Figure 8.1), probably from the Techinantitla compound (Berrin 1988: 187), when one realizes that the curved objects emanating from the claws are flames, it becomes a spine-tingling image of tensed and blazing fury. Understanding, in this image of the Storm God at Techinantitla (Figure 8.2), that the arch in the background is a portal through which the god emerges, the scene is filled with three-dimensional depth and motion. It is eventful, anything but static, and imagining it as enacted by a performer who either represents, or, more likely, for the moment *is* the Storm God, can be an emotion-laden experience. Teotihuacanos, from early childhood, and of all ranks in the society, must have found public religious pageantry intensely moving, and it would have gone far toward inculcating belief in messages intended by elites, whatever realities were.

Mention of Teotihuacan imagery calls to mind the paintings on the walls of rooms in some residential compounds. Miller (1973) illustrates many. Beatriz de la Fuente's volumes (1995) include many discovered later and have higher quality reproductions. Kathleen Berrin's edited volume (1988) concentrates on murals looted in and near the Techinantitla compound. It is hard to say what proportion of the 2,300 compounds at Teotihuacan enjoyed such decoration, since many compounds were

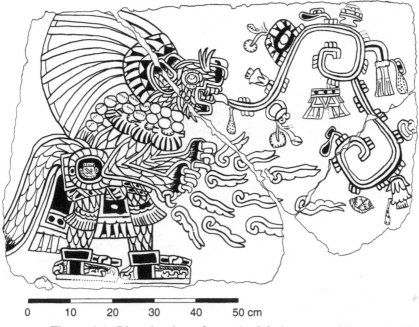

0   10   20   30   40   50 cm

Figure 8.1. Line drawing of mural of furious man-feline, probably from the Techinantitla compound.

After Berrin (1988: 188).

chosen for excavation precisely because there was evidence that murals were present. Including loose fragments of mural paintings encountered on the ground surface by the TMP, they are present in at least twenty or thirty compounds. This is a conservative estimate; further excavations would surely reveal many more. Nevertheless, some excavated compounds, such as Tlajinga 33, lack wall paintings, or have nothing more than red borders outlining edges of otherwise plain white plastered walls or floors.

Some murals occur on the exteriors of platforms and pyramids. The best example is a huge feline on a platform on the east side of the Avenue of the Dead in sector N4E1, a short distance north of the Sun Palace. Extremely faded traces of paintings can be made out on the fore-platform fronting the FSP. Many pyramids have traces of solid red surfaces. Probably most pyramids had painted decoration on their exteriors which, unlike those in room interiors, have been lost because of their much greater exposure to the elements.

Figure 8.2. Line drawing of the Storm God emerging from a portal, Techinantitla.

© Fine Arts Museums of San Francisco (1988).

Within rooms, most surviving paintings are from lower parts of walls. Murals can rarely be reconstructed from fragments of collapsed upper parts of walls. Few murals have been excavated by techniques that allow for unambiguous dating by associated ceramics or radiocarbon. Occasionally, architectural sequences permit a distinction between earlier and later murals in the same structure. Some of the earliest compounds whose walls were faced with Teotihuacan concrete and plaster had mural paintings. Murals may have been in use by 100 CE, but most surviving murals are from the Xolalpan-Metepec interval, because earlier ones were often obliterated by later construction stages. Efforts to date murals on stylistic grounds have had limited success so far. Clara Millon (1972) proposed a sequence but later repudiated it, perhaps too self-critically. Many of the earliest tend to have orangeish reds, few other colors except black, and motifs such as grecas, interlaces, and checkerboard patterns, while later ones tend to have redder reds whose shades intentionally vary from intense red to pale pink, a wider range of other colors (including blues, greens, and yellows), and figures of humans, animals, plants, and supernatural beings. There are exceptions to these generalizations, as in the polychrome "Mythological Animals" mural in 6:N4W1, which is probably quite early. A wide range of colors is also present in pre-Ciudadela murals.

Figure 8.3. Line drawing of dancing armed figures, "White Patio," Atetelco compound.

After Agustín Villagra (1971).

Figure 8.4. Line drawing of an anthropomorphic "net-jaguar" approaching a temple, Tetitla compound.

Courtesy of Annabeth Headrick.

Most murals show processions or other performances. It is unlikely that any of these performances took place within the confines of the rooms on whose walls the murals occur. Dancing armed figures at the Atetelco compound are either in a sunken courtyard or on a raised platform (Figure 8.3). A running man-feline at Tetitla (Figure 8.4) is outdoors. Almost the only Teotihuacan mural that doesn't depict ritual performance and pageantry is one from Tepantitla showing simply clad individuals, probably children, playing a variety of games (Figure 7.5). Why do the murals depict such a narrow range of topics? I doubt if any had a purely didactic purpose, yet perhaps one of their uses was as a model of the correct way of carrying out certain ceremonies.

Elaborately costumed processions of identical figures share a generic resemblance throughout the city, but details of regalia are different in every compound. It may be that many depict rituals whose right (and duty) to perform was "owned" by occupants of the compound. Perhaps occupants of a compound had a monopoly on certain sacred knowledge. It is not clear that shared specific knowledge crosscut residential units, but if any two compounds are ever found to share specific iconography, it would suggest the existence of such cross-cutting social units.

Other murals, such as a procession of named figures at Techinantitla, may have been historical commemoration of specific individuals. Such compound-specific practices, like those seen in burials by Clayton (2009, 2011), may have been complementary to other practices that pertained to cross-cutting social units (sodalities) that linked people in scattered parts of the city.

Many scenes show side views of figures in processions or emerging from frameworks that are portals to another world. Others are frontal tableaus of personages with spread arms bestowing objects from their hands or holding torches, shields, or other objects. Landscapes are rare, although at Tepantitla water flows onto cultivated fields from the base of a personified mountain. The squat appearance of human figures is to some extent intentional, for it shows up on stucco-painted vases where there was room to have made the figures taller. Nevertheless, it is often due to constraints of space, because so many of the surviving murals come from the lowest registers of walls, and had to fit a slightly sloping *talud* that is only about a meter high. In rare cases where upper parts of a wall have survived, as in Techinantitla, the figures in the upper register are much taller than those below (Figure 8.5).

Less successful in conveying motion, although that was certainly the intention of the painter, is a scene from Atetelco where the image looks static, in spite of the intricate pattern of footprints (Figure 8.3).

A prominent feature of Teotihuacan imagery is *multiplicity* and *replication*. Frequently a number of humans or other beings are shown in a mural or stone relief, all with the same attire and all in the same pose, as alike as could be made with freehand techniques. This contrasts markedly with the Maya emphasis on variety and individuality. At Monte Albán, no two of some 300 early carved *danzantes* are alike – repetition was avoided. Repetition similar to Teotihuacan does appear at some Andean sites in South America, such as Tiwanaku (Janusek 2008). At Teotihuacan it seems to be part of an ideology that represents specific social categories as very homogeneous, whatever the actual variation among their members. This is also seen in the tendency for similar attire within sets of victims at the FSP.

In Teotihuacan imagery, parts are often used as abbreviations for more complex entities. This is not an effort to be mysterious or esoteric: it is because many entities were so well known to everyone that shorthand

Figure 8.5. Line drawing of the Storm God, Techinantitla, showing taller figure in upper register above *talud*.

© Fine Arts Museums of San Francisco (Berrin 1988: 102).

representations were unambiguous, however baffling some of them may be to us. Think of how many wordless logos of manufactured brands are perfectly obvious to anyone today but would baffle future archaeologists, a point noted by Miller (1973: 26).

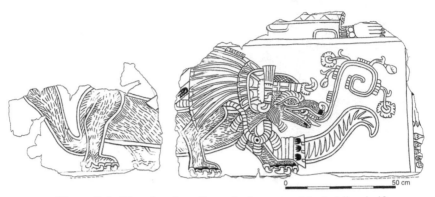

Figure 8.6. Line drawing of mural of coyote with obsidian knife, provenance unknown. Compare with real knife, Figure 7.9b.
© Fine Arts Museums of San Francisco (Berrin 1988: 123).

Sometimes we have clues to the meanings of objects in Teotihuacan imagery. For example, the objects carried by these canids (Figure 8.6) are surely obsidian knives – similar, although often smaller, bifacially flaked obsidian knives have been found in excavations (Figure 7.9b). From such paintings we learn how the Teotihuacanos represented bifacial flaking. Dissimilar figures are unlikely to represent flaked obsidian.

In Teotihuacan imagery, some humans wear nose pendants, objects that hang from the nose and cover the upper lip. Most fit one of three types: those often misunderstood as a butterfly but correctly identified as a rattlesnake's final rattle by Oralia Cabrera (2002) (Figure 6.15b), another type identified with the Storm God (Figure 6.15a), and those representing a *talud-tablero* platform, also sometimes called a butterfly. Butterflies are important in Teotihuacan imagery, but their representations are very different. The first two types of nose-pendants were objects actually worn by some victims in the FSP, Storm God in Burial 13, and rattlesnake elsewhere. They probably served as insignia of rank or office (Cowgill n.d.a.).

Creatures found in Teotihuacan imagery include fierce animals such as jaguars/pumas, coyotes/wolves, eagles/hawks, owls, and a variety of serpents in addition to the Feathered Serpent. These beings often have some human features and are seen doing things ordinarily restricted to humans, such as blowing conch shell trumpets, wearing feather headdresses, and standing or running on two legs. Three-dimensional stone felines of moderate size occur in several poses, some sphinx-like with forelegs extended, others rearing up on hind legs. Examples are known from the Sun Plaza (perhaps once attached to the fore-platform of the

Figure 8.7. Stone felines, Teotihuacan.
After Gamio (1922).

Sun Pyramid), the Xalla complex, the Quetzalpapalotl Palace, and else-where (Figure 8.7). A "net" jaguar, described by Pasztory (1997: 183) as transparent, is opaque, obscuring elements behind it (Figure 8.4). Cynthia Conides (2000) argues that the net pattern represents the way shadows of ripples intersect in clear standing water, one of several asso-ciations of jaguars with water.[1] This mural is also an excellent exam-ple of a depiction in which human and feline traits are combined. It is not a human in jaguar costume. Note also the temple with a large and ornate roof, atop a barely noticeable *talud-tablero* substructure. Only substructures survive along the Avenue of the Dead and elsewhere today in Teotihuacan. All the rest of what was once there has to be supplied by the visitor's imagination. Other murals, as in one from the Palace of the Sun (Figure 8.8) do show humans in costumes – in this case, a bird of prey, most likely an eagle. Even here, however, the humans are probably to be understood as no mere impersonators, but possessed by an eagle being. As at Atetelco (Figure 8.3), these celebrants carry what are prob-ably human hearts impaled on curved obsidian knives.

Other animals identifiable as to general kind, but rarely to specific species, include parrots, macaws, quails, quetzals, rabbits, fish, shellfish, butterflies, other insects, spiders, centipedes, snails, and crocodilians. Recognizable plants include maize, *magueys*, prickly pears, barrel cac-tuses, and many flowering plants.

Figure 8.8. Processing human in bird dress, heart impaled on obsidian knives, Sun Palace.
After Millon (1973).

Teotihuacan imagery is not restricted to wall paintings and sculpture. Other scenes are on stucco-covered direct-rim cylinder vases, jars and bowls, and on plano-relief vases. Their styles have much in common with the murals, but Conides (2001) has shown that the subject matter and techniques used in ceramics, both stucco-decorated and plano-relief, differ significantly from those in the murals, and were made by different schools of artisans. Many scenes mysterious to us probably depict episodes in myths well-known to Teotihuacanos.

Figurines made of clay, semiprecious stones, and obsidian are further sources of imagery. Although it suffers from lack of comprehensive study, there is a large body of stone sculpture at Teotihuacan. It ranges in size from the colossal monolith of Coatlinchán, the so-called *Diosa de Agua* and the carvings on the façades of the FSP, to medium-sized and smaller reliefs and three-dimensional carvings of skulls, serpents, felines, and humans, as well as stone masks that were probably attached to mortuary bundles. Stone skulls were found in the Sun Plaza, both full-face (Figure 8.9) and profile. These suggest that one of the associations of the Sun Pyramid was with death or a death god. So far as I know, similar

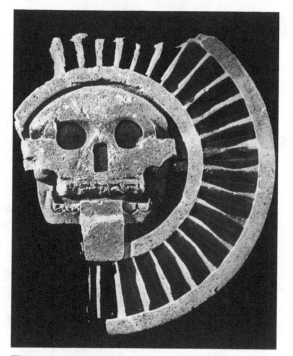

Figure 8.9. Frontal view of stone skull, Sun Plaza. A separate nose element is missing.

Courtesy of René Millon (1973).

imagery is not known anywhere else at Teotihuacan, although skulls appear on a Cholula mural.

Sometimes obsidian was flaked to represent humans, animals, or other objects. These have been lumped under the category of "eccentrics," but many categories are quite distinct. These include humans, serpents, objects that may be lightning bolts (Figure 6.4), and "trilobed" objects (Stocker and Spence 1974).

Teotihuacan Writing

Instead of writing in the strict sense, where words and grammatical sentences are represented with little ambiguity, Teotihuacanos relied on standardized signs. James Langley (1986) has very usefully cataloged 229 of them and discussed them further in subsequent publications (Langley 1991, 1992, 1993). Janet Berlo (1989b) discusses them, and Karl Taube (2000b) provides a comprehensive overview. It may seem strange that Teotihuacanos did not adopt anything more elaborate, since they were surely aware of the more elaborate systems of other Mesoamericans, such as Zapotecs and Maya. But the sixteenth-century Aztec Empire was able to conduct its business with standardized notation, based mainly on pictographic signs with few phonetic or syntactic elements. The Aztecs occasionally made use of puns, as when a toothed jaw element (the Náhuatl word for tooth is *tlantli*) stood for the place-indicating suffix *tlan*, as in *Mictlan*: place of the dead. Since such puns work in only certain languages and not in others, their occurrence in Aztec writing means that even if we didn't already know it we could identify Aztec inscriptions as written by Nahua speakers. No such puns have yet been surely identified in Teotihuacan inscriptions, which is one reason there is so much dispute about the principal language of the Teotihuacanos. I (Cowgill 1992c) pointed out that some of the flowering plants in a mural at Techinantitla bear juxtaposed pictures of a flower and a bone, readily readable as bone-flower. However, a word translatable into English as bone-flower occurs in many Mesoamerican languages, so this is no help in identifying a Teotihuacan language.

Surviving examples of Teotihuacan signs are found primarily in murals and decorated ceramics, and rarely in stone carvings. However, I cannot believe that the Teotihuacan state and other large Teotihuacan organizations could have done their business without forms of record keeping, most likely paper or skin documents whose sheets could be folded like a screen ("codices") such as were used by Aztecs, Maya, and other Mesoamericans. Given their perishable nature, it is not surprising that no clear traces of Teotihuacan codices have been found.

The meanings of many Teotihuacan standardized signs are still unknown. A few continued in use at sites such as Xochitécatl-Cacaxtla (Figure 1.4/17) and Xochicalco for a few centuries after the fall of Teotihuacan, but many went out of use long before Aztec times. This not only adds to the difficulty of deciphering them, it also indicates that some symbolism current in Central Mexico as late as the 800s CE did not survive into historic times. An example is the so-called *ojo de reptil* (reptile's eye) sign, which is surely not a reptilian eye (Figure 8.10). It appears often at Teotihuacan and in Teotihuacan-related imagery abroad.

At Teotihuacan, standardized signs often occur as elements in pictures. One example is in looted wall paintings of a procession of figures at Techinantitla. The elaborately costumed figures are as nearly identical to one another as could be expected in freehand drawings, but each is identified by a different composite sign. In this instance, replication of images did not mean suppression of distinct identities. A few lend themselves to interpretation, such as the head of a feathered serpent on a mat (Figure 8.11), since being seated on a mat is a symbol of rulership

Figure 8.10. So-called *Ojo de reptil* signs.
After von Winning (1987).

Figure 8.11. Line drawing of processing figure at Techinantitla with Feathered Serpent on a mat.
© Fine Arts Museums of San Francisco. (Berrin 1988: 117).

Figure 8.12. Signs painted on the floor of the Patio of the Glyphs, La Ventilla district.
After Taube (2000).

widely shared in Mesoamerica, but most remain mysterious. Are they names of individuals, names of offices, or names of places associated with the individuals?

Painted signs stand alone on the floor of a courtyard in the Compound of the Glyphs, a structure in the La Ventilla district (Cabrera and Gómez 2008) (Figure 8.12). Taube (2011) calls attention to their resemblance to figures in sixteenth-century documents and suggests they may represent named spatial-social units such as apartment compounds, identified for taxation and/or other administrative purposes. I wonder if the units might be districts or neighborhoods rather than individual compounds, or perhaps provinces of the Teotihuacan state. Nielsen and Helmke (2011) argue that the signs may instead relate to disease and curing, another plausible possibility.

Calendars, Astronomy, and Cosmograms

Teotihuacanos must have kept track of the seasons, and they surely had origin myths. The Feathered Serpent may have been associated with the beginning of time. But it is not clear that Teotihuacanos elaborated concepts of time to the extent that the Classic Maya did. Teotihuacan calendars were probably more comparable to those used by the Aztecs. Today many indigenous communities in Mesoamerica use a ritual calendar for divination that is composed of combinations of twenty names of objects and thirteen numbers. In the Aztec codices, the objects are represented by pictures and the numbers by dots. For example, 1 House is followed by 2 Lizard, etc., until all the 260 possible combinations have occurred ($20 \times 13 = 260$). On the 261st day, the cycle begins to repeat, with 1 House again. Since 260 is not close to the number of days in a year, this ritual cycle is not related to the annual seasons. But in the past the 260-day interval was followed by a 105-day interval, and since $260 + 105 = 365$, the combination adds to one year.[2]

The 260-day interval began August 12 (or 13) and ended April 29 (or 30), giving 105 days for the summer period from April 29 to August 12 and 260 days for the fall, winter, and spring. These dates may have been chosen because, at the latitude of Maya sites such as Copán and Izapa, these are the only two days in the year when the sun is directly overhead at noon. The most important of these dates was August 12, because that was also the date when, in Classic Maya belief, the present world was created, in 3114 BCE. It may also be related to the time of year when the compact constellation called the Pleiades first rose or set far enough from the sun to be visible.

At the latitude of Teotihuacan, the sun is not overhead on August 12. It sets about 15.5 degrees north of west on that day. This may explain the canonical orientation of Teotihuacan streets and structures. Many large features are extremely close to this skewing, not just approximately, but within about a fifth of a degree, showing that Teotihuacanos could consistently achieve that accuracy when it was important to them. However, some east-west features are closer to a 16.5 degree orientation, and less well-built structures such as Tlajinga 33 are less accurately aligned (Figure 7.8d).

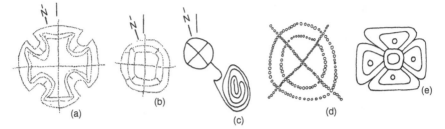

Figure 8.13. Teotihuacan figures composed of pecked dots, including cross in circles and Maltese crosses.
After von Winning (1987).

Alfonso Caso (1937) demonstrated that Teotihuacanos observed a combination of thirteen numbers and twenty day signs. At least seven of their signs can be equated with sixteenth-century day names, although several others cannot be (Taube 2011).

Mesoamerican counting systems were usually vigesimal (base-20). Numbers larger than nineteen were represented by a sequence of positions; multiples of 1 in the last position, up to nineteen, multiples of twenty in the next-to-last position, multiples of 400 (20×20) before that, and so on. Thus, the number twenty would be represented by a sign for one (i.e., 1×20) in the second position and a sign for nothing (zero) in the first position. The number 853 would be 2.2.13, that is, two 400s, two twenties, and thirteen ones. I know of no Teotihuacan inscription showing a number larger than nineteen, but Teotihuacanos probably used positional notation in keeping perishable tallies of large quantities for economic and governmental purposes.

Cross-in-circles motifs consisting of dots pecked in stone or concrete also frequently contain 260 dots (Aveni 2000) (Figure 8.13). There are many of these figures at Teotihuacan and they are found widely in central and northern Mexico, as far north as Alta Vista in Zacatecas (Aveni et al. 1982), and there is one at Uaxactún in the Maya area. Most are not well situated for city planning. There is a concentration of them and other pecked-dot figures, including Maltese crosses, on the south enclosing platform of the Sun Pyramid precinct (Aveni 2005). Most likely they were used for divination or games.

Teotihuacanos probably also shared with other Mesoamericans a "vague year" of eighteen "months" of twenty days each, adding to 360 days, plus an extra five days to bring the total to 365 days. One standardized sign, the so-called trapeze and ray (Figure 8.14) appears to be associated with the year, but it often occurs in headdresses and other

Figure 8.14. The "trapeze and ray" sign.
After von Winning (1987).

contexts suggestive of political power. It is widespread in Mesoamerica. They probably also recognized, like the Aztecs, a "calendar round" of 52 years, which is the time needed for all possible combinations of the 260-day cycle and the 365-day year to occur (365 × 52 = 260 × 73). Evidence is doubtful for other calendrical units at Teotihuacan, such as the Maya Long Count.

Box 8.1 The Long Count

The Long Count, rather than being cyclical, starts from a unique starting day, most likely August 13, 3114 BCE. It counts elapsed time in a modified vigesimal system, consisting of days (*kins* in Yucatec Maya), multiples of twenty days (*uinals*), multiples of eighteen uinals (*tuns*), multiples of twenty tuns (*katuns*), multiples of twenty katuns (*baktuns*), and so on.

Teotihuacanos shared with other Mesoamericans, as well as many other peoples in the New and Old Worlds, the concept of four cardinal axes (east, north, west, and south) that divided the cosmos into symbolically meaningful quarters. These axes converged at the cosmic center, where they intersected a vertical axis that led upward from the surface layer occupied by humans into multiple celestial layers and downward into underworld layers (Wheatley 1971). Often 45-degree intercardinal directions were also recognized, as is particularly clear in some sixteenth-century Mesoamerican codices. At Teotihuacan, in addition to East and West avenues and the north-south Street of the Dead, the notion of four cardinal directions (and sometimes four intercardinal directions) can be seen in early murals at 1B-prime:N1E1 in the Ciudadela plaza (Figure 6.19), in the Building of the Altars in the Moon Plaza, and in pecked dot images of four-lobed objects (Figure 8.13). Occupants of numerous major centers, and even minor ones (e.g., Gossen 1974: 8, 16, 23) view their community as *the* cosmic center, and surely Teotihuacanos believed this with especial confidence. Nevertheless, I cannot see that the entire city was viewed as a replica of the cosmos.

Structure 1B-prime:N1E1 presents a special problem, because of its asymmetrical location in the southern part of the Ciudadela Plaza. It has no counterpart in the northern part of the plaza, and thus violates the usual Teotihuacan emphasis on symmetry. Yet, because of its mural motifs, it seems especially linked with the concept of the cosmic center. I would expect the material manifestation of the cosmic center to have been at the Temple of Quetzalcóatl, the Sun Pyramid, or the Building of the Altars, and 1B-prime seems an unlikely place for the cosmic center. There is a long sequence of construction stages at this structure. Perhaps it was established as a marker of the center for the pre-Ciudadela city, and then was kept in place even when the layout of the civic-ceremonial center was changed.

There is a strong case for a Teotihuacan measurement unit (TMU) of about 81–83 cm. In 1864, Ramón Almaraz proposed a unit of 1.65 m, or about half that (i.e., 82.5 cm). Bruce Drewitt (1987) proposed 80.5 cm, based on many features within and outside the civic-ceremonial core, including stairways in the Ciudadela and streets throughout the city separated by multiples of 400 TMU. Based on survey of the Tepantitla compound by G. Raymond Krotser, David Drucker proposed 80.5 cm (Drucker 1974: 129–31). Sugiyama (1993), restricting himself to the core, argues for a unit of about 83 cm. He makes a good case that multiples of 260 TMU spatially materialized the 260-day cycle. The Sun Pyramid, later slightly enlarged, was originally close to 260 TMU on all four sides, and the distance from the rear of Stage 4 of the Moon Pyramid to the south side of the Ciudadela is close to 2,600 TMU, ten times 260. This is not an arbitrary selection of reference points, because Stage 4 is the first major enlargement of the Moon Pyramid, built about the same time as the Ciudadela. It looks as if the designers marked out the north-south extent of the civic-ceremonial zone and various features within the zone in multiples of 260 TMU. Sugiyama (2013) makes less compelling arguments for other distances of astronomic significance, including the 584-day Venus cycle and the 173.31-day eclipse cycle.

I add that the distance along the Avenue of the Dead from the Moon Pyramid to the Sun is roughly 1,000 TMU, from the Sun to the Río San Juan another 1,000 TMU, and from the Río San Juan to the Río San

Lorenzo another 2,000 TMU, distances in the simple ratios of 1:1:2. Some Teotihuacan features fit a decimal system more easily than a vigesimal system. Evidence for planning extends as far west as a north-south watercourse in sector N2W8 that is 4,500 TMU from the Avenue of the Dead (Cowgill 2007: 273). A measurement unit of around 80–84 cm is common worldwide, based on the distance from the center of the human chest to the outstretched hand. Features outside the civic-ceremonial core of Teotihuacan tend to be simple multiples of this unit. I suspect the layout of the city outside its core was based on quite mundane thinking.

Teotihuacan Religion

Teotihuacanos worked with practices and concepts they inherited from earlier times or (probably less often) borrowed from neighbors and, to judge from some new kinds of figurines and novel artifacts like *candeleros*, they sometimes invented new ones. But they reworked old practices and concepts to serve the needs and interests of various elements of their own changing society, and in reaction to new issues they had to confront. Nothing would have been inherited unchanged from previous less complex situations. Practices and concepts of commoners as well as elites were affected by the kind of society in which they now lived.

It is useful to distinguish the *settings* in which objects employed in rituals were used, the *topics* to which they refer, and *whose interests* they represented. Settings include major civic-ceremonial structures and spaces related to them, lesser civic-ceremonial structures (likely of significance for specific neighborhoods or districts), apartment compounds, single apartments within compounds ("domestic" settings), and individuals. Interests represented include those of the Teotihuacan state or highest elites, lesser elites, districts or neighborhoods within the city, perhaps sodalities or other cross-cutting entities such as gender categories and occupational groups, possibly large descent groups ("clans"), occupants of specific apartment compounds, occupants of apartments (households), and individuals.

These distinctions are not mere hairsplitting; they are needed for clear thinking about how religion worked at Teotihuacan. It is important to ask *where* certain things were done, but it is not enough; we also have to ask *whose interests* were served. For example, it is likely that individuals participated in ceremonial events carried out in the civic-ceremonial core partly as a civic duty, but also in part to serve their personal interests, and not necessarily only on occasions when large crowds gathered. On the other hand, while much of the ritual carried out in apartments or by individuals served household or individual interests, there is reason to think that some of the rituals carried out in these small-scale contexts also served state interests and were carried out in compliance with dictates of the state.

Likely topics of ritual carried out in various contexts and by various practitioners include good weather, good harvests, good fortune in general, military success, human and cosmic order, health and healing, good afterlife, relations with ancestors, human fertility, childbirth, good outcomes from childrearing, domestic harmony and prosperity, reverence for the state and obedience to it, divination, and witchcraft.

Some Teotihuacan beliefs and practices, and perhaps deities and whole systems of belief, may have been adopted by people elsewhere, but it is not clear whether there was anything like proselytizing, let alone missionaries. Teotihuacan is often called a pilgrimage center. People traveled from near and far to visit the city for a variety of purposes, and there may have been pilgrims among them, but I see no persuasive evidence for this. Some of the stone monuments at the fore-platform of the Sun Pyramid probably represent "new fire" ceremonies observed at beginnings of fifty-two-year calendrical cycles. Related imagery at Copán and elsewhere in the Maya area was intended to evoke Teotihuacan connections (Fash et al. 2009). But the argument that Maya rulers traveled to Teotihuacan for investiture is less convincing.

Teotihuacan Deities

It is difficult to get a clear image of ancient pantheons in the absence of texts. Numerous authors since Seler (1915) have struggled with this topic. What we call deities were not necessarily quite like human persons, but represented sentient natural forces. One recent synthesis is by Hasso von Winning (1987). It is useful, although I sometimes disagree with him. Some deities stand out clearly, while others are harder to define and tend to blend with one another. Probably to some extent this accurately reflects ancient beliefs and practices. It is unlikely that any social entity could rule on orthodoxy versus heresy. Probably different people held somewhat different notions of their deities, and likely the same person was not consistent from time to time. Probably many ritual performances had to be carried out in rigidly specified ways, but I doubt if anyone could decide on points of doctrine.

Part of our problem in recognizing deities lies in techniques for identification. Especially mischievous is reasoning that goes "A has some features in common with B, B shares some features with C, and C shares features with D; therefore D and A can be considered representations of 'the same' deity," when in fact A and D have nothing in common.

In trying to escape from this problem of method, I suggest four concepts: *polythetic core entity* (or *PCE*) *diagnostic feature, abbreviation,* and *qualifier*. I believe these are more useful than the linguistic approach used by George Kubler (1967: 5) in which he interpreted imagery in terms of "nouns," "adjectives," and "verbs."

A *polythetic core entity* (PCE) is an entity represented by images that share a polythetic core of features. By "polythetic" (a term borrowed from taxonomists) I mean that not every image exhibits every one of the core features, but they all exhibit at least most of these features. A PCE can have somewhat fuzzy edges, so there can be borderline cases, but many examples clearly and closely relate to the same definable core. Nevertheless, there are also images that have something in common with the core entity, but only a small subset of the core features, and perhaps also some features of other PCEs. That is why further concepts are needed.

A *diagnostic feature* is uniquely associated with a specific PCE. However, diagnostics can be dependent on the context in which they appear. For example, in contexts that are clearly related to Christian saints, keys are diagnostic of Saint Peter. In the contexts of locksmiths' ads, no connection with Saint Peter is intended or perceived.

An *abbreviation* is a small subset of the features of one (and only one) PCE, intended to stand unambiguously for the whole. Teotihuacanos often used parts to stand for wholes, so abbreviations are common in Teotihuacan imagery. Abbreviations stand alone, without features of other polythetic core entities. We find some abbreviations puzzling, but to any competent member of Teotihuacan society, an abbreviation would unambiguously represent the full PCE.

A *qualifier* is an element of one PCE that is present in an image that mainly represents something else (usually a different PCE). The qualifier is in the image in order to indicate that the central PCE has, in this particular case, some aspects in common with the PCE represented by the qualifying element. The distinction between abbreviation and qualifier is critical. An element of a PCE that stands alone is an abbreviation; when it is added to a different PCE, it is a qualifier.

The Storm God was one of the principal deities of Teotihuacan, as he was throughout much of Mesoamerica.[3] He can be used to illustrate these concepts. Core elements include a human figure with an unhumanly large and curled upper lip, fangs protruding from the upper jaw, a reduced or absent lower jaw, a snub nose, prominent rings around the eyes (they are often called "goggles," but this is anachronistic; the Teotihuacanos did not have goggles or eyeglasses), a large split tongue, large green earspools, and male attire. He often holds an undulating

Figure 8.15. Line drawing of the Storm God in a Tetitla mural, holding a Storm God jar and wavy spear with atlatl.
Courtesy of Annabeth Headrick.

lightning serpent in his right arm or in his mouth, or a flower depending from his mouth. Some images of the Storm God emphasize beneficent aspects and are linked to water, gentle rain, and flourishing crops, while others have a more threatening aspect and are linked to violent lightning storms and war. But there are too many images with intergrading combinations of features to allow for more than one Storm God PCE.

I know of no chronological distinctions among representations of the Storm God in murals or painted or incised ceramics. Storm God jars, however, change over time, as I have described in previous chapters. These jars represent the same PCE, but some features differ from painted versions. They must derive from a tradition somewhat different from that seen in the paintings. Notably, they have well-defined eyebrows, rather than rings encircling their eyes. Frequently, three tabs project from the rim of a Storm God jar, the Teotihuacan "three mountain" sign (Langley 1986: 274, sign 135). This fits with modern Mesoamerican beliefs in sacred water-filled mountains. Some painted images show the Storm God holding a Storm God jar (Figure 8.15). In these cases the jar looks like a painted version of the Storm God, rather than accurately portraying such a jar. This is partly because Storm God jars and paintings of the Storm God were made by different artisans, but it shows that

Figure 8.16. Line drawing of a late Feathered Serpent, Palace of the Sun.
Courtesy of R. Millon (1973).

Teotihuacanos were interested in portraying concepts, rather than anything like photographic realism. This is why many pictures of creatures can readily be identified as to broad category (bird, felid, canid, serpent, arthropod, etc.) but are hard to pin down more exactly.

The other principal deity of Teotihuacan was the Feathered Serpent. So much has been written about this PCE that I discuss it only briefly. It is surely related to Quetzalcóatl, a major Aztec deity. However, not all features of Aztec Quetzalcóatl can be safely projected back onto the Teotihuacan Feathered Serpent. Stories about the quasi-historical personage Ce Acatl Topiltzin Quetzalcóatl possibly preserve faint echoes of events at Teotihuacan, but more likely they refer to post-Teotihuacan events if they are not wholly mythical. The Teotihuacan Feathered Serpent has been linked to the beginning of time (López Austin et al. 1991), but it is not clear to me that it was ever linked to a human, or to a Wind God (Ehecatl), as it was among the Aztecs.

The Feathered Serpent and the Storm God seem to have been partners. Feathered Serpent imagery is prominent early and continues throughout the history of the city, as in a late mural fragment from the Palace of the Sun (Figure 8.16). In the West Plaza Group of the Avenue of the Dead Complex, the stone figures on the balustrade of an early stairway emphasize reptilian features, while those on the stairway belonging to a later stage show more of a mix of feline and reptilian

Figure 8.17. Landscape with sacred mountain and trees, Tepantitla compound.
After Headrick (2007).

features. It has been suggested that the Feathered Serpent may have lost some importance relative to jaguars, but the Feathered Serpent never became insignificant.

Peter Furst (1974), Esther Pasztory (1997), Berlo (1992b) and others have seen a "Great Goddess" as the principal deity of Teotihuacan, although, by 1997, Pasztory seemed equivocal about the concept, as was Clara Millon (1988). I and others have been skeptical of this concept for some time. There were important female deities at Teotihuacan, such as the one represented by the monumental *Diosa de Agua* (Figure 6.9), but it is highly unlikely that there was a single overarching goddess who took precedence over the Storm God and the Feathered Serpent. Paulinyi (2006) has tellingly critiqued the Great Goddess concept.

A particularly important figure of the alleged Great Goddess is in a mural at Tepantitla (Figure 8.17). Landscapes are rare in Teotihuacan imagery, but in this case no one questions that a mountain is represented. What needs more emphasis is that this is not the image of a human with "mountainy" features. The mountain itself is the PCE. It is a mountain that exhibits some human *qualifiers*, including arms. First and foremost, it belongs to the "flowery mountain" concept that Kelley Hays-Gilpin and Jane Hill (1999) discuss with regard to Uto-Aztecan speakers in Mesoamerica and the southwestern United States, which is

Figure 8.18. Detail of Figure 8.17 showing fire symbols and Storm God nose pendant.

widespread in Mesoamerica among other language groups. The flowery mountain is associated with fertility and seen as a source of life-giving water. At Tepantitla, the flowery aspect is represented by the plants or trees that spring from its peak, while water gushes from a cave-like opening at its base and onto cultivated fields. This orifice is often interpreted as a vagina, although the physical resemblance seems remote to me. To be sure, caves tend to be thought of throughout Mesoamerica as entrances to the womb of an Earth Mother, but how could a flow of water emanating from the earth be depicted otherwise? I do not think this orifice has much bearing on the gender of the mountain. I find its gender unclear, and perhaps gender is not even an applicable aspect of identity here.

More significant is the band of diamond or rhomboidal elements that runs across the front of the mountain (Figure 8.18). These are a diagnostic feature of Old God sculptures ("*Huehueteotls*") (see Figure 8.22), and are generally accepted as a standardized sign for fire (Langley 1986: 252, sign 72). Here they are *qualifiers*, indicating that the mountain has fiery aspects – it is a volcano as well as a source of flowing water. It is not clear whether the Tepantitla mountain represents any specific volcano or just volcanoes in general. In any case, this takes us far from the "Great Goddess" concept. The Storm God nose pendant seen in this figure is also a qualifier, not a diagnostic of a Great Goddess.

The human celebrants in profile on each side of the mountain have been described as wearing female dress, but I find their attire ambiguous. Men in Teotihuacan imagery often wear capes that cover their shoulders but are open in front, while women wear a more encompassing garment that covers front as well as back, as seen on the *Diosa de Agua*.

Figure 8.19. Figure with flaming bundle torches in outstretched hands, "tassel" headdress, eye-rings, and Storm God nose pendant, plaque in burial B-V, Kaminaljuyú.
Kidder et al. 1946 © Carnegie Institution of Washington.

The methodological misstep in many proposed identifications of other images as representations of a "Great Goddess" is that they take features of the Tepantitla mountain or some other PCE as *diagnostics* of the Great Goddess, when in fact they are *qualifiers* embedded in images of other PCEs. A prominent example is the carved stone frieze in the Avenue of the Dead Complex (Figure 7.4). I see no evidence that it represents a female. More likely it is a PCE whose typical attributes include a frontal spread-armed posture, often holding a flaming bundle torch[4] in each hand and wearing a Storm God nose pendant. Figures in the same posture, carrying bundle torches in both hands and wearing a Storm God nose pendant occur outside Teotihuacan, notably on a slate plaque in tomb B-V at Mound B in Kaminaljuyú (Kidder et al. 1946: 130 and figure 175a). This personage wears eye-rings and a variant of the "tassel" headdress (Figure 8.19). Probably this PCE has something to do with the power of the Teotihuacan state. It may represent Teotihuacan rulership.

Figure 8.20. Flaming bundle torch motifs in mural border, Tetitla compound.
After Miller (1973).

A related recurrent image is that of a person in the same spread-arm posture but holding two shields instead of flaming bundle torches, as on the splendid cylinder vase found in the Margarita tomb at Copán (although there are flames atop the building that encloses the human figure) (Figure 7.27). Instead of a Storm God nose pendant, this figure wears a rattlesnake pendant. The pose and the paired shields also appear on an exceptional composite censer lid found in Oztoyahualco 15B:N6W3, a modest apartment compound, where the individual wears a *talud-tablero* nose pendant. Perhaps these are variants of the same PCE, referring to somewhat lower ranks in the Teotihuacan political system; those bearing the rattlesnake pendant of relatively high rank and those with the *talud-tablero* of more modest rank. Found abroad, on fine objects like slate plaques or cylinder vases, these images seem to refer to emissaries of the Teotihuacan state, rather than merchants or independent adventurers.

Flaming bundle torches can appear by themselves at Teotihuacan, as in a mural border in the Tetitla compound (Figure 8.20) and, inconspicuously, in the headdress of the Teotihuacan-related person holding an atlatl on the right side of Stela 31 at Tikal (Figure 8.21). David Grove (1987b) suggests that torches were an early symbol of rulership in Mesoamerica. They are probably distinct from tied bundles representing

Figure 8.21. Flaming bundle torch motifs in headdress, Tikal Stela 31. After Berrin (1988: 126).

completion of the fifty-two-year cycle in many Mesoamerican calendars (Cowgill n.d.a). Clara Millon (1973) identified a distinctive "tassel" headdress as a marker of high office. These items of regalia often appear in Teotihuacan imagery abroad.

A cult of sacred war was probably important at Teotihuacan for indoctrinating and motivating young Teotihuacan men (and possibly women) to serve as well-disciplined soldiers. This can be seen in warlike aspects of major deities, representations of armed figures, "portrait" figurines, and sacrificial burials of humans and fierce animals.

Another relatively well-defined Teotihuacan deity, a good PCE, is the so-called "Old God," an equivalent of the Aztec *Huehueteotl*. He takes the form of a bent and wrinkled old man, seated in tailor fashion, one hand clenched while the other is cupped, with prominent upper canine teeth, and with a circular basin on his head. The basin is ringed by the same lozenge-shaped "fire" signs seen in the Tepantitla mountain mural (Figure 8.22). Within Teotihuacan, his images are quite standardized, although some are considerably larger than others. Most are of andesitic stone, although at least one is of unfired earth. They are common in residential compounds and are often the only stone ritual object present. They derive from pre-Teotihuacan antecedents. It seems likely that they were used in rituals pertaining to the whole compound, probably domestic observances not connected with the state. Their

Figure 8.22. "Old God" stone brazier (*Huehueteotl*).
Photo by author.

occurrence spans nearly the full socioeconomic range of Teotihuacan
society, although maybe not in insubstantial structures. They occur in
humble compounds such as Tlajinga 33 and also in the "palaces" in the
Ciudadela.

Another Teotihuacan deity or sacred symbol is the butterfly (some
may be moths). It often appears among the *adornos* attached to composite censers, used in rituals for commemorating and communing with
the dead. In this context it probably represents deceased souls. It is discussed by Paulinyi (1995). Berlo (1983, 1984, 1989a) notes its presence
in Teotihuacan-derived censers in highland Guatemala, and Conides
(2001) discusses its frequent occurrence on stuccoed and plano-relief
decorated ceramics, in contrast to its scarcity in murals. It is a good
PCE: other figures are sometimes incorrectly identified as butterflies,
but real butterflies in Teotihuacan imagery are unmistakable, even when
abbreviated to a part, such as a proboscis.

A human figure whose head is covered by a mask with holes through
which eyes and mouth are exposed is represented by clay figurines

(Figure 7.20e) and sometimes on stuccoed cylinder vases. These figures have been called "xipes," from a supposed connection with *Xipe Totec*, the Aztec flayed god, celebrated in rites in which the skin of a sacrificial victim was worn by a priest. But Hasso von Winning (1987: volume 1, pp. 147–49) is very skeptical of this interpretation, and Sue Scott (1993) argued convincingly against it. More likely these figures depict soldiers wearing leather armor, which would have offered some protection, especially against club-wielding opponents. Some may represent ball players, but this seems less likely, given the limited evidence for ball games at Teotihuacan. A few, shown at the center of Maltese crosses on cylinder vases (von Winning 1987: Figure 2, following p. 149) could possibly represent an earth deity, since the Maltese cross can be a cosmogram. Several other deities are described by von Winning (1987) and others. Taube (1986, 1992a, 1992b) interprets other Teotihuacan imagery.

9 "Interesting Times":
Teotihuacan Comes Apart and a New Story Begins: 550 CE and After

The Decline and Fall of Teotihuacan: 500/550–550/650 CE

By 550 CE or perhaps a little earlier, the population of the city seems to have begun to decline, and parts apparently began to be abandoned, especially around its edges (Figure 9.1). The specifics are still unclear, especially because the Metepec ceramic complex needs better definition. However, the population probably decreased by at least a third, and possibly by more than half. There are other suggestions of decline. Thin Orange Ware continued to be imported, but now there were locally made hemispherical bowls that resemble Thin Orange bowls in shape, although readily distinguishable in fabric and surface appearance, so they could not have fooled any Teotihuacano. They were poor makeshifts for the genuine article. This suggests foreign goods were becoming harder to obtain. In the La Ventilla district, garbage accumulated in streets, ultimately blocking drains, and some streets were blocked by gates (Cabrera and Gómez 2008). Séjourné (1966a: 21) reports over two meters of midden in a street outside the Yayahuala compound. Seemingly, civic services were breaking down in Teotihuacan's last years and people were more wary of their neighbors.

Then, around 600/650 CE, major structures in the civic-ceremonial core, and some structures elsewhere, were burned. Martínez and Jarquín (1982) report a 6 cm layer of ash and charcoal atop the eastern outer platform of the Ciudadela, where a 60 cm stone male statuette was smashed and its fragments widely scattered. Some researchers (e.g., Beramendi-Orosco et al. 2009) think the burning happened around 550 CE and the Metepec phase represents post-burning occupation. This depends on the validity of a few archaeomagnetic dates. However, I have observed composite censers, whose flush rim flanges are diagnostically Metepec, smashed in place atop the latest concrete floor at the rear of the FSP, as part of the final destruction. This and other evidence places the burning at or near the end of the Metepec phase, rather than its beginning.

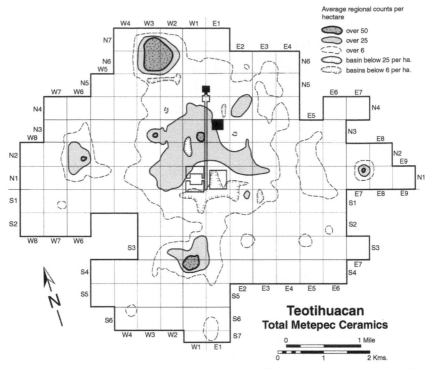

Figure 9.1. A smoothed contour map of Metepec phase sherd densities per hectare, collected by the TMP.

By S. Vaughn after original by author & W. Powell.

Somewhat outside the burned areas of the city, Cabrera and Gómez (2008) found signs of rapid abandonment in the La Ventilla district – artisans' tools and partly finished objects were left in place rather than carried away. Many earlier excavations at Teotihuacan were not of a quality to have detected this kind of evidence. It looks as if decline of the city terminated in catastrophic burning of major structures and hasty departures.

Causes of the decline and ultimate catastrophe remain controversial. They can be grouped into three broad categories: relations with the natural environment, internal sociopolitical and economic problems, and troubles with outsiders. Perhaps the climate became drier and less favorable for agriculture, but evidence for this is conflicting. Lachniet et al. (2012) neglect sociopolitical factors and see a sequence of wet and dry periods that conflicts with some other studies and does not correlate well with political rises and falls. Some see drought at this time in lake basins in western Mexico. However, Michelle Elliott (2007) finds no evidence for climatic change before the 1500s at La Quemada (Figure 1.2/6), in Zacatecas. In the Teotihuacan Valley, collecting firewood or other practices might have eventually led to serious environmental damage, but it is not clear why such damage would have appeared after what seems like centuries of sustainable use of resources. Barba et al. (2009) argue that most lime burning took place outside the Teotihuacan Valley. Within the valley, Emily McClung (2009) sees evidence that relatively high humidity persisted, and she does not see evidence of major deforestation or other environmental degradation. She finds the clearest suggestions of a major drought several centuries later, around the time when the Tula state collapsed. Severe erosion and deep down-cutting of barrancas appear to have begun in Colonial times. There was another major eruption of ash from Popocatépetl around 650–850 CE (Siebe 2000). It is unlikely that it had a role in the collapse of the Teotihuacan state, but it may have contributed to turbulent conditions in the ensuing Epiclassic interval.

Increased factionalism among ruling elites is possible. However, I know of no evidence for elite factionalism after desecration of the FSP around 300/350 CE. Growing class conflict is more likely. Ian Robertson's (2001, 2005) study of Teotihuacan neighborhoods found evidence that differences among them in markers of wealth were greater in the Tlamimilolpa phase than in Miccaotli, and this trend continued into the Xolalpan phase (Robertson, personal communication 2008). Martha Sempowski's (1992; Sempowski and Spence 1994: 268–72) study of grave offerings in several apartment compounds suggests that late in Teotihuacan's history these compounds increasingly differed from one another in the wealth deposited in burials. In some, although not all, grave offerings were markedly impoverished relative to those of the Xolalpan phase. Growing disparities in wealth among the city's residents could have provided a reason for widespread discontent that may have boiled over into violent rebellion.

Bureaucratic proliferation could also have been a factor in Teotihuacan's decline and collapse. Parkinson's (1957) critique of bureaucracies is instructive. Among other things, he wrote that "work expands to fill the time available for its completion." Perhaps because what he wrote was often funny, rather than deadly academic prose, and because his examples were chosen a bit informally, his writings have been largely ignored by archaeologists. But irreversible bureaucratic proliferation seems to me one of the closest approximations to a real "law" that social scientists have. It explains far more about so-called evolutionary changes, such as from "chiefdom" to "state," than do notions such as adaptive responses to stress. As to its validity, how can anyone dealing with universities or other large organizations doubt it? Much as we might wish it otherwise, bureaucracies are indispensable in complex organizations. Yet bureaucratic proliferation has its costs, and one of the principal tasks of "agency" is devising ways to circumvent bureaucracy in order to actually get anything done.

Applying Parkinson's ideas to Teotihuacan, it is easy to imagine that at first bureaucracies were weakly developed and could do little to impede the efforts of powerful and imaginative leaders to mobilize the resources and enthusiasm to lay out the vast ceremonial center, build the immense pyramids, and expand the Teotihuacan state. But, as we have seen, after the widespread construction of architecturally sub-stantial residential compounds, materially tangible innovation almost ceased, and it seems that Teotihuacan coasted for several centuries with little change. Perhaps bureaucracies continued to proliferate to a point where they seriously impeded political and even economic functioning.

Millon (1988a:156) has proposed growing ideological rigidity and resistance to change as a possible source of trouble for Teotihuacan. He wrote "the price paid for political continuity may have been the suppres-sion of the potential for radical internal change and transformation." While bureaucratic proliferation is a structural factor, Millon's sugges-tion is in the ideational realm, and perhaps applies to elites more than to bureaucrats, only a few of whom would have been of high status.

Based especially on her work at the Teopancazco apartment com-pound, Manzanilla (2006, 2009, 2012) has suggested that late in Teotihuacan's history the growing power of "intermediate" elites (Elson and Covey 2006) may have significantly impeded the ability of the state to function effectively. Intermediate elites are different from bureau-crats. By bureaucrats I mean servants of the state, persons often with little independent wealth or claims to high status, while by intermediate elites I mean persons with some degree of status and wealth that is not derived from the state and which can be in competition with the central authority. The distinction is not always clear – an independently pow-erful person can also be a servant of the state, and service to the state can become an avenue toward independent power – but in many states, ancient as well as modern, the distinction is often fairly clear. In feudal polities the categories are merged, but it is unlikely that Teotihuacan was feudally organized.

The topic of provincial elites is important, but my concern here is with intermediate elites who resided within the city. Persons or families may have gained increasing control over sources of wealth that had formerly accrued to the state, thus weakening the resources of the state and at the same time gaining wealth that they could use for their own purposes, often conflicting with state purposes. Manzanilla's idea derives from the wealth and apparent control over persons and trade at Teopancazco, and is independent of the data used by Sempowski and Robertson. But it is consonant with their interpretations, since the growing differences they suggest are not between the highest elites and everyone else, but between intermediate elites and those of lower status.

I turn to possible external human sources of trouble for Teotihuacan. During most of the time when Teotihuacan flourished there were no other major centers within a radius of at least 200 km. Cholula, about a hundred km away, may have doubled in size, to about eight square kilometers (Geoffrey McCafferty, personal communication 2007), but was still considerably smaller than Teotihuacan. Whether or not Teotihuacan politically controlled this whole region, it at least had the power to discourage the creation of rivals. Cantona, about 164 km east of Teotihuacan, near the eastern edge of the central highlands, was culturally distinct from Teotihuacan. It may have already existed before the decline of Teotihuacan, but its best days were later. Other centers that primarily flourished soon after the fall of Teotihuacan include Xochicalco in the valley of Morelos (Hirth 2000a, 2000b), Cacaxtla-Xochitécatl in Puebla, and possibly Tula Chico (the small center that preceded Tula Grande), which may have been larger at this time than previously thought (Suárez et al. 2007). Farther away, there was El Tajín in northern Veracruz. Because of poor chronologies, it is unclear whether any of these centers began to be serious competitors with Teotihuacan before the fall of that city. Did their growth contribute to the decline and collapse of the Teotihuacan state, through economic and political competition and possibly even military action, or did they only arise after Teotihuacan had collapsed? If their growth began before Teotihuacan's destruction, did they grow simply because Teotihuacan was in decline, or were there other factors? Did they adopt innovations in economic and/or political practices that Teotihuacan was too rigid, too wedded to what had worked in the past, to accept? This is Millon's notion of ideological rigidity.

Large-scale invasions are another possibility. A few decades ago, many thought that "civilization" did not extend far northwest of Central Mexico. Ragged nomads, the Chichimecs described in some sixteenth century sources, were thought typical of the whole region. This was perhaps why many doubted that invaders from the west or northwest would have stood a chance against such a mighty city as Teotihuacan. But there is now good evidence of sizable polities in many parts of western Mexico well before 500 CE. It is not hard to imagine successful invasion by a coordinated group from this region, possibly a coalition of several small polities, attacking a Teotihuacan already in decline and diminished in population. (If they weren't keeping garbage out of the streets, in what condition were their defenses?)

A major reason for suspecting a sizable invasion by outsiders is that the next abundantly represented style of decorated ceramics in Central Mexico, called Coyotlatelco, differs considerably from Teotihuacan styles. Some archaeologists, including Sanders (2006), have argued that the Coyotlatelco style is derived mainly from Teotihuacan antecedents. But discontinuities between Teotihuacan ceramics and the Coyotlatelco complex are pronounced (Cowgill 2013). Mastache and Cobean (1989) see antecedents to Coyotlatelco in areas several hundred kilometers to the west, including the Bajío, and Healan and Hernandez (2012) see especially close resemblances in ceramics from around Ucareo.

There may be partial continuity with some Teotihuacan plainwares. Barbour (1998) sees some continuity in certain figurine types. Ritual wares changed drastically. *Candeleros* disappeared. Composite censers disappeared and were replaced by large hourglass censers and by portable censers consisting of a shallow bowl to which a long tubular handle is attached (*sahumadores*).

There is no necessary correspondence between spreads of styles and movements of people: new styles can be adopted without the arrival of migrants, and migrants can abandon their old styles and adopt new ones. Nevertheless, many independent kinds of evidence suggest a significant migration around the time of Teotihuacan's collapse. Christopher Beekman and Andrew Christensen (2003) combine linguistic, biological, archaeological, and ethnohistoric evidence to argue for a sizable migration of Náhuatl speakers into Central Mexico at about this time. Náhuatl is the southeasternmost member of the Uto-Aztecan family of languages. Its original homeland was somewhere west or northwest of Central Mexico (Hill 2001). Náhuatl dialects eventually spread as far south as Nicaragua. Many scholars have believed that the dominant language of Teotihuacan was Náhuatl. But linguists Terrence Kaufman and John Justeson (2007) argue against supposed Náhuatl loan words in Classic Maya inscriptions and do not see good evidence that Náhuatl was influential in Central or Eastern Mesoamerica before the collapse of Teotihuacan. They argue that the primary language of Teotihuacan was a member of the Mixe-Zoque family, the family that probably includes the language of the much earlier Olmecs of the southern Gulf

Coast. Perhaps so, but there are other good candidates, including the Otomanguean languages, many of whose speakers, such as the Otomí, still live in Central Mexico.

Explanations for the decline and fall of the state and city of Teotihuacan are varied and not mutually exclusive. I suspect that internal social, political, and economic troubles, perhaps especially growing power of intermediate elites, weakened the Teotihuacan state to an extent that made it vulnerable and an attractive target for invasion by people from West Mexico. Increasing competition from nearby polities in Central Mexico may also have played a role. But this is just my current best guess. We need far more problem-oriented research on this topic.

Aftermath of Collapse

The period between about 550/650 and 850 CE is called Epiclassic in Central Mexico. It roughly corresponds to the interval called Late Classic elsewhere in Mesoamerica. The Central Mexican terminology confusingly jumps from Early Classic to Epiclassic, with no Late Classic. Whatever the exact sequence of events and their causes, the Teotihuacan state had come to an end. Later occupants of the city left few remains in the former civic-ceremonial core and mostly lived a little outside it, although there is a small concentration of Coyotlatelco ceramics at 6:N5W1, adjoining the Moon Pyramid. Richard Diehl's (1989b) account is faulty. Teotihuacan was still one of the most populous places in Central Mexico, but its political reach was limited. During the Teotihuacan Period, other settlements in the Basin of Mexico had been much smaller than the city, but now a more dispersed settlement pattern reappeared and other sizable centers arose.

Some archaeologists seem to take persistence of identity for granted, treating it as an unquestioned axiom rather than a postulate that needs testing. We cannot assume that Teotihuacan survivors who remained in the city or migrated elsewhere would have retained their identity in archaeologically visible ways for more than a generation or two. Identities are most likely to persist when there are perceived advantages in maintaining the ethnic identity of one's ancestors and/or when host groups place obstacles in the way of adopting a new identity. It helps if the number of survivors is reasonably large. It is unlikely that any of these conditions applied to descendants of Teotihuacan survivors. We cannot rule out the possibility of large-scale loss of life. Failure to find great numbers of skeletons scattered about is inconclusive; their slayers might well have removed most of the bodies, or left them without burial, to decompose in the open. And even if many survived and possibly

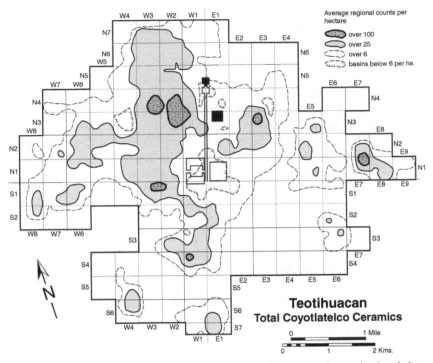

Figure 9.2. A smoothed contour map of Coyotlatelco style sherd densities per hectare, collected by the TMP.

By S. Vaughn after original by author & W. Powell.

emigrated, within a generation or two their descendants may have shed any archaeologically visible markers of Teotihuacan identity.

Limited occupation of the former civic-ceremonial core of the city by the makers of Coyotlatelco ceramics suggests that they wanted to dissociate themselves symbolically from the Teotihuacan state. If so, why did they settle in the city at all? Perhaps it was simply because they found it advantageous to make use of ruins in the residential areas of the city. Multiple high-density areas of Coyotlatelco ceramics within the former city suggest it was not highly centralized politically (Figure 9.2). Coyotlatelco civic-ceremonial structures have not been identified at Teotihuacan, but I suspect some modest ones existed. The picture at Teotihuacan contrasts strangely with the relatively elaborate architecture (including polychrome murals) found with Coyotlatelco ceramics at Xico in the southeastern Basin (Raúl García, personal communication, 2005). Possibly many of the people at Teotihuacan were descendants of earlier Teotihuacanos, still attached to their city, if not to the Teotihuacan state, but politically marginalized by newcomers.

The Coyotlatelco style of serving wares did not spread much east or south of the Basin of Mexico. One cannot assume a simple relation between pots and people, but it suggests that, for the time being, newcomers didn't get much past the Basin. Large scale movements of people continued in Postclassic times, and by the 1400s Náhuatl speakers were numerous in Puebla-Tlaxcala and Morelos, although there were also many speakers of Otomí and other languages.

Elsewhere in Mesoamerica

Monte Albán apparently flourished a couple of centuries longer than did Teotihuacan, perhaps benefiting from Teotihuacan's fall. But that state also gradually collapsed, probably by 800 CE (Blomster 2008). Perhaps Teotihuacan's decline was accelerated by western invaders whose conquests stopped short at the Basin of Mexico. In contrast, in the southern Maya Lowlands the period from around 600 to 850 CE saw the largest populations ever and a climax in art and monumental architecture, followed by a rapid drop in population and a cultural collapse in many parts of the area. There was far greater continuity in the northern Maya Lowlands.

Since 850 CE

In the Central Mexican Highlands, Tula reached a climax in the Early Postclassic or "Toltec" Period, which lasted from about 850 to 1050 CE, or perhaps somewhat later (Mastache et al. 2002). At this time, Tula was a sizable city that covered around twelve square kilometers. Its civic-ceremonial center was considerably smaller than Teotihuacan's had been, but it was a major power, and the area it controlled qualifies it as a regional state, if not an empire. Smith and Montiel (2001) underestimate the area it dominated and do not think it extended to the Basin of Mexico. But, at least judging by ceramic styles, its influence was strong in the northern Basin, including the Teotihuacan region (Crider 2013). This was roughly the Mazapan phase at Teotihuacan, with a peak density of ceramics in the Las Palmas area in sector N3E3 where Linné and Vaillant excavated in the 1930s (Figure 9.3). To the southeast, Cholula was flourishing and its sphere of influence reached into the southern Basin of Mexico, where it confronted that of Tula. At roughly the same time, insofar as can be judged from present chronologies, Chichén Itzá (Figure 1.2/32), in northern Yucatán, showed remarkable similarities to

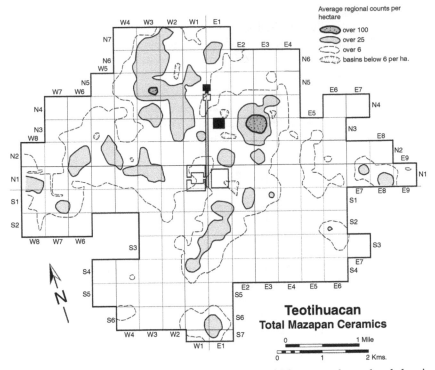

Figure 9.3. A smoothed contour map of Mazapan phase sherd densities per hectare, collected by the TMP.

By S. Vaughn after original by author & W. Powell.

Tula in some iconographic and architectural features. It is likely that there was some kind of significant central Mexican presence at Chichén Itzá.

A Middle Postclassic Period in the Basin of Mexico sees the beginning of the "Aztec" style of ceramics, during a period of numerous small states. In the late 1300s, the Tepanec state, centered at Azcapotzalco, conquered a significant part of Central Mexico. It was defeated in 1428 by a small state centered on the twin cities of Tenochtitlan and Tlatelolco, and the Mexica began an expansionist career, in alliance with the small states of Texcoco and Tlacopan (a little south of Azcapotzalco) that led to Late Postclassic conquests and, by the late 1400s, political and economic domination of most of Mesoamerica west of Tehuantepec, plus a few strategic areas farther east, including much of Pacific coastal Chiapas and Guatemala, which earlier was of interest to Teotihuacanos (Berdan et al. 1996). Figure 9.4 shows Aztec sherd densities in the TMP

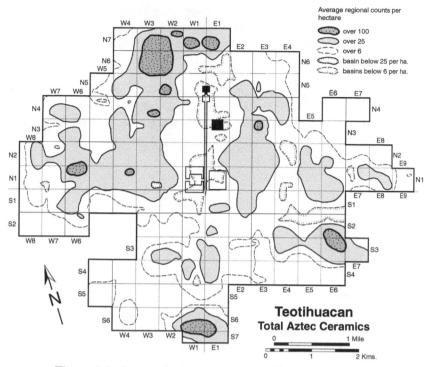

Figure 9.4. A smoothed contour map of Aztec phase sherd densities per hectare, collected by the TMP.

By S. Vaughn after original by author & W. Powell.

survey area, primarily Late Postclassic. In some places, occupation runs off the TMP map, but occupation in the central part of the ancient city was lighter than ever.

To the west, in Michoacán, the Tarascan (Purépecha) state successfully held off the Aztecs, and there were pockets of resistance elsewhere, notably in Tlaxcala. The situation was still very fluid when the arrival of Hernando Cortés and his party of conquistadores in 1519 abruptly initiated a very different chapter in Mesoamerican history. Mesoamerica remained a part of the Spanish colonial empire until 1821, when Mexico gained its independence. Guatemala and other Central American republics soon followed, although Belize did not gain full independence from the British Empire until 1981.

Ever since the Teotihuacan Period, a substantial population has lived in the Teotihuacan Valley, including the outer parts of the ancient city. After the Spanish Conquest the former urban zone of Teotihuacan was divided between the municipalities of San Juan Teotihuacán on the west and San Martín de las Pirámides on the east. This is the case today. It may have been appropriate to refer to them as villages at the beginning of the twentieth century, but by late in that century they had grown into sizable towns, offering a wide variety of goods and services, within an hour from Mexico City by four-lane highway. The archaeological zone, now a UNESCO World Heritage site, is a significant source of local employment, although agriculture and commerce are also important.

Urban developments were underway in Central Mexico at least as early as 400 BCE, at Cuicuilco and probably at Cholula and elsewhere in Puebla/Tlaxcala. By 100 BCE, Teotihuacan began to grow rapidly, and by 100 CE it covered about 20 square km, with a population probably close to 60,000. Thereafter, the spatial extent of the city changed little, although the southern part of the city filled in more. The rate of population growth slowed, and the city seems to have leveled off at around 70,000–100,000. The Teotihuacan polity continued to expand, and the scale and complexity of the political system increased.

Early political institutions and ethics may have been collective, but the scale of civic-ceremonial structures in the city's core and the rapidity of developments suggest the leadership of some talented, charismatic, and highly motivated individuals. I suspect that by the first century CE the system was subverted by more despotic leaders who were responsible for the largest pyramids and an increased scale of human sacrifice. The Teotihuacan polity soon began to reach beyond the Basin of Mexico, and by 200 CE, if not earlier, there were Teotihuacan presences, probably primarily to obtain materials not available in Central Mexico, as far away as Pacific coastal Guatemala, 1,100 km from the city. No other Mesoamerican polity before the Aztecs had comparably distant outposts. It is unclear how directly they were administered from the city, and it seems unlikely that Teotihuacan ever directly administered large blocks of territory far from the capital. However, Teotihuacanos or people with strong Teotihuacan connections intervened directly in the politics of some Early Classic Maya polities, and apparently founded new dynastic lines at Tikal and Copán.

Sometime in the 300s there may have been a shift in ideology, marked by desecration of the FSP, and perhaps new political institutions that returned to a more collective ethos that provided an arena for "corporate" strategies and practices. The city continued to do well for a few centuries, and apparently was not having any disastrous impact on its environment. Most people lived in commodious multi-apartment walled compounds. Insubstantial structures housed perhaps as much as 15 percent of the people (Robertson 2008). Then, by about 550 CE, there are signs of trouble. The population of the city decreased, the city shrank toward its core, and foreign imports became harder to obtain. The reasons for decline are not clear, but I suspect that growing power of intermediate elites was one important factor. They may have increasingly siphoned off surpluses that would formerly have accrued to the state. It is also possible that centers not far outside the Basin of Mexico whose growth had formerly been suppressed by the power of Teotihuacan, such as Xochicalco, Xochitécatl-Cacaxtla, and possibly Tula Chico were beginning to develop and compete with Teotihuacan, but vague chronologies leave this uncertain. By 650 CE and possibly as early as 550, major civic-ceremonial structures and some elite residences were systematically burned, the Teotihuacan state collapsed, and the city was probably briefly abandoned. Ceramic styles changed drastically and there was probably an influx of people from the west. Teotihuacan survivors probably mingled with newcomers and soon lost their identity as Teotihuacanos.

If we had no written records for the Roman state and no more archaeological data than we have for Teotihuacan, the course of Roman history between 100 BCE and 400 CE might look as uneventful as Teotihuacan's history looks now, except for the possible revolution marked by desecration of the FSP. Yet we know what troubled times there were for Romans: slave revolts, civil wars between factions, dynastic usurpations and assassinations (often led by generals), occasional madmen in power, chronic financial problems for the state, drastic sociopolitical reorganizations, and the rise of new religions. Was Teotihuacan's actual career anywhere near as tempestuous?

I will not compare Teotihuacan with other ancient polities in any systematic or detailed way. I only offer a few thoughts. Today we know too much about different early states for any one person to do a satisfactory job of comparison. Even as heroic an effort as Bruce Trigger's (2003) massive and in-depth comparison of seven cases leaves me uncomfortable, since my image of Teotihuacan does not fit easily into either of the two major types he identifies – territorial states and city-states. Teotihuacan dominated too large an area with too many secondary and tertiary centers, and without nearby peers, to be considered part of a city-state system, but the city was too large and too compact to fit his description of typical capitals of territorial states (Trigger 2003: 120–41).

Notions about the decline and fall of Teotihuacan invite comparison with the dynastic cycles of imperial China and ancient Egypt. In China, the cyclic rise and fall of dynasties over the past 2,200 years is well-documented (e.g., Fairbank et al. 1973) and the notion of cycles superposed on cumulative change is old hat, but there are various proposed explanations. Traditionally, much was attributed to the moral qualities of emperors: virtuous emperors enjoyed the Mandate of Heaven and founded dynasties, while increasingly degenerate successors forfeited the Mandate and provoked rebellions leading to chaos and eventual reestablishment of centralized authority by the worthy founder of a new dynasty. Nowadays more weight is given to political and economic processes. A new regime was able to gain income by taxing "free" peasants, but over time some persons were increasingly able to lend money at exorbitant rates to distressed peasants, foreclosing on debts and converting them to tenants owing rent to rich landlords rather than taxes to the state. The landlords themselves were increasingly able to escape taxation, thus cutting off state revenues at the same time that they gained resources for their own purposes. Something like this may have happened at Teotihuacan.

Ancient Egypt offers other examples. By the Fourth Dynasty, in the Old Kingdom, political centralization was very strong, but it weakened, and the Sixth Dynasty collapsed into an era of political fragmentation and death from warfare and famine. In this case, environmental factors may have been important. But another factor was the extent to which control over resources was diverted from the central government to untaxed priestly establishments.

The number of people subjugated by the Teotihuacan state was likely no more than a half-million, in a territory that could have only briefly been larger than 100,000 square kilometers, plus a few distant strategic outposts, and it may have covered much less. By 1500 CE the Aztec Empire was much larger in both area and population. Other early empires, with metals, beasts of burden, and (except in the Andes) long rivers for transport, tended to be larger. Individual city-states in pre-Sargonic Mesopotamia and Classical Greece were generally much smaller, but they were components in regional or macroregional *systems* of small polities. (The key concept is the *system* of polities, and the concept of an isolated city-state is as anomalous as the concept of one hand clapping.)

Differences between the Indus civilization (Wright 2009) and Teotihuacan are greater than they seem at first sight. The scale of civic-ceremonial structures was far greater at Teotihuacan, while the spatial extent of Teotihuacan culture was far smaller. There also seems to be a certain austerity to Indus material culture, a term one would not apply to Teotihuacan.

One of the most fruitful sources for thinking about ancient cities is our experience in contemporary cities. A problem for studies of hunter-gatherer societies is that so few of them still exist, but today cities encompass most of the world's population, and we cannot get away from them. There is a large literature on problems and issues concerning contemporary cities, and this literature is a fertile source for thinking about the past (York et al. 2011). For any salient topic of research on twenty-first-century cities, we can address the same topic in thinking about Teotihuacan. To neglect information about ancient cities is to needlessly diminish the database for considering today's cities. We can get a clearer idea of the ways in which ancient cities such as Teotihuacan both resembled and differed from various types of modern cities. We can get more of an idea of which features have a long history and are widespread and which are genuinely unprecedented. By getting some idea of what worked and didn't work for Teotihuacan, we can improve the quality of present-day planning efforts (Smith 2010).

I cannot offer any neatly packaged prescriptions for remedies for currently perceived problems. Yet I follow the maxim that those who are ignorant of the past are doomed to repeat it, although I would modify it to say that ignorance can lead to *avoidable* mistakes, for some things seem unavoidable. I agree with Karl Marx, who said "men make their own history, but they do not make it just as they please ..." (McLellan 1977: 300). Still, accurate knowledge of Teotihuacan cannot help but be of some use in gaining perspective on the world in which we now live. I have emphasized aspects of Teotihuacan that call for more research and that can lead to more accurate knowledge, if economic, political, and ideological conditions prove to be favorable for well-funded further archaeological research. To have lasted as long as the Teotihuacan polity did, Teotihuacanos must have been doing some things right. But the question then arises "why didn't it last even longer?" In the present state of our knowledge, it is too simplistic to point to any single cause of collapse. I have evaluated a set of "usual suspects": tensions arising from growing wealth differences, state access to resources weakened by "intermediate elites," sheer bureaucratic proliferation and rigidity, droughts or other climatic changes, gradually increasing human-induced environmental damage, growing competition from neighboring polities, and large scale invasions. There may be other factors I haven't considered.

Further research addressed to these questions should at least narrow the range of plausible possibilities, even if it doesn't provide definitive answers. It would be unrealistic to expect that, even if we knew much more about Teotihuacan than we do now, it would furnish us with any clear and simple guidelines for how to cope with practical problems we face today. But it can correct simplistic and often plain wrong "lessons from the past." Together with the study of other ancient and historic societies, it can enrich our wisdom about human affairs, in all their unpredictability and untidiness, perhaps give us some warnings about things to avoid, and hopefully induce an attitude that is suspicious of "quick fixes" and easy solutions to complex problems.

But I end on a note of urgency. The outer parts of ancient Teotihuacan are not within the well-protected archaeological zone, and they are rapidly disappearing as a result of population growth and mechanized agriculture. Elsewhere, more than half the archaeological sites in the Basin of Mexico have disappeared within the past fifty years, most never excavated and known only through the surface surveys of Sanders, Parsons, and their colleagues (Sanders et al. 1979). Surviving sites rapidly continue to disappear, and resources for archaeological salvage work are desperately limited. Unless more funding can be found very soon, almost nothing will be left of the archaeological record in the Basin of Mexico, including much of Teotihuacan. Many important questions that still might be answered risk becoming forever unanswerable.

Notes

1 Preliminaries

1 Bayesian methods make systematic use of multiple kinds of prior information, which makes them generally superior to traditional methods of statistical inference.
2 This and similar platforms attached to the fronts of major Teotihuacan pyramids have generally been called *plataformas adosadas*, but I am uncomfortable with that term, and I prefer to call them "fore-platforms."
3 I use a slash (/) to designate a specific item within a figure.

2 Situating Teotihuacan

1 I am indebted to Glenn Stuart for the felicitous term "wetland agriculture," which involves all the techniques for using or removing excess water, in contrast to "irrigation," which involves bringing water to plots otherwise short of moisture.

3 Urbanism Begins in Central Mexico: 500–100 BCE

1 Sanders et al. (1979: 98–105) assert that Bennyhoff (1967) reports Tezoyuca ceramics at Cuicuilco, but I can find no mention of this in Bennyhoff's paper.

6 Great Pyramids and Early Grandeur: 100–250 CE

1 Burial 1 was a neonate with no offerings found in a recent layer near the northwest corner of the Moon Pyramid.
2 Just this was done at the opening of the 1968 Olympics in Mexico City, when a runner carried the Olympic torch up the Avenue of the Dead and onto the Moon Pyramid.
3 Grave numbers at the Feathered Serpent Pyramid are confusing because those found in the 1980–82 excavations were assigned relatively high numbers, since many graves were found in other operations of this project. Those discovered in the 1988–94 excavations began again with the number 1. Fortunately, there

is no duplication of numbers for the graves at this pyramid, so identifications are unambiguous.

4 The wall is preserved up to 2.5 m, but my observations in 1964 of the amount of debris before excavation imply an original height of at least 3–4 m.

7   Teotihuacan at Its Height: 250–550 CE

1 Some years ago I suggested that the entire adult population of the city might have fitted into the Ciudadela plaza (Cowgill 1983: 322). This seemed such an obvious point for anyone capable of long division and willing to make a guess about how closely people would be willing to be packed that I almost didn't bother to mention it. To my chagrin, it seems to have come as a fascinating surprise to many archaeologists and has since been frequently mentioned by writers who paid little heed to what I thought were more important points. Such is the state of quantitative imagination in the archaeological community.

2 Paddock (1983) was only aware of three of these structures and erroneously believed that the enclave only covered about 1.5 ha.

3 Adoption of the term "trade diaspora" by archaeologists is unfortunate, because the term primarily refers to enforced dispersion or exile of populations.

4 Carballo and Hirth began excavations in 2013 at an obsidian workshop in the Tlajinga district.

5 Borowicz's new drawing of Tikal Stela 4 wisely omits the very problematic dashed lines in a badly damaged area, in the widely copied version drawn by William Coe. There is little doubt that the figure is in full frontal standing position, probably a bust.

8   Teotihuacan Ideation and Religion: Imagery, Meanings, and Uses

1 I have verified this in my swimming pool, a tough job, but someone had to do it.

2 Actually the year is about 365.242 days, which is why we have leap years. It is not clear how Mesoamericans handled this problem.

3 The Teotihuacan Storm God is often called "Tlaloc," the name of an Aztec deity. Tlaloc derived in large part from the Teotihuacan Storm God, but the derivation was not simple or direct, so I avoid that name in referring to the Teotihuacan deity.

4 Langley (1986: 238–40), identifies sign 30 as "bundle," without distinguishing cases where flames appear.

Glossary

Adorno	A ceramic object of symbolic significance, often mold-made, attached to a composite censer or other vessel.
Andesite	Compact volcanic rock, lighter in color than basalt and often of visibly granular composition.
Almena	A tabular ornament rising from the outer margin of the flat roof of residential structures, smaller ones usually ceramic, larger ones often of stone.
Ashlar	Cut stone masonry, "*cantera*" in Spanish.
Basalt	Compact volcanic rock, dark in color, usually fine-grained but sometimes with open cavities or voids.
Candelero	A small, often crude, ceramic object for burning incense. Some earlier ones have a single chamber, and a few have three or more chambers, but the vast majority have two chambers. Teotihuacan-style *candeleros* are quite different from other styles and are very rare outside Teotihuacan, except at Matacapan in southern Veracruz and in Pacific coastal Guatemala.
Cascajo	Gravel-sized fragments of volcanic rock, much more porous than andesite or basalt, often with the appearance of solidified froth. Colors vary from reddish to black.
Ceramic complex	The full repertoire of ceramics in use by a community during a limited time interval.

253

Collection tract	The actual patch of ground from which a TMP collection was made.
Comal	A large, flat ceramic griddle, often used for toasting tortillas or other food.
Courtyard	In this book, a relatively large unroofed rectangular space within an apartment compound, usually only one per compound, usually architecturally linked to the compound as a whole rather than to any specific apartment.
Fabric	In ceramic contexts, this refers to the entire composition of the vessel, including the paste of microscopic clay and other particles, and larger objects that occur naturally in source clays or were intentionally added.
Fill	Earth, rubble, and other materials used to provide solid substance under floors and in cores of walls.
Fore-platform	In this book, a smaller platform attached to the front of a larger pyramid. Often called *plataforma adosada*.
FSP	The Feathered Serpent Pyramid (Temple of Quetzalcóatl).
Handled cover	See *tapaplato*.
Hegemonic	Indirect rule, as opposed to direct administration.
INAA	See NAA.
NAA	Neutron Activation Analysis.
Mano	A stone object used for grinding maize or other materials on a *metate*, usually made of basalt.
Metate	A stone slab on which maize or other materials are ground, usually made of basalt. Varieties include those with a trough into which the *mano* fits and those without a trough, for which a longer *mano* is used that overhangs the *metate*. Some *metates* have three supports, others lack supports.

Patio	In this book, a relatively small unroofed space that pertains to one apartment within an apartment compound.
Plaza	In this book, a relatively large unroofed space, usually outside any structure, although some are within large civic-ceremonial structures, such as triadic groups and the Ciudadela.
Polythetic	A category which is not defined by any single attribute, but by its members possessing at least most of some set of attributes.
Sector	In this book, a 500 by 500 meter square in the TMP map. Each sector comprises 250,000 square meters (25 hectares).
Tablero	A vertical architectural panel much wider from side to side than top to bottom. Most *tableros* in Teotihuacan structures have projecting moldings on all four sides. Some lack a projecting molding on the bottom. *Tableros* occur atop *talud*s. See Figures 5.3 and 5.4.
Talud	Architecturally, a sloping panel, often but not always topped by a *tablero*. See Figures 5.3, 5.4, and 6.25.
Tapaplato	Also called handled cover. A medium-sized, shallow ceramic bowl, usually with an unsmoothed surface, with three loop handles on the convex side. The handles typically have wear facets, indicating their use on a hard, flat surface. Often shallow motifs made by a mold occur on the convex surface. The concave surface is often sooted, probably from burning incense. They were probably used in rituals, but perhaps had additional uses. See Figure 6.28.
Tepetate	Volcanic ash subsoil, often nearly rock-hard. *Tepetate* blocks were often used in the interiors of Teotihuacan concrete-faced walls, and crushed *tepetate* was used as a subsurface for concrete floors.

Tezcacuitlapilli	Shiny fragments of iron pyrites attached to a slate disk to make a mirror, worn on their lower back by soldiers.
Tezontle	Porous volcanic rock. *Cascajo* is crushed *tezontle*.
Three-prong burner	A coarse conical bowl with flat bottom, and three hollow prongs that project upwardly and inwardly from the otherwise plain rim. Interiors are often sooted. Possibly the prongs were used to support other vessels during cooking, but there is never any sign of wear on the prongs. Probably their main use was for indoor heating, especially in rooms lacking hearths (Figure 7.18).
TMP	The Teotihuacan Mapping Project.

Bibliography

Abbreviations

ENAH: Escuela Nacional de Antropología e Historia, Mexico City.
FAMSI: Foundation for the Advancement of Mesoamerican Studies, Inc., Chrystal River, FL.
INAH: Instituto Nacional de Antropología e Historia, Mexico City.
UNAM: Universidad Nacional Autónoma de México, Mexico City.

Acosta, Jorge R. 1940. Exploraciones en Tula, Hgo., 1940. *Revista Mexicana de Estudios Antropológicos* 4:172–94.

1964a. La Decimotercera Temporada de Exploraciones en Tula; Hgo. *Anales del Instituto Nacional de Antropología e Historia* 16:45–76.

1964b. *El Palacio del Quetzalpapalotl.* INAH.

Agrinier, Pierre. 1970. *Mound 20, Mirador, Chiapas, Mexico.* New World Archaeological Foundation, Brigham Young University, Paper 28, Provo, UT.

1975. *Mounds 9 and 10 at Mirador, Chiapas, Mexico.* New World Archaeological Foundation, Provo, UT.

Allen, Lawrence P. 1980. Intra-Urban Exchange at Teotihuacan: Evidence from Mold-Made Figurines. In *Models and Methods in Regional Exchange,* Ed. by R. E. Fry, pp. 83–94. Society for American Archaeology, Washington, DC.

Almaraz, Ramón. 1865. *Memoria de los Trabajos Ejecutacos por la Comisión Científica de Pachuca en el Año 1864.* Mexico.

Andrews, Bradford W. 1999. *Craftsman Skill and Specialization: Investigating the Craft Production of Prehispanic Obsidian Blades at Xochicalco and Teotihuacan, Mexico.* Doctoral Thesis, Department of Anthropology, Pennsylvania State University, University Park.

2002. Stone Tool Production at Teotihuacan: What More Can We Learn from Surface Collections? In *Pathways to Prismatic Blades: A Study in Mesoamerican Obsidian Core-Blade Technology,* Ed. by K. Hirth and B. Andrews, pp. 47–60. The Cotsen Institute of Archaeology, University of California, Los Angeles.

2006. Skill and the Question of Blade Crafting Intensity at Classic Period Teotihuacan. In *Skilled Production and Social Reproduction: Aspects of Traditional Stone-Tool Technologies,* Ed. by J. Apel and K. Knutsson, pp. 263–75. Societas Archaeologica Upsaliensis & The Department of Archaeology and Ancient History, Uppsala University, Uppsala.

Angulo Villaseñor, Jorge. 1987. Nuevas Consideraciones sobre los Llamados Conjuntos Departamentales, Especialmente Tetitla. In *Teotihuacan: Nuevos Datos, Nuevas Síntesis, Nuevos Problemas*, Ed. by E. McClung de Tapia and E. C. Rattray, pp. 275–315. Instituto de Investigaciones Antropológicas, UNAM.

Armillas, Pedro. 1944. Exploraciones Recientes en Teotihuacán, Mexico. *Cuadernos Americanos* 16(4):121–36.

1945. Los Dioses de Teotihuacán. *Anales del Instituto de Etnología Americana* 6:35–61. Universidad Nacional de Cuyo, Mendoza, Argentina.

1947. La Serpiente Emplumada, Quetzalcóatl y Tláloc. *Cuadernos Americanos* 31(1):161–78.

1948. A Sequence of Cultural Development in Meso-America. In *A Reappraisal of Peruvian Archaeology*, Ed. by W. C. Bennett. Society for American Archaeology, Memoir 4.

1950. Teotihuacán, Tula, y los Toltecas: Las Culturas PostArcaicas y PreAztecas del Centro de México. Excavaciones y Estudios, 1922–1950. *Runa* 3(part 1):37–70. Buenos Aires.

1951. Technología, Formaciones Socio-Económicas y Religión en Mesoamérica. In *The Civilizations of Ancient America*, Ed. by S. Tax. University of Chicago Press, Chicago.

1964. Northern Mesoamerica. In *Prehistoric Man in the New World*, Ed. by J. D. Jennings and E. Norbeck, pp. 291–321. University of Chicago Press, Chicago.

Arnold, Philip J. III, and Robert S. Santley. 2008. Classic Currents in the West-Central Tuxtlas. In *Classic Period Cultural Currents in Southern and Central Veracruz*, Ed. by P. J. Arnold III and C. A. Pool, pp. 293–321. Dumbarton Oaks, Washington, DC.

Aveleyra Arroyo de Anda, Luis. 1963a. *La Estela Teotihuacana de la Ventilla.* INAH.

1963b. An Extraordinary Composite Stela from Teotihuacán. *American Antiquity* 29(2):235–37.

Aveni, Anthony F. 2000. Out of Teotihuacan: Origins of the Celestial Canon in Mesoamerica. In *Mesoamerica's Classic Heritage: From Teotihuacan to the Aztecs*, Ed. by D. Carrasco, L. Jones, and S. Sessions, pp. 253–68. University Press of Colorado, Boulder.

2005. Observations on the Pecked Cross and Other Figures Carved on the South Platform of the Pyramid of the Sun at Teotihuacan. *Journal for the History of Astronomy* 36: 31–47.

Aveni, Anthony F., Horst Hartung, and J. Charles Kelley. 1982. Alta Vista (Chalchihuites): Astronomical Implications of a Mesoamerican Ceremonial Outpost at the Tropic of Cancer. *American Antiquity* 47: 316–35.

Barba, Luis, J. Blancas, Linda R. Manzanilla, A. Ortiz, D. Barca, G. M. Crisci, D. Miriello, A. Pecci. 2009. Provenance of the Limestone Used in Teotihuacan (Mexico): a Methodological Approach. *Archaeometry* 51(4):525–45.

Barba, Luis, and José Luis Córdova Frunz. 1999. Estudios Energéticos de la Producción de Cal en Tiempos Teotihuacanos y sus Implicaciones. *Latin American Antiquity* 10: 168–79.

Barba, Luis, Agustin Ortiz, and Linda Manzanilla. 2007. Commoner Ritual at Teotihuacan, Central Mexico: Methodological Considerations. In *Commoner Ritual and Ideology in Ancient Mesoamerica*, Ed. by N. Gonlin and J. C. Lohse, pp. 55–82. University Press of Colorado, Boulder.

Barbour, Warren D. 1976. *The Figurines and Figurine Chronology of Ancient Teotihuacan, Mexico*. PhD diss., Dept. of Anthropology, University of Rochester, NY.

1998. The Figurine Chronology of Teotihuacan, Mexico. In *Los Ritmos de Cambio en Teotihuacan: Reflexiones y Discusiones de su Cronología*, Ed. by R. Brambila and R. Cabrera, pp. 243–53. INAH.

Batres, Leopoldo.1906. *Teotihuacán*. Fidencio S. Soria, Mexico City.

Beekman, Christopher S. and Alexander F. Christensen. 2003. Controlling for Doubt and Uncertainty through Multiple Lines of Evidence: A New Look at the Mesoamerican Nahua Migrations. *Journal of Archaeological Method and Theory* 10: 111–64.

Bennyhoff, James A. 1967. Continuity and Change in the Teotihuacan Ceramic Tradition. In *Teotihuacan. Onceava Mesa Redonda*, pp. 19–29. Sociedad Mexicana de Antropología, Mexico City.

Bennyhoff, James A., and Robert F. Heizer. 1965. Neutron Activation Analysis of Some Cuicuilco and Teotihuacan Pottery: Archaeological Interpretation of Results. *American Antiquity* 30(3):348–49.

Bentley, R. A. 2006. Strontium Isotopes from the Earth to the Archaeological Skeleton: A Review. *Journal of Archaeological Method and Theory* 13(3): 135–87.

Beramendi-Orosco, Laura E., Galia González-Hernández, Jaime Urrutia-Fucugauchi, Linda R. Manzanilla, Ana M. Soler-Arechalde, Avto Goguitchaishvili, and Nick Jarboe. 2009. High-Resolution Chronology for the Mesoamerican Urban Centre of Teotihuacan Derived from Bayesian Statistics of Radiocarbon and Archaeological Data. *Quaternary Research* 71:99–107.

Berdan, Frances F., Richard E. Blanton, Elizabeth H. Boone, Mary G. Hodge, Michael E. Smith, and Emily Umberger. 1996. *Aztec Imperial Strategies*. Dumbarton Oaks, Washington, DC.

Berlo, Janet C. 1983. The Warrior and the Butterfly: Central Mexican Ideologies of Sacred Warfare and Teotihuacan Iconography. In *Text and Image in PreColumbian Art: Essays on the Interrelationship of the Verbal and Visual Arts*, Ed. by J. C. Berlo, pp. 79–117. British Archaeological Reports, Oxford, UK.

1984. *Teotihuacan Art Abroad: A Study of Metropolitan Style and Provincial Transformation in Incensario Workshops*. British Archaeological Reports, Oxford, UK.

1989a. Art Historical Approaches to the Study of TeotihuacánRelated Ceramics from Escuintla, Guatemala. In *New Frontiers in the Archaeology of the Pacific Coast of Southern Mesoamerica*, Ed. by F. Bove and L. Heller, pp. 147–65. Anthropological Research Papers, No. 39, Arizona State University, Tempe.

1989b. Early Writing in Central Mexico: In Tlilli, in Tlapalli before AD 1000. In *Mesoamerica after the Decline of Teotihuacan: AD 700–900*, Ed. by R. A. Diehl and J. C. Berlo, pp. 19–47. Dumbarton Oaks, Washington, DC.

1992a. (ed.) *Art, Ideology, and the City of Teotihuacan*. Dumbarton Oaks, Washington, DC.

1992b. Icons and Ideologies at Teotihuacan: The Great Goddess Reconsidered. In *Art, Ideology, and the City of Teotihuacan*, Ed. by J. C. Berlo, pp. 129–68. Dumbarton Oaks, Washington, DC.

Bernal, Ignacio. 1963. *Teotihuacan: Descubrimientos, Reconstrucciones*. INAH.

Berrin, Kathleen, (ed.) 1988. *Feathered Serpents and Flowering Trees: Reconstructing the Murals of Teotihuacan*. The Fine Arts Museums of San Francisco, San Francisco.

Berrin, Kathleen, and Esther Pasztory, (eds.) 1993. *Teotihuacan: Art from the City of the Gods*. Thames & Hudson, New York.

Blanton, Richard E. 1972. *Prehispanic Settlement Patterns of the Ixtapalapa Peninsula Region, Mexico*. Department of Anthropology, Occasional Papers in Anthropology, No. 6. Pennsylvania State University, University Park.

Blanton, Richard E., and Lane F. Fargher. 2011. The Collective Logic of Pre-Modern Cities. *World Archaeology* 43(3):505–22.

Blanton, Richard E., Gary M. Feinman, Stephen A. Kowalewski, and Linda M. Nicholas. 1999. *Ancient Oaxaca: The Monte Albán State*. Cambridge University Press, Cambridge, UK.

Blanton, Richard E., Gary M. Feinman, Stephen A. Kowalewski, and Peter N. Peregrine. 1996. A Dual-Processual Theory for the Evolution of Mesoamerican Civilization. *Current Anthropology* 37(1):1–14.

Blanton, Richard E., Stephen A. Kowalewski, Gary M. Feinman, and Laura M. Finsten. 1993. *Ancient Mesoamerica: A Comparison of Change in Three Regions* (2nd edition). Cambridge University Press, Cambridge, UK.

Blomster, Jeffrey P. (ed.). 2008. *After Monte Albán: Transformation and Negotiation in Oaxaca, Mexico*. University Press of Colorado, Boulder.

2010. Complexity, Interaction, and Epistemology: Mixtecs, Zapotecs, and Olmecs in Early Formative Mesoamerica. *Ancient Mesoamerica* 21(1):135–49.

Blucher, Darlena K. 1971. *Late Preclassic Cultures in the Valley of Mexico: PreUrban Teotihuacan*. PhD diss., Brandeis University, Waltham, MA. Xerox University Microfilms, Ann Arbor, MI.

1983. *Patlachique Phase Ceramics*. Unpublished manuscript.

Borowicz, James. 2003. Images of Power and the Power of Images: Early Classic Iconographic Programs of the Carved Monuments of Tikal. In *The Maya and Teotihuacan: Reinterpreting Early Classic Interaction*, Ed. by G. E. Braswell, pp. 217–34. University of Texas Press, Austin.

Bourdieu, Pierre. 1977. *Outline of a Theory of Practice*. Cambridge University Press, Cambridge, UK.

1990. *The Logic of Practice*. Stanford University Press, Stanford, CA.

Bove, Frederick J., and Sonia Medrano Busto. 2003. Teotihuacan, Militarism, and Pacific Guatemala. In *The Maya and Teotihuacan*, Ed. by G. E. Braswell, pp. 45–79. University of Texas Press, Austin.

Bracamontes, Sonia. 2001. *Las Vasijas Tlaloc de Teotihuacan*. Departamento de Antropología, Universidad de las Américas, Puebla, Mexico.

Brambila, Rosa, and Rubén Cabrera, (eds.) 1998. *Los Ritmos de Cambio en Teotihuacán: Reflexiones y Discusiones de su Cronología*. INAH.

Braswell, Geoffrey E., ed. 2003. *The Maya and Teotihuacan: Reinterpreting Early Classic Interaction*. University of Texas Press, Austin.

Brumfiel, Elizabeth M. 1995. Heterarchy and the Analysis of Complex Societies: Comments. In *Heterarchy and the Analysis of Complex Societies*, Ed. by R. R. Ehrenreich, C. L. Crumley, and J. E. Levy, pp. 125–31. American Anthropological Association, Arlington, VA.

Cabrera Castro, Rubén. 1982. El Proyecto Arqueológico Teotihuacan. In *Teotihuacan 80–82: Primeros Resultados*. Ed. R. Cabrera, I. Rodríguez G., and N. Morelos G., pp. 7–40. INAH.

1991. Secuencia Arquitectónica y Cronológica de la Ciudadela. In *Teotihuacan 1980–1982: Nuevas Interpretaciones*, coordinated by Rubén Cabrera Castro, Ignacio Rodríguez García, and Noel Morelos García, pp. 31–60. INAH.

1995. Catalog of Murals in the Ciudadela. In *La Pintura Mural Prehispánica en México I: Teotihuacan: Tomo 1: Catálogo*, coordinated by Beatriz de la Fuente, pp. 3–17. Instituto de Investigaciones Estéticas, UNAM.

Cabrera Castro, Rubén, and Sergio Gómez Chávez. 2008. La Ventilla: A Model for a Barrio in the Urban Structure of Teotihuacan. In *El Urbanismo en Mesoamérica/Urbanism in Mesoamerica, Volume 2*, Ed. by A. G. Mastache, R. H. Cobean, Á. García Cook, and K. G. Hirth, pp. 37–83. INAH, and Pennsylvania State University, University Park.

Cabrera Castro, Rubén, Ignacio Rodríguez G., and Noel Morelos G., (eds.) 1982a. *Memoria del Proyecto Arqueológico Teotihuacan 80–82*. INAH.

Cabrera Castro, Rubén, Ignacio Rodríguez G., and Noel Morelos G. 1982b. *Teotihuacan 80–82: Primeros Resultados*. INAH.

1991. *Teotihuacan 1980–1982: Nuevas Interpretaciones*. INAH.

Cabrera Castro, Rubén, Saburo Sugiyama, and George L. Cowgill. 1991. The Templo de Quetzalcoatl Project at Teotihuacan: A Preliminary Report. *Ancient Mesoamerica* 2(1):77–92.

Cabrera Cortés, M. Oralia. 1995. *La Lapidaria del Proyecto Templo de Quetzalcoatl 1988–1999*. ENAH.

2001. *Textile Production at Teotihuacan, Mexico*. Department of Anthropology, Arizona State University, Tempe.

2002. Ideología y Política en Teotihuacan. Ofrendas de Rocas Semipreciosas de la Pirámide de la Serpiente Emplumada. In *Ideología y Política a Través de Materiales, Imágenes y Símbolos: Memoria de la Primera Mesa Redonda de Teotihuacan*, Ed. by M. E. Ruiz Gallut, pp. 75–99. UNAM and INAH.

2006. *Craft Production and Socio-Economic Marginality: Living on the Periphery of Teotihuacan, Mexico*. FAMSI.

2011. *Craft Production and Socio-Economic Marginality: Living on the Periphery of Urban Teotihuacan*. PhD diss., Arizona State University, Tempe.

Carballo, David M. 2005. *State Political Authority and Obsidian Craft Production at the Moon Pyramid, Teotihuacan, Mexico*. PhD diss., Department of Anthropology, University of California, Los Angeles.

2007. Implements of State Power: Weaponry and Martially Themed Obsidian Production near the Moon Pyramid, Teotihuacan. *Ancient Mesoamerica* 18(1):173–90.

2011. *Obsidian and the Teotihuacan State: Weaponry and Ritual Production at the Moon Pyramid/La Obsidiana y el Estado Teotihucano: La Producción Militar y Ritual en la Pirámide de la Luna.* University of Pittsburgh and UNAM, Pittsburgh and Mexico City.

2012. Public Ritual and Urbanization in Central Mexico: Temple and Plaza Offerings from La Laguna, Tlaxcala. *Cambridge Archaeological Journal* 22(3):329–52.

2013. The Social Organization of Craft Production and Interregional Exchange at Teotihuacan. In *Merchants, Markets, and Exchange in the Pre-Columbian World,* Ed. by K. G. Hirth and J. Pillsbury, pp. 113–40. Dumbarton Oaks, Washington, DC.

Carballo, David M., Jennifer Carballo, and Hector Neff. 2007. Formative and Classic Period Obsidian Procurement in Central Mexico: A Compositional Study Using Laser Ablation-Inductively Coupled Plasma-Mass Spectrometry. *Latin American Antiquity* 18(1):27–43.

Carballo, David, and Thomas Pluckhahn. 2007. Transportation Corridors and Political Evolution in Highland Mesoamerica: Settlement Analyses Incorporating GIS for Northern Tlaxcala, Mexico. *Journal of Anthropological Archaeology* 26:607–29.

Caso, Alfonso. 1937. ¿Tenian los Teotihuacanos Conocimiento del Tonalpohualli? *El México Antiguo* 4:131–43.

Caso, Alfonso, and Ignacio Bernal. 1952. *Urnas de Oaxaca.* INAH.

Charlton, Thomas H. 1978. Teotihuacan, Tepeapulco, and Obsidian Exploitation. *Science* 200(4347):1227–36.

Charlton, Thomas H., Raúl García Chávez, Cynthia L. Otis Charlton, Verónica Ortega C., David Andrade O., and Teresa Palomares R. 2005. Salvamento Arqueológico Reciente en el Valle de Teotihuacan. Sitio TC-83; San Bartolomé el Alto. La Arquitectura Teotihuacana. In *Arquitectura y Urbanismo: Pasado y Presente de los Espacios en Teotihuacan: Memoria de la Tercera Mesa Redonda de Teotihuacan,* Ed. by M. E. Ruiz Gallut and J. Torres Peralta, pp. 343–71. INAH.

Charlton, Thomas H., and Cynthia L. Otis Charlton. 2007. En las Cercanías de Teotihuacan. Influencias Urbanas dentro de Comunidades Rurales. In *Arqueología y Complejidad Social,* Ed. by P. Fournier, W. Wiesheu and T. H. Charlton, pp. 87–106. ENAH and INAH.

Charnay, Désiré. 1887. *Ancient Cities of the New World.* Harper and Brothers, New York.

Cheetham, David. 2010. Cultural Imperatives in Clay: Early Olmec Carved Pottery from San Lorenzo and Cantón Corralito. *Ancient Mesoamerica* 21(1):165–85.

Clark, John E. 1986. From Mountains to Molehills: A Critical Review of Teotihuacan's Obsidian Industry. In *Economic Aspects of Prehispanic Highland Mexico,* Ed. by B. L. Isaac, pp. 23–74. JAI Press, Greenwich, CT.

2007. Mesoamerica's First State. In *The Political Economy of Ancient Mesoamerica: Transformations during the Formative and Classic Periods,* Ed. by V. L. Scarborough and J. E. Clark, pp. 11–46. University of New Mexico Press, Albuquerque.

Clayton, Sarah C. 2005. Interregional Relationships in Mesoamerica: Interpreting Maya Ceramics at Teotihuacan. *Latin American Antiquity* 16: 427–48.

2009. *Ritual Diversity and Social Identities: A Study of Mortuary Behaviors at Teotihuacan.* PhD diss., Arizona State University, Tempe.

2011. Gender and Mortuary Ritual at Ancient Teotihuacan, Mexico: A Study of Intrasocietal Diversity. *Cambridge Archaeological Journal* 31(1):31–52.

2013. Measuring the Long Arm of the State: Teotihuacan's Relations in the Basin of Mexico. *Ancient Mesoamerica* 24(1):87–105.

Conides, Cynthia A. 2000. *The Shape of Water at Teotihuacan: Demystifying the Netted Jaguar.* Presented at the International Congress of Americanists, Warsaw, Poland.

2001. *The Stuccoed and Painted Ceramics from Teotihuacan, Mexico: A Study of Authorship and Functions of Works of Art from an Ancient Mesoamerican City.* PhD diss., Columbia University, New York, NY.

Cook de Leonard, Carmen. 1957. Excavaciones en la Plaza No. 1, "Tres Palos," Ostoyahualco, Teotihuacan. (Informe Preliminar). *Boletín del Centro de Investigaciones Antropológicas de México,* no. 4, pp. 3–5.

Córdova, Carlos, Ana Lilian Martín del Pozzo, and Javier López Camacho. 1994. Paleolandforms and Volcanic Impact on the Environment of Prehistoric Cuicuilco, Southern Mexico City. *Journal of Archaeological Science* 21:585–96.

Cowgill, George L. 1974. Quantitative Studies of Urbanization at Teotihuacan. In *Mesoamerican Archaeology: New Approaches,* Ed. by N. Hammond, pp. 363–96. Duckworth, London.

1977. Processes of Growth and Decline at Teotihuacan: The City and the State. In *Los Procesos de Cambio en Mesoamérica y Areas Circunvecinas,* Mesa Redonda 15, pp. 183–93. Sociedad Mexicana de Antropología, Mexico City.

1979. Teotihuacan, Internal Militaristic Competition, and the Fall of the Classic Maya. In *Maya Archaeology and Ethnohistory,* Ed. by N. Hammond and G. R. Willey, pp. 51–62. University of Texas Press, Austin.

1983. Rulership and the Ciudadela: Political Inferences from Teotihuacan Architecture. In *Civilization in the Ancient Americas: Essays in Honor of Gordon R. Willey,* Ed. by R. M. Leventhal and A. L. Kolata, pp. 313–43. University of New Mexico Press and Peabody Museum of Archaeology and Ethnology, Harvard University, Cambridge, MA.

1987. Métodos para el Estudio de Relaciones Espaciales en los Datos de la Superficie de Teotihuacan. In *Teotihuacan: Nuevos Datos, Nuevas Síntesis, Nuevos Problemas,* Ed. by E. McClung de Tapia and E. C. Rattray, pp. 161–89. UNAM.

1992a. Social Differentiation at Teotihuacan. In *Mesoamerican Elites: An Archaeological Assessment,* Ed. by D. Z. Chase and A. F. Chase, pp. 206–20. University of Oklahoma Press, Norman.

1992b. Toward a Political History of Teotihuacan. In *Ideology and PreColumbian Civilizations,* Ed. by A. A. Demarest and G. W. Conrad, pp. 87–114. School of American Research Press, Santa Fe, NM.

1992c. Teotihuacan Glyphs and Imagery in the Light of Some Early Colonial Texts. In *Art, Ideology, and the City of Teotihuacan,* Ed. by J. C. Berlo, pp. 231–46. Dumbarton Oaks, Washington, DC.

1993a. Distinguished Lecture in Archeology: Beyond Criticizing New Archeology. *American Anthropologist* 95(3):551–73.

1993b. What We Still Don't Know about Teotihuacan. In *Teotihuacan: Art from the City of the Gods*, Ed. by K. Berrin and E. Pasztory, pp. 116–25. Thames & Hudson, New York.

1997. State and Society at Teotihuacan, Mexico. *Annual Review of Anthropology* 26:129–61.

1998. Nuevos Datos del Proyecto Templo de Quetzalcóatl Acerca de la Cerámica Miccaotli Tlamimilolpa. In *Los Ritmos de Cambio en Teotihuacán: Reflexiones y Discusiones de su Cronología*, Ed. by R. Brambila and R. Cabrera, pp. 185–99. INAH.

2000a. The Central Mexican Highlands from the Rise of Teotihuacan to the Decline of Tula. In *The Cambridge History of the Native Peoples of the Americas, Volume II: Mesoamerica, Part 1*, Ed. by R. E. W. Adams and M. J. MacLeod, pp. 250–317. Cambridge University Press, Cambridge, UK.

2000b. Intentionality and Meaning in the Layout of Teotihuacan, Mexico. *Cambridge Archaeological Journal* 10(2):358–61.

2000c. "Rationality" and Contexts in Agency Theory. In *Agency in Archaeology*, Ed. by M. A. Dobres and J. Robb, pp. 51–50. Routledge, London and New York.

2002. Contextos Domésticos en Teotihuacan. In *Ideología y Política a Través de Materiales, Imágenes, y Símbolos: Memoria de la Primera Mesa Redonda de Teotihuacan*, Ed. by M. E. Ruiz Gallut, pp. 61–74. UNAM and INAH.

2003a. Teotihuacan and Early Classic Interaction: A Perspective from Outside the Maya Region. In *The Maya and Teotihuacan: Reinterpreting Early Classic Interaction*, Ed. by G. E. Braswell, pp. 315–35. University of Texas Press, Austin.

2003b. Teotihuacan: Cosmic Glories and Mundane Needs. In *The Social Construction of Ancient Cities*, Ed. by M. L. Smith, pp. 37–55. Smithsonian Institution Press, Washington, DC.

2005. Planeamiento a Gran Eescala en Teotihuacan: Implicaciones Religiosas y Sociales. In *Arquitectura y Urbanismo: Pasado y Presente de los Espacios en Teotihuacan*, Ed. by M. A. Ruiz Gallut and J. Torres Peralta, pp. 21–40. INAH.

2006. Using Numerous Cases to Extract Valid Information from Noisy Surface Data at Teotihuacan. In *Managing Archaeological Data: Essays in Honor of Sylvia W. Gaines*, Ed. by J. L. Hantman and R. Most, pp. 147–54. Arizona State University Anthropological Research Papers No. 57. Tempe.

2007. The Urban Organization of Teotihuacan, Mexico. In *Settlement and Society: Essays Dedicated to Robert McCormick Adams*, Ed. by E. L. Stone, pp. 261–95. Cotsen Institute of Archaeology, University of California, Los Angeles, and the Oriental Institute of the University of Chicago.

2008. Teotihuacan as an Urban Place. In *El Urbanismo en Mesoamérica/ Urbanism in Mesoamerica, Volume 2*, Ed. by A. G. Mastache, R. H. Cobean, Á. García Cook, and K. G. Hirth, pp. 85–112. INAH, and Pennsylvania State University, University Park.

2013. Possible Migrations and Shifting Identities in the Central Mexican Epiclassic. *Ancient Mesoamerica* 24(1):131–49.

n.d.a. Nose Pendants: Signs of Rank and Office in the Political System of Teotihuacan? In *The Art of Teotihuacan and Its Sphere of Influence*. Denver Art Museum, Denver, CO. Being revised for publication.

n.d.b. Hints of Hierarchies in Teotihuacan Insignia and Ritual Contexts. In *Rituals and Power at Teotihuacan*, Musée du Quai Branly, Paris. Being revised for publication.

Cowgill, George L., Jeffrey H. Altschul, and Rebecca S. Sload. 1984. Spatial Analysis of Teotihuacan: A Mesoamerican Metropolis. In *Intrasite Spatial Analysis in Archaeology*, Ed. by H. J. Hietala, pp. 154–95. Cambridge University Press, Cambridge, UK.

Cowgill, George L., and Oralia Cabrera. 1991. Excavaciones en el Frente B y Otros Materiales del Análisis de la Cerámica. *Arqueología* 6:41–52. INAH.

Cowgill, George L., and Hector Neff. 2004. Algunos Resultados del Análisis por Activación Neutrónica de la Cerámica Foránea de Teotihuacan. In *La Costa del Golfo en Tiempos Teotihuacanos: Propuestas y Perspectivas*, Ed. by Ma. Elena Ruiz Gallut and A. Pascual Soto, pp. 63–75. INAH.

Cowgill, George L., Ian G. Robertson, and Rebecca S. Sload. *Electronic Files from the Teotihuacan Mapping Project*. In preparation.

Crider, Destiny. 2013. Shifting Alliances: Epiclassic and Early Postclassic Interactions at Cerro Portezuelo. *Ancient Mesoamerica* 24(1):107–30.

Croissier, Michelle M. 2006. *Excavations at Structure L5 (N1W6) in the Oaxaca Barrio, Teotihuacan*. FAMSI.

Cummings, Byron. 1933. *Cuicuilco and the Archaic Culture of Mexico*. University of Arizona Bulletin 4, Tucson.

Cyphers, Ann, and Kenneth G. Hirth. 2000. Ceramics of Western Morelos: The Cañada through Gobernador Phases at Xochicalco. In *Archaeological Research at Xochicalco, Volume Two: The Xochicalco Mapping Project*, Ed. by K. Hirth, pp. 102–35. University of Utah Press, Salt Lake City.

Darras, Véronique, and Brigitte Faugère. 2007. Chupícuaro, entre el Occidente y el Altiplano Central. Un Balance de los Conocimientos y las Nuevas Aportaciones. In *Dinámicas Culturales entre el Occidente, el Centro-Norte y la Cuenca de México, del Preclásico al Epiclásico*, pp. 51–83. El Colegio de Michoacán, Zamora.

David, Cybèle, Diana Platas, and Luis Manuel Gamboa Cabezas. 2007. Estudio Comparativo de las Prácticas Funerarias en Chupícuaro, Guanajuato, y Buenaventura, Estado de México, durante la Fase Ticomán. In *Dinámicas Culturales entre el Occidente, el Centro-Norte y la Cuenca de México, del Preclásico al Epiclásico*, pp. 85–110. El Colegio de Michoacán, Zamora.

de la Fuente, Beatriz, (ed.) 1995. *La Pintura Mural Prehispánica en México. I: Teotihuacán*. Instituto de Investigaciones Estéticas, UNAM.

Demarest, Arthur. 2004. *Ancient Maya: The Rise and Fall of a Rainforest Civilization*. Cambridge University Press, Cambridge, UK.

Díaz Oyarzábal, Clara Luz. 1980. *Chingú: Un Sitio Clásico del Area de Tula, Hgo*. INAH.

Diehl, Richard A. 1989a. The Physical Setting. In *Tula of the Toltecs: Excavation and Survey*, Ed. by D. M. Healan, pp. 7–12. University of Iowa Press, Iowa City.

1989b. A Shadow of Its Former Self: Teotihuacan during the Coyotlatelco Period. In *Mesoamerica after the Decline of Teotihuacan: A.D. 700–900*, Ed. by R. A. Diehl and J. C. Berlo, pp. 9–18. Dumbarton Oaks, Washington, DC.

Dobres, Marcia-Anne. 2010. Archaeologies of Technology. *Cambridge Journal of Economics* 34:103–14.

Dozal, Pedro. 1925. Descubrimientos Arqueológicos en el Templo de Quetzalcoatl. *Anales del Museo Nacional de Arqueología, Historia, y Etnografía* Época IV(3):216–19.

Drennan, Robert D., and Christian E. Peterson. 2004. Comparing Archaeological Settlement Systems with Rank-Size Graphs: A Measure of Shape and Statistical Significance. *Journal of Archaeological Science* 31:533–49.

Drewitt, R. Bruce. 1987. Measurement Units and Building Axes at Teotihuacan. In *Teotihuacan: Nuevos Datos, Nuevas Síntesis, Nuevos Problemas,* Ed. by E. McClung de Tapia and E. C. Rattray, pp. 389–98. Instituto de Investigaciones Antropológicas, UNAM.

Drucker, R. David. 1974. *Renovating a Reconstruction: The Ciudadela at Teotihuacan, Mexico: Construction Sequence, Layout, and Possible Uses of the Structure.* PhD diss., University of Rochester, Rochester, NY. Xerox University Microfilms, Ann Arbor, MI.

Duncan, William N., Christina Elson, Charles S. Spencer, and Elsa M. Redmond. 2009. A Human Maxilla Trophy from Cerro Tilcajete, Oaxaca, Mexico. *Mexicon* 31(5):108–13.

Elliott, Michelle. 2007. *Human Occupation and Landscape Change in the Malpaso Valley, Zacatecas, Mexico.* PhD diss., Arizona State University, Tempe.

Elson, Christina M., and R. Alan Covey, (eds.) 2006. *Intermediate Elites in Pre-Columbian States and Empires.* The University of Arizona Press, Tucson.

Elson, Christina M., and Kenneth Mowbray. 2005. Burial Practices at Teotihuacan in the Early Postclassic Period: The Vaillant and Linné Excavations (1931–1932). *Ancient Mesoamerica* 16(2):195–211.

Estrada-Belli, Francisco, Alexandre Tokovinine, Jennifer Foley, Heather Hurst, Gene A. Ware, David Stuart, and Nikolai Grube. 2009. A Maya Palace at Holmul, Peten, Guatemala and the Teotihuacan "Entrada": Evidence from Murals 7 and 9. *Latin American Antiquity* 20(1):228–59.

Fairbank, John K., Edwin O. Reischauer, and Albert M. Craig. 1973. *East Asia: Tradition and Transformation.* Houghton Mifflin Company, Boston, MA.

Falkenhausen, Lothar von. 2006. *Chinese Society in the Age of Confucius (1000–250 BC).* Cotsen Institute of Archaeology, University of California, Los Angeles.

Fargher, Lane F., Richard E. Blanton, Verenice Y. Heredia Espinoza, John Millhauser, Nezahualcoyotl Xiuhtecutli, and Lisa Overholtzer. 2011. Tlaxcallan: The Archaeology of an Ancient Republic in the New World. *Antiquity* 85:172–86.

Fash, William L., Alexandre Tokovinine, and Barbara W. Fash. 2009. The House of New Fire at Teotihuacan and Its Legacy in Mesoamerica. In *The Art of Urbanism: How Mesoamerican Kingdoms Represented Themselves in Architecture and Imagery,* Ed. by W. L. Fash and L. López Luján, pp. 201–29. Dumbarton Oaks, Washington, DC.

Fernández Mendiola, S. E., and L. Jiménez Hernández. 1997. Restauración de la Ofrenda Cerámica Teotihuacana. *Arqueología* 18:23–28.

Filini, Agape, and Efraín Cárdenas García. 2007. El Bajío, la Cuenca de Cuitzeo y el Estado Teotihuacano. In *Dinámicas Culturales entre el Occidente, el Centro-Norte y la Cuenca de México, del Preclásico al Epiclásico,* Ed. by

B. Faugère, pp. 137–54. El Colegio de Michoacán and Centro de Estudios Mexicanos y Centroamericanos. Zamora, Michoacán, Mexico.

Florance, Charles A. 2000. The Late and Terminal Preclassic in Southeastern Guanajuato: Heartland or Periphery? In *Greater Mesoamerica: The Archaeology of West and Northwest Mexico*, Ed. by M. S. Foster and S. Gorenstein, pp. 21–33. University of Utah Press, Salt Lake City.

Furst, Peter T. 1974. Morning Glory and Mother Goddess at Tepantitla, Teotihuacan: Iconography and Analogy in Pre-Columbian Art. In *Mesoamerican Archaeology: New Approaches*, Ed. by N. Hammond, pp. 187–215. Duckworth, London.

Gamio, Manuel.1979[1922]. *La Población del Valle de Teotihuacán*. Secretaria de Agricultura y Fomento, Dirección de Antropología, Mexico City.

García Chávez, Raúl E. 1991. *Desarrollo Cultural en Azcapotzalco y el Area Suroccidental de la Cuenca de México, Desde el Preclásico Medio hasta el Epiclásico*. ENAH.

1995. *Variabilidad Cerámica en la Cuenca de México durante el Epiclásico*. ENAH.

2002. La Relación entre Teotihuacan y los Centros Provinciales del Clásico en la Cuenca de México. In *Ideología y Política a Través de Materiales, Imágenes y Símbolos: Memoria de la Primera Mesa Redonda de Teotihuacan*, Ed. by M. E. Ruiz Gallut, pp. 501–27. UNAM and INAH.

García Chávez, Raúl E., Luis M. Gamboa Cabezas, and Nadia V. Vélez Saldaña. 2005. Excavaciones Recientes en un Sitio de la Fase Tlamimilolpa en Cuautitlan, Izcalli, Estado de México. In *Arquitectura y Urbanismo: Pasado y Presente de los Espacios en Teotihuacan: Memoria de la Tercera Mesa Redonda de Teotihuacan*, Ed. by María Elena Ruiz Gallut and Jesús Torres Peralta, pp. 487–506. INAH.

García Cook, Ángel. 1981. The Historical Importance of Tlaxcala in the Cultural Development of the Central Highlands. In *Supplement to the Handbook of Middle American Indians: Volume One: Archaeology*, Ed. by V. R. Bricker and J. A. Sabloff, pp. 244–76. University of Texas Press, Austin.

2003. Cantona: The City. In *Urbanism in Mesoamerica, Volume 1*, Ed. by W. T. Sanders, A. G. Mastache, and R. H. Cobean, pp. 311–43. INAH and Pennsylvania State University, University Park, PA.

García-Des Lauriers, Claudia. 2007. *Proyecto Arqueológico Los Horcones: Investigating the Teotihuacan Presence on the Pacific Coast of Chiapas, Mexico*. PhD diss., University of California, Riverside.

2008. *The Early Classic Obsidian Trade at Los Horcones, Chiapas, Mexico*. FAMSI.

Gazzola, Julie. 2008. *The Project for the Investigation and Conservation of the Feathered Serpent Pyramid, Teotihuacan, Mexico*. FAMSI.

2012. Nuevos Datos sobre el Proceso de Desarrollo del Complejo Urbano de Teotihuacán en Fases Tempranas. *Fifth Mesa Redonda de Teotihuacan*. INAH.

Gazzola, Julie, and Sergio Gómez. 2009. Características Generals de la Primera Ocupación en el Espacio de la Ciudadela, Teotihuacan. *Arqueología 42*.

Gibbs, Kevin T. 2001. *Time and Ethnicity in the Oaxaca Barrio, Teotihuacan: The TL6 Ceramics*. MA Thesis, Department of Anthropology, University of Western Ontario, London, ON.

2010. Pottery and Ethnic Identity in the Oaxaca Barrio, Teotihuacan. In *The "Compleat Archaeologist": Papers in Honour of Michael W. Spence*, Ed. by

C. J. Ellis, N. Ferris, P. A. Timmins, and C. D. White, pp. 255–63. London Chapter, Ontario Archaeological Society, London, ON.

Giddens, Anthony. 1979. *Central Problems in Social Theory: Action, Structure, and Contradiction in Social Analysis*. University of California Press, Berkeley.

1984. *The Constitution of Society: Outline of the Theory of Structuration*. Polity Press, Cambridge, UK.

1991. Structuration Theory: Past, Present, and Future. In *Giddens' Theory of Structuration: A Critical Appreciation*, Ed. by C. G. A. Bryant and D. Jary, pp. 201–21. Routledge, London.

Goldsmith, Kim C. 2000. *Forgotten Images: A Study of the Ceramic Figurines from Teotihuacan, Mexico*. PhD diss. Department of Anthropology, University of California, Riverside.

Gómez Chávez, Sergio. 2000. *La Ventilla: Un Barrio de la Antigua Ciudad de Teotihuacán*. ENAH.

2002. Presencia del Occidente de México en Teotihuacan. Aproximaciones a la Política Exterior del Estado Teotihuacano. In *Ideología y Política a Través de Materiales, Imágenes, y Símbolos: Memoria de la Primera Mesa Redonda de Teotihuacan*, Ed. by M. E. Ruiz Gallut, pp. 563–625. UNAM and INAH.

Gómez Chávez, Sergio, and Julie Gazzola. 2007. Análisis de las Relaciones entre Teotihuacán y el Occidente de México. In *Dinámicas Culturales Entre el Occidente, el Centro-Norte y la Cuenca de México, del Preclásico al Epiclásico*, Ed. by B. Faugère, pp. 113–35. El Colegio de Michoacán, Zamora, Michoacán.

Gossen, Gary H. 1974. *Chamulas in the World of the Sun: Time and Space in a Maya Oral Tradition*. Waveland Press, Prospect Heights, IL.

Grove, David C. 1984. *Chalcatzingo: Excavations on the Olmec Frontier*. Thames & Hudson, New York.

1987a. (ed.) *Ancient Chalcatzingo*. University of Texas Press, Austin.

1987b. "Torches," "Knuckle Dusters," and the Legitimization of Formative Period Rulership. *Mexicon* 9(3):60–65.

Hays-Gilpin, Kelley, and Jane H. Hill. 1999. The Flower World in Material Culture: an Iconographic Complex in the Southwest and Mesoamerica. *Journal of Anthropological Research* 55(1):1–37.

Headrick, Annabeth. 1999. The Street of the Dead. It Really Was: Mortuary Bundles at Teotihuacan. *Ancient Mesoamerica* 10: 69–85.

2001. Merging Myth and Politics: The Three Temple Complex at Teotihuacan. In *Landscape and Power in Ancient Mesoamerica*, Ed. by R. Koontz, K. Reese-Taylor and A. Headrick, pp. 169–95. Westview Press, Boulder, CO.

2007. *The Teotihuacan Trinity: The Sociopolitical Structure of an Ancient Mesoamerican City*. University of Texas Press, Austin.

Healan, Dan, and Christine L. Hernandez. 2012. The Role of Migration in Shaping Trans-Regional Interaction in Post-Classic Central and Near West Mexico. Annual Meeting of the Society for American Archaeology, Memphis, TN.

Heizer, Robert F., and James A. Bennyhoff. 1958. Archaeological Investigation of Cuicuilco, Valley of Mexico, 1957. *Science* 127(3292):232–33.

1972. Archaeological Excavations at Cuicuilco, Mexico 1957. *National Geographic Reports, 1955–60*:93–104.

Heyden, Doris. 1975. An Interpretation of the Cave underneath the Pyramid of the Sun at Teotihuacan, Mexico. *American Antiquity* 40(2):131–47.

Hill, Jane. 2001. Proto-Uto-Aztecan: A Community of Cultivators in Central Mexico? *American Anthropologist* 103(4):913–34.

Hirth, Kenneth G. 1978. Teotihuacan Regional Population Administration in Eastern Morelos. *World Archaeology* 9(3):320–33.

2000a (ed.) *Archaeological Research at Xochicalco. Volume I, Ancient Urbanism at Xochicalco: The Evolution and Organization of a Pre-Hispanic Society.* The University of Utah Press, Salt Lake City.

2000b (ed.). *Archaeological Research at Xochicalco. Volume 2, The Xochicalco Mapping Project.* The University of Utah Press, Salt Lake City.

2009 (ed.). Craft Production, Household Diversification, and Domestic Economy in Prehispanic Mesoamerica. In *Housework: Craft Production and Domestic Economy in Ancient Mesoamerica*, Ed. by K. G. Hirth, pp.13–32. Archeological Papers of the American Anthropological Association, Number 19.

Hirth, Kenneth, and Jorge Angulo Villaseñor. 1981. Early State Expansion in Central Mexico: Teotihuacan in Morelos. *Journal of Field Archaeology* 8(2):135–50.

Hirth, Kenneth G., Mari Carmen Serra Puche, Jesús Carlos Lazcano Arce, and Jason De León. 2009. Intermittent Domestic Lapidary Production at Nativitas, Tlaxcala, Mexico. In *Housework: Craft Production and Domestic Economy in Ancient Mesoamerica*, Ed. by K. G. Hirth, pp. 157–73. Archaeological Papers of the American Anthropological Association, Number 19.

Higham, Charles. 2002. *The Civilization of Angkor.* Berkeley: University of California Press.

Hopkins, Mary R. 1987a. An Explication of the Plans of Some Teotihuacan Apartment Compounds. In *Teotihuacan: Nuevos Datos, Nuevas Síntesis, Nuevos Problemas*, Ed. by E. McClung de Tapia and E. C. Rattray, pp. 369–88. Instituto de Investigaciones Antropológicas, UNAM.

1987b. Network Analysis of the Plans of Some Teotihuacan Apartment Compounds. *Environment and Planning B* 14:387–406.

1995. *Teotihuacan Cooking Pots: Scale of Production and Product Variability.* PhD diss., Department of Anthropology, Brandeis University, Waltham, MA.

Hosler, Dorothy. 1994. *The Sounds and Colors of Power: The Sacred Metallurgical Technology of Ancient West Mexico.* MIT Press, Cambridge, MA.

Janusek, John. 2008. *Ancient Tiwanaku.* Cambridge University Press, Cambridge, UK.

Jarquín Pacheco, Ana María, and Enrique Martínez Vargas. 1982. Exploraciones en el Lado este de la Ciudadela (Estructuras: 1G, 1R, 1Q, y 1P). In *Memoria del Proyecto Arqueológico Teotihuacan 80–82*, coordinated by R. Cabrera Castro, I. Rodríguez, and N. Morelos, pp. 19–47. INAH.

Jenkins, R. 1992. *Pierre Bourdieu.* Routledge, London and New York.

Jiménez Moreno, Wigberto. 1941. Tula y los Toltecas Según las Fuentes Históricas. *Revista Mexicana de Estudios Antropológicos* 5:79–83.

Joyce, Arthur A. 2003. Interregional Interaction and Social Development on the Oaxaca Coast. *Ancient Mesoamerica* 4: 67–84.

Joyce, Rosemary A., and Susan D. Gillespie (eds). 2000. *Beyond Kinship: Social and Material Reproduction in House Societies.* University of Pennsylvania Press, Philadelphia.

Kaufman, Terrence, and John Justeson. 2007. The History of the Word for Cacao in Ancient Mesoamerica. *Ancient Mesoamerica* 18(2):193–237.

Kertzer, David I. 1988. *Ritual, Politics, and Power.* Yale University Press, New Haven, CT.

Kidder, Alfred V., Jesse D. Jennings, and Edwin M. Shook. 1946. *Excavations at Kaminaljuyu, Guatemala.* Carnegie Institution of Washington, Washington, DC.

Kirchhoff, Paul. 1943. Mesoamérica: sus Límites Geográficas, Composición Étnica y Carácteres Culturales. *Acta Americana* 1:92–107.

Knudson, Kelly J. 2009. Oxygen Isotope Analysis in a Land of Environmental Extremes: The Complexities of Isotope Work in the Andes. *International Journal of Osteoarchaeology* 19(2):171–91.

Kolb, Charles C. 1987. *Marine Shell Trade and Classic Teotihuacan, Mexico.* BAR International Series 364, Oxford, UK.

—— 1995. Teotihuacan Period Figurines: A Typological Classification, Their Spatial and Temporal Distribution in the Teotihuacan Valley. In *The Teotihuacan Valley Project. The Teotihuacan Occupation of the Valley. Part 2. Artifact Analyses*, Ed. by W. T. Sanders, pp. 275–468. Pennsylvania State University, University Park.

Kowalski, Jeff Karl. 1999. Natural Order, Social Order, Political Legitimacy, and the Sacred City: The Architecture of Teotihuacan. In *Mesoamerican Architecture as a Cultural Symbol*, Ed. by J. K. Kowalski, pp. 76–109. Oxford University Press, New York and Oxford.

Kroeber, Alfred L. 1925. Archaic Culture Horizons in the Valley of Mexico, pp. 373–408. University of California Publications in American Archaeology and Ethnology, vol. 17, No. 7. University of California, Berkeley.

Krotser, Paula H. 1987. Levels of Specialization among Potters of Teotihuacan. In *Teotihuacan: Nuevos Datos, Nuevas Síntesis, Nuevos Problemas*, Ed. by E. McClung de Tapia and E. C. Rattray, pp. 417–27. Instituto de Investigaciones Antropológicas, UNAM.

Kubler, George. 1967. *The Iconography of the Art of Teotihuacán.* Dumbarton Oaks, Washington, DC.

Lachniet, Matthew S., Juan Pablo Bernal, Yemane Asmerom, Victor Polyak, and Dolores Piperno. 2012. A 2400-Yr Mesoamerican Rainfall Reconstruction Links Climate and Cultural Change. *Geology* 40:259–62.

Langley, James C. 1986. *Symbolic Notation of Teotihuacan: Elements of Writing in a Mesoamerican Culture of the Classic Period.* BAR International Series 313, Oxford, UK.

—— 1991. The Forms and Usage of Notation at Teotihuacan. *Ancient Mesoamerica* 2(2):285–98.

—— 1992. Teotihuacan Sign Clusters: Emblem or Articulation? In *Art, Ideology, and the City of Teotihuacan*, Ed. by J. C. Berlo, pp. 247–80. Dumbarton Oaks, Washington, DC.

—— 1993. Symbols, Signs, and Writing Systems. In *Teotihuacan: Art from the City of the Gods*, Ed. by K. Berrin and E. Pasztory, pp. 128–39. Thames and Hudson, New York.

Lee-Thorp, Julia A. 2008. On Isotopes and Old Bones. *Archaeometry* 50(6):925–50.

Linné, Sigvald. 2003a[1934]. *Archaeological Researches at Teotihuacan, Mexico.* University of Alabama Press, Tuscaloosa.

2003b[1942]. *Mexican Highland Cultures: Archaeological Researches at Teotihuacan, Calpulalpan, and Chalchicomula in 1934–35.* University of Alabama Press, Tuscaloosa.

Lira López, Yamile. 2004. Presencia Teotihuacana en el Valle de Maltrata, Veracruz. In *La Costa del Golfo en Tiempos Teotihuacanos: Propuestas y Perspectivas,* Ed. by Ma. E. Ruiz Gallut and A. Pascual Soto, pp. 5–22. INAH.

López Austin, Alfredo, Leonardo López Luján, and Saburo Sugiyama. 1991. The Temple of Quetzalcoatl at Teotihuacan: Its Possible Ideological Significance. *Ancient Mesoamerica* 2(1):93–105.

López Luján, Leonardo. 1989. *La Recuperación Mexica del Pasado Teotihuacano.* INAH.

n.d. Life after Death in Teotihuacan: The Moon Plaza's Monoliths in Colonial and Modern Mexico. In *An Uncommon Legacy: Essays in Ancient American and World Art History in Honor of Esther Pasztory,* Ed. by Andrew Finegold and Ellen Hoober. University of Oklahoma Press, Norman.

López Luján, Leonardo, Laura Filloy Nadal, Barbara W. Fash, William L. Fash, and Pilar Hernández. 2006. The Destruction of Images in Teotihuacan: Anthropomorphic Sculpture, Elite Cults, and the End of a Civilization. *Res: Anthropology and Aesthetics* 49/50:13–39.

Ma, Marina K. S. 2003. *Examining Prehispanic Ceramic Exchange in the Basin of Mexico—A Chemical Source Analysis from Azcapotzalco.* Senior Honors Thesis, Dartmouth College, Hanover, NH.

Manzanilla, Linda, (ed.) 1993. *Anatomía de un Conjunto Residencial Teotihuacano en Oztoyahualco.* Instituto de Investigaciones Antropológicas, UNAM.

Manzanilla, Linda. 2006. Estados Corporativos Arcaicos. Organizaciones de Excepción en Escenarios Excluyentes. *Cuicuilco* 13(36):13–45.

2009. Corporate Life in Apartments and Barrio Compounds at Teotihuacan, Central Mexico: Craft Specialization, Hierarchy, and Ethnicity. In *Domestic Life in Prehispanic Capitals: A Study of Specialization, Hierarchy, and Ethnicity,* Ed. by L. R. Manzanilla and C. Chapdelaine, pp. 21–42. Memoirs of the Museum of Anthropology, University of Michigan, Number 46, Ann Arbor.

2012. Teopancazco, un Centro de Barrio Multiétnico de Teotihuacan. In *Estudios Arqueométricos del Centro de Barrio de Teopancazco en Teotihuacan,* ed. Linda Manzanilla, pp. 17–66. UNAM.

Manzanilla, Linda, Luis Barba, R. Chávez, A. Tejero, G. Cifuentes, and N. Peralta. 1994. Caves and Geophysics: An Approximation to the Underworld of Teotihuacan, Mexico. *Geophysics* 36(1):141–57.

Manzanilla, Linda, Claudia López, and AnnCorinne Freter. 1996. Dating Results from Excavations in Quarry Tunnels behind the Pyramid of the Sun at Teotihuacan. *Ancient Mesoamerica* 7(2):245–66.

Manzanilla, Linda, and Carlos Serrano, (eds.) 1999. *Prácticas Funerarias en la Ciudad de los Dioses: Los Enterramientos Humanos de la Antigua Teotihuacan.* Instituto de Investigaciones Antropológicas, UNAM.

Marcus, Joyce, and Kent V. Flannery. 1996. *Zapotec Civilization*. Thames & Hudson, London, UK.

2000. Cultural Evolution in Oaxaca. In *The Cambridge History of the Native Peoples of the Americas, Volume II: Mesoamerica, Part 1*, Ed. by R. E. W. Adams and M. J. MacLeod, pp. 358–406. Cambridge University Press, Cambridge, UK.

Marquina, Ignacio. 1979[1922]. Arquitectura y Escultura. In *La Población del Valle de Teotihuacán*, Ed. by M. Gamio, pp. 99–164. Secretaria de Agricultura y Fomento, Dirección de Antropología, Mexico City.

1951. *Arquitectura Prehispánica*. INAH.

Martínez V., Enrique, and Ana María Jarquín P. 1982. Arquitectura y Sistemas Constructivos de la Fachada Posterior de la Ciudadela. Analisis Preliminar. In *Teotihuacan 80–82: Primeros Resultados*, coordinated by R. Cabrera Castro, I. Rodríguez García, and N. Morelos García, pp. 41–47. INAH.

Massey, Douglas S. 1999. Why Does Immigration Occur? A Theoretical Synthesis. In *The Handbook of International Migration: The American Experience*, Ed. by C. Hirschman, P. Kasinitz, and J. DeWind, pp. 34–52. Russell Sage Foundation, New York.

Mastache, Alba Guadalupe, and Robert H. Cobean. 1989. The Coyotlatelco Culture and the Origins of the Toltec State. In *Mesoamerica after the Decline of Teotihuacan: A.D. 700–900*, Ed. by R. A. Diehl and J. C. Berlo, pp. 49–67. Dumbarton Oaks, Washington, DC.

Mastache, Alba Guadalupe, Robert H. Cobean, and Dan M. Healan. 2002. *Ancient Tollan: Tula and the Toltec Heartland*. University Press of Colorado, Boulder.

Matos, Eduardo. 1980. Teotihuacan: Excavaciones en la Calle de los Muertos (1964). *Anales de Antropología* 17(1):69–90.

Mayer-Oakes. William J. 1959. A Stratigraphic Excavation at El Risco, Mexico. *Proceedings of the American Philosophical Society* 103(3):332–73.

McBride, Harold W. 1974. *Formative Ceramics and Prehistoric Settlement Patterns in the Cuauhtitlan Region, Mexico*. University Microfilms, Ann Arbor, MI.

McClung de Tapia, Emily. 2009. Los Ecosistemas del Valle de Teotihuacan a Lo Largo de su Historia. In *Teotihuacan: Ciudad de los Dioses*, pp. 37–45. INAH.

McClung de Tapia, Emily, and Evelyn C. Rattray, (eds.) 1987. *Teotihuacan: Nuevos Datos, Nuevas Síntesis, Nuevos Problemas*. Instituto de Investigaciones Antropológicas, UNAM.

McLellan, David. 1977. *Karl Marx: Selected Writings*. Oxford University Press, Oxford, UK.

Michelet, Dominique, and Grègory Pereira. 2009. Teotihuacan y el Occidente de México. In *Teotihuacan: Ciudad de los Dioses*, pp. 79–83. INAH.

Miller, Arthur G. 1973. *The Mural Painting of Teotihuacan*. Dumbarton Oaks, Washington, DC.

Miller, Mary Ellen. 1991. Rethinking the Classic Sculptures of Cerro de las Mesas, Veracruz, Mexico. In *Settlement Archaeology of Cerro de las Mesas, Veracruz, Mexico*, Ed. by B. L. Stark, pp. 26–38. Institute of Archaeology, University of California, Los Angeles.

Millon, Clara. 1972. The History of Mural Art at Teotihuacan. In *Teotihuacan, XI Mesa Redonda*, pp. 1–16. Sociedad Mexicana de Antropología, Mexico City.

1973. Painting, Writing, and Polity in Teotihuacan, Mexico. *American Antiquity* 38(3):294–314.

1988. A Reexamination of the Teotihuacan Tassel Headdress Insignia. In *Feathered Serpents and Flowering Trees: Reconstructing the Murals of Teotihuacan*, Ed. by K. Berrin, pp. 114–34. The Fine Arts Museums of San Francisco, San Francisco.

Millon, René. 1960. The Beginnings of Teotihuacan. *American Antiquity* 26(1):1–10.

1973. *The Teotihuacan Map. Part One: Text.* University of Texas Press, Austin.

1974. The Study of Urbanism at Teotihuacan, Mexico. In *Mesoamerican Archaeology: New Approaches*, Ed. by N. Hammond, pp. 335–62. Duckworth, London.

1976a. Chronological and Developmental Terminology: Why They Must Be Divorced. In *The Valley of Mexico: Studies in Pre-Hispanic Ecology and Society*, Ed. by E. R. Wolf, pp. 23–27. University of New Mexico Press, Albuquerque.

1976b. Social Relations in Ancient Teotihuacan. In *The Valley of Mexico: Studies in Pre-Hispanic Ecology and Society*, Ed. by E. R. Wolf, pp. 205–48. University of New Mexico Press, Albuquerque.

1981. Teotihuacan: City, State, and Civilization. In *Supplement to the Handbook of Middle American Indians, Volume One: Archaeology*, Ed. by V. R. Bricker and J. A. Sabloff, pp. 198–243. University of Texas Press, Austin.

1988a. The Last Years of Teotihuacan Dominance. In *The Collapse of Ancient States and Civilizations*, Ed. by N. Yoffee and G. L. Cowgill, pp. 102–64. University of Arizona Press, Tucson.

1988b. Where Do They All Come From? The Provenance of the Wagner Murals from Teotihuacan. In *Feathered Serpents and Flowering Trees: Reconstructing the Murals of Teotihuacan*, Ed. by K. Berrin, pp. 78–113. The Fine Arts Museums of San Francisco, San Francisco.

1991. Descubrimiento de la Procedencia de las Pinturas Murales Saqueadas con Representaciones de Personajes que Llevan el Tocado de Borlas. In *Teotihuacan 1980–1982: Nuevas Interpretaciones*, Ed. by R. Cabrera, I. Rodríguez, and N. Morelos, pp. 185–92. INAH.

1992. Teotihuacan Studies: From 1950 to 1990 and Beyond. In *Art, Ideology, and the City of Teotihuacan*, Ed. by J. C. Berlo, pp. 339–429. Dumbarton Oaks, Washington, DC.

1993. The Place Where Time Began: An Archaeologist's Interpretation of What Happened in Teotihuacan History. In *Teotihuacan: Art from the City of the Gods*, Ed. by K. Berrin and E. Pasztory, pp. 16–43. Thames & Hudson, New York.

Millon, René, and James A. Bennyhoff. 1961. A Long Architectural Sequence at Teotihuacan. *American Antiquity* 26(4):516–23.

Millon, René, Bruce Drewitt, and James A. Bennyhoff. 1965. The Pyramid of the Sun at Teotihuacan: 1959 Excavations. *Transactions of the American Philosophical Society* 55(part 6). Philadelphia.

Millon, René, Bruce Drewitt, and George L. Cowgill. 1973. *The Teotihuacan Map. Part Two: Maps.* University of Texas Press, Austin.

Mock, Shirley B. (ed.). 1998. *The Sowing and the Dawning: Termination, Dedication, and Transformation in the Archaeological and Ethnographic Record of Mesoamerica.* University of New Mexico Press, Albuquerque.

Moholy-Nagy, Hattula. 1999. Mexican Obsidian at Tikal, Guatemala. *Latin American Antiquity* 10: 300–13.

Montiel, Lisa M. 2010. *Teotihuacan Imperialism in the Yautepec Valley, Morelos.* PhD diss., University at Albany, State University of New York.

Moore, Frank W. 1966. An Excavation at Tetitla, Teotihuacan. *Mesoamerican Notes* 7–8:69–85.

Morelos García, Noel. 1993. *Proceso de Producción de Espacios y Estructuras en Teotihuacan: Conjunto Plaza Oeste y Complejo Calle de los Muertos.* INAH.

Müller, Florencia. 1978. *La Cerámica del Centro Ceremonial de Teotihuacan.* INAH.

1990. *La Cerámica de Cuicuilco B: Un Rescate Arqueológico.* INAH.

Múnera Bermúdez, L. Carlos. 1985. *Un Taller de Cerámica Ritual en La Ciudadela, Teotihuacan.* ENAH.

Múnera Bermúdez, L. Carlos, and Saburo Sugiyama. 1993. *Cerámica Ritual del Taller de la Ciudadela, Teotihuacan: Catálogo.* Ms.

Murakami, Tatsuya. 2010. *Power Relations and Urban Landscape Formation: A Study of Construction Labor and Resources at Teotihuacan.* PhD diss., Arizona State University, Tempe.

Nalda H., Enrique. 1997. El Noreste de Morelos y la Desestabilización Teotihuacana. *Arqueología* 18:103–17.

Nelson, Ben A. 1995. Complexity, Hierarchy, and Scale: A Controlled Comparison between Chaco Canyon, New Mexico, and La Quemada, Zacatecas. *American Antiquity* 60(4):597–618.

Nichols, Deborah L.1982. A Middle Formative Irrigation System near Santa Clara Coatitlan in the Basin of Mexico. *American Antiquity* 47(1):133–44.

Nichols, Deborah L., Hector Neff, and George L. Cowgill. 2013. Cerro Portezuelo: States and Hinterlands in the Pre-Hispanic Basin of Mexico. *Ancient Mesoamerica* 24(1):47–71.

Nichols, Deborah L., Michael W. Spence, and Mark D. Borland. 1991. Watering the Fields of Teotihuacan: Early Irrigation at the Ancient City. *Ancient Mesoamerica* 2(1):119–29.

Nielsen, Jesper, and Christophe Helmke. 2011. Reinterpreting the Plaza de los Glifos, La Ventilla, Teotihuacan. *Ancient Mesoamerica* 22(2):345–70.

Noguera, Eduardo. 1935. Antecedentes y Relaciones de la Cultura Teotihuacana. *El México Antiguo* 3(5–8):3–95.

Nuttall, Zelia. 1926. Official Reports on the Towns of Tequizistlan, Tepechpan, Acolman, and San Juan Teotihuacan Sent by Francisco de Castañeda to His Majesty, Philip II, and the Council of the Indies in 1580. *Papers of the Peabody Museum of American Archaeology and Ethnology, Harvard University* 11(2), Cambridge, MA.

Ortiz, Ponciano, and Robert Santley. 1998. Matacapan: Un Ejemplo de Enclave Teotihuacano en la Costa del Golfo. In *Los Ritmos de Cambio en Teotihuacán*, Ed. by R. Brambila and R. Cabrera, pp. 377–460. INAH.

Paddock, John. 1983. Topic 52: The Oaxaca Barrio in Teotihuacan. In *The Cloud People: Divergent Evolution of the Zapotec and Mixtec Civilizations*, Ed. by K. V. Flannery and J. Marcus, pp. 170–75. Academic Press, New York.

Padilla Gutiérrez, Eliseo Francisco. 2009. *La Cerámica Blanco Granular de Guerrero, Implicaciones de su Distribución Temporal y Espacial.* UNAM.

Palerm, Angel. 1972. Sistemas de Regadío Prehispánico en Teotihuacán y en el Pedregal de San Angel. In *Agricultura y Civilización en Mesoamérica. SepSetentas* 32:95–108.

Palomares Rodríguez, María Teresa. 2006. *Ocupación Zapoteca en Tlailotlacan, Teotihuacan: Un Estudio de Identidad y Adaptación en la Unidad Doméstica TL1.* ENAH.

2013. *The Oaxaca Barrio in Teotihuacan: Mortuary Customs and Ethnicity in Mesoamerica's Greatest Metropolis.* Southern Illinois University, Carbondale.

Parkinson, C. Northcote. 1957. *Parkinson's Law and other Studies in Administration.* Houghton Mifflin, Boston, MA.

Parkinson, William A., and Michael L. Galaty (eds). 2010. *Archaic State Interaction: The Eastern Mediterranean in the Bronze Age.* School for Advanced Research Press, Santa Fe, NM.

Parry, William J., and Shigeru Kabata. 2004. *Chronology of Obsidian Artifacts from the Moon Pyramid, Teotihuacan, Mexico.* Paper presented at the Annual Meeting of the Society for American Archaeology, Montreal.

Parsons, Jeffrey R. 1971. *Prehistoric Settlement Patterns in the Texcoco Region, Mexico.* Memoirs of the Museum of Anthropology, University of Michigan, No. 3, Ann Arbor.

2008. *Prehispanic Settlement Patterns in the Northwestern Valley of Mexico: The Zumpango Region.* Museum of Anthropology, University of Michigan, Memoirs, Number 45. Ann Arbor.

Parsons, Jeffrey R., Elizabeth Brumfiel, Mary H. Parsons, and David J. Wilson. 1982. *Prehispanic Settlement Patterns in the Southern Valley of Mexico: The Chalco-Xochimilco Region.* Memoirs of the Museum of Anthropology, University of Michigan, No. 14, Ann Arbor.

Parsons, Jeffrey R., Keith W. Kintigh, and Susan A. Gregg. 1983. *Archaeological Settlement Pattern Data from the Chalco, Xochimilco, Ixtapalapa, Texcoco, and Zumpango Regions, Mexico.* Museum of Anthropology, The University of Michigan, Ann Arbor.

Parsons, Mary H. 1972. Spindle Whorls from the Teotihuacan Valley, Mexico. In *Miscellaneous Studies in Mexican Prehistory*, Ed. by M. W. Spence, J. R. Parsons, and M. H. Parsons, pp. 45–80. Anthropological Papers 45. Museum of Anthropology, University of Michigan, Ann Arbor.

Pastrana, Alejandro. 2009. Obsidiana. In *Teotihuacan: Ciudad de los Dioses*, pp. 233–43. INAH.

Pastrana, Alejandro, and Felipe Ramírez. 2012. *Reinterpretando Cuicuilco.* Paper for the Annual Meeting of the Society for American Archaeology, Memphis, TN.

Pasztory, Esther. 1973. The Gods of Teotihuacan: A Synthetic Approach in Teotihuacan Iconography. *Proceedings of the 40th International Congress of Americanists*, 1:147–59. Rome.

1997. *Teotihuacan: An Experiment in Living.* University of Oklahoma Press, Norman.

Paulinyi, Zoltán. 1995. El Pájaro del Dios Mariposa de Teotihuacan: Análisis Iconográfico a Partir de una Vasija de Tiquisate, Guatemala. *Boletín del Museo Chileno de Arte Precolumbino* 6:71–110.

2006. The "Great Goddess" of Teotihuacan: Fiction or Reality? *Ancient Mesoamerica* 17(1):1–15.

2013. The Maize Goddess in the Teotihuacan Pantheon. *Mexicon* 35(4):86–90.

Peeler, Damon E., and Marcus Winter. 1993. *Tiempo Sagrado, Espacio Sagrado: Astronomía, Calendario y Arquitectura en Monte Albán y Teotihuacan.* Instituto Oaxaqueño de las Culturas, Oaxaca, Mexico.

Pendergast, David M. 1990. *Excavations at Altun Ha, Belize, 1964–1970, Volume 3.* Royal Ontario Museum, Toronto.

2003. Teotihuacan at Altun Ha: Did It Make a Difference? In *The Maya and Teotihuacan: Reinterpreting Early Classic Interaction,* Ed. by G. E. Braswell, pp. 235–47. University of Texas Press, Austin.

Pérez, José R. 1935. Unpublished manuscript on Sun Pyramid tunnel.

Plunket, Patricia, and Gabriela Uruñuela. 1998. Cholula y Teotihuacan: Una Consideración del Occidente de Puebla Durante el Clásico. In *Rutas de Intercambio en Mesoamérica,* Ed. by E. C. Rattray, pp. 101–14. Instituto de Investigaciones Antropológicas, UNAM.

2002. Shrines, Ancestors, and the Volcanic Landscape at Tetimpa, Puebla. In *Domestic Ritual in Ancient Mesoamerica,* Ed. by P. Plunket, pp. 32–42. The Cotsen Institute of Archaeology, University of California, Los Angeles.

Porter, Muriel Noé. 1956. Excavations at Chupícuaro, Guanajuato, Mexico. *Transactions of the American Philosophical Society* 46(5):515–637.

Price, Barbara J. 1976. A Chronological Framework for Cultural Development in Mesoamerica. In *The Valley of Mexico: Studies in Pre-Hispanic Ecology and Society,* Ed. by E. R. Wolf, pp. 13–21. University of New Mexico Press, Albuquerque.

Price, T. Douglas, James H. Burton, P. D. Fullagar, Lori E. Wright, Jane Buikstra, and V. Tiesler. 2008. Strontium Isotopes and the Study of Human Mobility in Ancient Mesoamerica. *Latin American Antiquity* 19(2):167–80.

Price, T. Douglas, Linda Manzanilla, and William D. Middleton. 2000. Immigration and the Ancient City of Teotihuacan in Mexico: A Study Using Strontium Isotope Ratios in Human Bone and Teeth. *Journal of Archaeological Science* 27: 903–13.

Quilter, Jeffrey, and Michele L. Koons. 2012. The Fall of the Moche: A Critique of Claims for South America's First State. *Latin American Antiquity* 23(2):127–43.

Quintanilla Mtz., Patricia E. 1982. Estructura 69. In *Memoria del Proyecto Arqueológico Teotihuacan 80–82.* Ed. by R. Cabrera, I. Rodríguez G., and N. Morelos G., pp. 355–60. INAH.

Rattray, Evelyn C. 1981. Anaranjado Delgado: Cerámica de Comercio de Teotihuacán. In *Interacción Cultural en México Central,* Ed. by E. C. Rattray, J. Litvak King, and C. Díaz Oyarzábal, pp. 55–80. UNAM.

1983. La Industria de Obsidian durante el Periodo Coyotlatelco. *Revista Mexicana de Estudios Antropológicos* 27(2):213–23.

1987. Los Barrios Foráneos de Teotihuacan. In *Teotihuacan: Nuevos Datos, Nuevas Síntesis, Nuevos Problemas,* Ed. by E. McClung de Tapia and E. C. Rattray, pp. 243–73. Instituto de Investigaciones Antropológicas, UNAM.

1989. El Barrio de los Comerciantes y el Conjunto Tlamimilolpa: Un Estudio Comparativo. *Arqueología* 5:105–29.

1990a. The Identification of Ethnic Affiliation at the Merchants' Barrio, Teotihuacan. In *Etnoarqueología: Primer Coloquio Bosch-Gimpera*, Ed. by Y. Sugiura Y. and M. C. Serra P., pp. 113–38. Instituto de Investigaciones Antropológicas, UNAM.

1990b. New Findings on the Origins of Thin Orange Ceramics. *Ancient Mesoamerica* 1(2):181–95.

1992. *The Teotihuacan Burials and Offerings: A Commentary and Inventory*. Vanderbilt University, Publications in Anthropology, No. 42, Nashville, TN.

1993. *The Oaxaca Barrio at Teotihuacan*. Universidad de las Américas, Puebla, Mexico.

2001. *Teotihuacan: Ceramics, Chronology, and Cultural Trends*. INAH and University of Pittsburgh, Mexico City and Pittsburgh.

Reyna Robles, Rosa Ma., and Paul Schmidt Schoenberg. 2004. Diversidad de la Cerámica Blanco Granular. In *Homenaje a Jaime Litvak*, Ed. by A. Benavides, L. Manzanilla, and L. Mirambell, pp. 217–34. INAH and UNAM.

Rice, Don S. (ed.). 1983. *Latin American Horizons*. Dumbarton Oaks. Washington, DC.

Robertson, Ian G. 1999. Spatial and Multivariate Analysis, Random Sampling Error, and Analytical Noise: Empirical Bayesian Methods at Teotihuacan, Mexico. *American Antiquity* 64: 137–52.

2001. *Mapping the Social Landscape of an Early Urban Center: SocioSpatial Variation in Teotihuacan*. PhD diss., Department of Anthropology, Arizona State University, Tempe.

2005. Patrones Diacrónicos en la Constitución de los Vecindarios Teotihuacanos. In *Arquitectura y Urbanismo: Pasado y Presente de los Espacios en Teotihuacan: Memoria de la Tercera Mesa Redonda de Teotihuacan*, Ed. by Ma. E. Ruiz Gallut and J. Torres Peralta, pp. 277–94. INAH.

2008. *'Insubstantial' Residential Structures at Teotihuacán, Mexico*. FAMSI, Chrystal River.

Rodríguez, Ana Mónica. 2009. Hallazgo de Murales Teotihuacanos en El Rosario, Querétaro, Mexico. *Mexicon* 31(4):83–84.

Rodríguez García, Ignacio. 1982. Zona de la Ciudadela: Frente 2. In *Memoria del Proyecto Arqueológico Teotihuacan 80–82*, Ed. by R. Cabrera Castro, I. Rodríguez G., and N. Morelos G., pp. 55–73. INAH.

Rodríguez Sánchez, E. A., and Jaime Delgado Rubio. 1997. Una Ofrenda Cerámica al Este de la Antigua Ciudad de Teotihuacan. *Arqueología* 18:17–22.

Rubel, Meagan A. 2009. *Assessing Musculoskeletal Markers Characteristic of Military Activities: An Analysis of Sacrificial Victims from Teotihuacan*. Senior Honors Thesis, Arizona State University, Tempe.

Rubín de la Borbolla, Daniel F. 1947. Teotihuacan: Ofrendas de los Templos de Quetzalcóatl. *Anales del Instituto Nacional de Antropología e Historia* 2:61–72.

Ruiz Gallut, María Elena, (ed.) 2002. *Ideología y Política a Través de Materiales, Imágenes y Símbolos*. UNAM and INAH.

Ruiz Gallut, María Elena, and Arturo Pascual Soto, (eds.) 2004. *La Costa del Golfo en Tiempos Teotihuacanos: Propuestas y Perspectivas*. INAH.

Ruiz Gallut, María Elena, and Jesús Torres P., (eds.) 2005. *Arquitectura y Urbanismo: Pasado y Presente de los Espacios en Teotihuacan.* INAH.

Sanders, William T. 1956. The Central Mexican Symbiotic Region: A Study in Prehistoric Settlement Patterns. In *Prehistoric Settlement Patterns in the New World,* Ed. by G. R. Willey, pp. 115–27. Viking Publications in Anthropology No. 23, New York.

1965. *The Cultural Ecology of the Teotihuacan Valley.* Department of Sociology and Anthropology, Pennsylvania State University, University Park.

1967. Life in a Classic Village. In *Teotihuacan: Onceava Mesa Redonda,* pp. 123–48. Sociedad Mexicana de Antropología, Mexico City.

1981. Ecological Adaptation in the Basin of Mexico: 23,000 B.C. to the Present. In *Supplement to the Handbook of Middle American Indians. Volume One: Archaeology,* Ed. by V. R. Bricker and J. A. Sabloff, pp. 147–97. University of Texas Press, Austin.

1986. Ceramic Chronology. In *The Teotihuacan Valley Final Report: 4. The Toltec Period Occupation of the Valley: Part 1 – Excavations and Ceramics,* Ed. by W. T. Sanders. Department of Anthropology, Pennsylvania State University, University Park.

1995. Ceramic Vessels, Function and Chronology. In *The Teotihuacan Valley Project Final Report – Volume 3, The Teotihuacan Period Occupation of the Valley, Part 2 Artifact Analyses,* Ed. by W. T. Sanders, pp. 140–274. Matson Museum of Anthropology, Pennsylvania State University, University Park.

2006. Late Xolalpan-Metepec/Oxtotipac-Coyotlatelco; Ethnic Succession or Changing Patterns of Political Economy: A Reevaluation. In *El Fenómeno Coyotlatelco en el Centro de México: Tiempo, Espacio, y Significado,* Ed. by L. Solar V., pp. 183–200. INAH.

Sanders, William T., Jeffrey R. Parsons, and Robert S. Santley. 1979. *The Basin of Mexico: Ecological Processes in the Evolution of a Civilization.* Academic Press, New York.

Santley, Robert S. 1983. Obsidian Trade and Teotihuacan Influence in Mesoamerica. In *Highland-Lowland Interaction in Mesoamerica: Interdisciplinary Approaches,* Ed. by A. G. Miller, pp. 69–124. Dumbarton Oaks, Washington, DC.

Sarabia González, Alejandro. 2013. *Reporte de Resultados de la Temporada 2012.* Report submitted to INAH.

Scarborough, Vernon L., and David R. Wilcox (eds). 1991. *The Mesoamerican Ballgame.* University of Arizona Press, Tucson.

Schávelzon, Daniel. 1983. La Primera Excavación Arqueológica de América: Teotihuacan en 1675. *Anales de Antropología I: Arqueología y Antropología Física* 20:121–34.

Schortman, Edward M., and Patricia A. Urban. 2004. Modeling the Roles of Craft Production in Ancient Political Economies. *Journal of Archaeological Research* 12(2):185–226.

Scott, Sue. 1993. *Teotihuacan Mazapan Figurines and the Xipe Totec Statue: A Link between the Basin of Mexico and the Valley of Oaxaca.* Vanderbilt University Publications in Anthropology, No. 44, Nashville, TN.

2001. *The Corpus of Terracotta Figurines from Sigvald Linné's Excavations at Teotihuacan, Mexico (1932 and 1934–35) and Comparative Material.* Monograph Series 18, The National Museum of Ethnography, Stockholm.

Séjourné, Laurette. 1959. *Un Palacio en la Ciudad de los Dioses: Exploraciones en Teotihuacan, 1955–58*. INAH.

1966a. *Arqueología de Teotihuacan. La Cerámica*. Fondo de Cultura Económica, Mexico City.

1966b. *Arquitectura y Pintura en Teotihuacan*. Siglo Veintiuno, Mexico City.

1966c. *El Lenguaje de las Formas en Teotihuacan*. Publisher not indicated, Mexico City, Gabriel Mancera 65.

Seler, Eduard. 1915. Die TeotihuacanKultur des Hochlands von Mexico. In *Gesammelte Abhandlungen zur Amerikanischen Sprach- und Alterthumskunde*, pp. 405–585. Unger, Berlin.

Sempowski, Martha L. 1992. Economic and Social Implications of Variations in Mortuary Practices at Teotihuacan. In *Art, Ideology, and the City of Teotihuacan*, Ed. by J. C. Berlo, pp. 27–58. Dumbarton Oaks, Washington, DC.

Sempowski, Martha L., and Michael W. Spence. 1994. *Mortuary Practices and Skeletal Remains at Teotihuacan*. University of Utah Press, Salt Lake City.

Sharer, Robert J., and David C. Grove (eds.). 1989. *Regional Perspectives on the Olmec*. Cambridge University Press, Cambridge, UK.

Sheehy, James J. 1988. Ceramic Ecology and the Clay-Fuel Ratio: Modeling Fuel Consumption in Tlajinga 33, Teotihuacan, Mexico. In *Ceramic Ecology Revisited, 1987: The Technology and Socioeconomics of Pottery, Part I*, Ed. by C. C. Kolb, pp. 199–226. BAR International Series 436(ii), Oxford, UK.

1992. *Ceramic Production in Ancient Teotihuacan, Mexico: A Case Study of Tlajinga 33*. PhD diss., Pennsylvania State University, University Park. University Microfilms International, Ann Arbor.

1998. Chronological Trends in the Ceramics of Tlajinga 33. In *Los Ritmos de Cambio en Teotihuacán: Reflexiones y Discusiones de su Cronología*, Ed. by R. Brambila and R. Cabrera, pp. 299–315. INAH.

Siebe, Claus. 2000. Age and Archaeological Implications of Xitle Volcano, Southwestern Basin of MexicoCity. *Journal of Volcanology and Geothermal Research* 104:45–64.

Sload, Rebecca. 1987. The Great Compound: A Forum for Regional Activities. In *Teotihuacan: Nuevos Datos, Nuevas Síntesis, Nuevos Problemas*, Ed. by E. McClung de Tapia and E. C. Rattray, pp. 219–41. Instituto de Investigaciones Antropológicas, UNAM.

Smith, Adam T. 2003. *The Political Landscape: Constellations of Authority in Early Complex Societies*. University of California Press, Berkeley.

Smith, Michael E. 2008. *Aztec City-State Capitals*. University Press of Florida, Gainesville.

2010. Sprawl, Squatters, and Sustainable Cities: Can Archaeological Data Shed Light on Modern Urban Issues? *Cambridge Archaeological Journal* 20(2):229–53.

Smith, Michael E., and Lisa Montiel. 2001. The Archaeological Study of Empires and Imperialism in Pre-Hispanic Central Mexico. *Journal of Anthropological Archaeology* 20:245–84.

Smith, Michael E., Juliana Novic, Angela Huster, and Peter C. Kroefges. 2009. Reconocimiento Superficial y Mapeo en Calixtlahuaca. *Expresión Antropológica* 36:39–55.

280   Bibliography

Smith, Robert E. 1987. *A Ceramic Sequence from the Pyramid of the Sun, Teotihuacan, Mexico,* Papers of the Peabody Museum of Archaeology and Ethnology: 75. Harvard University, Cambridge, MA.

Sotomayor, Eduardo, and Noemí Castillo Tejero. 1963. *Estudio Petrográfico de la Cerámica Anaranjado Delgado.* INAH.

Spence, Michael W. 1974. Residential Practices and the Distribution of Skeletal Traits in Teotihuacan, Mexico. *Man* 9(2):262–73.

   1981. Obsidian Production and the State in Teotihuacan. *American Antiquity* 46:769–88.

   1984. Craft Production and Polity in Early Teotihuacan. In *Trade and Exchange in Early Mesoamerica,* Ed. by K. G. Hirth, pp. 87–114. University of New Mexico Press, Albuquerque.

   1987. The Scale and Structure of Obsidian Production in Teotihuacan. In *Teotihuacan: Nuevos Datos, Nuevas Síntesis, Nuevos Problemas,* Ed. by E. McClung de Tapia and E. C. Rattray, pp. 429–50. Instituto de Investigaciones Antropológicas, UNAM.

   1992. Tlailotlacan, a Zapotec Enclave in Teotihuacan. In *Art, Ideology, and the City of Teotihuacan,* Ed. by J. C. Berlo, pp. 59–88. Dumbarton Oaks, Washington, DC.

   2002. Domestic Ritual in Tlailotlacan, Teotihuacan. In *Domestic Ritual in Ancient Mesoamerica,* Ed. by P. Plunket, pp. 53–66. Cotsen Institute of Archaeology, University of California, Los Angeles.

   2005. A Zapotec Diaspora Network in Classic-Period Central Mexico. In *The Archaeology of Colonial Encounters: Comparative Perspectives,* Ed. by G. J. Stein, pp. 173–205. School of American Research Press, Santa Fe, NM.

Spence, Michael W., and Luis M. Gamboa Cabezas. 1999. Mortuary Practices and Social Adaptation in the Tlailotlacan Enclave. In *Prácticas Funerarias en la Ciudad de los Dioses,* Ed. by L. Manzanilla and C. Serrano, pp. 173–201. UNAM.

Spence, Michael W., Christine D. White, Fred J. Longstaffe, and Kimberly R. Law. 2004. Victims of the Victims: Human Trophies Worn by Sacrificed Soldiers from the Feathered Serpent Pyramid, Teotihuacan. *Ancient Mesoamerica* 15: 1–15.

Stark, Barbara L. 2012. Canchas de la Mixtequilla. *Primer Coloquio Temas Selectos del Centro-Sur de Veracruz: El Juego de Pelota,* Ed. by A. Daneels, N. R. Donner, and J. Hernández Arana. UNAM.

Stark, Barbara L., and Philip J. Arnold III (eds.). 1997. *Olmec to Aztec: Settlement Patterns in the Ancient Gulf Lowlands.* University of Arizona Press, Tucson.

Stark, Barbara L., and L. Antonio Curet. 1994. The Development of the Classic-Period Mixtequilla in South-Central Veracruz, Mexico. *Ancient Mesoamerica* 5(2:267–87).

Stark, Barbara L., Lynette Heller, Michael D. Glascock, J. Michael Elam, and Hector Neff. 1992. Obsidian-Artifact Source Analysis for the Mixtequilla Region, South-Central Veracruz, Mexico. *Latin American Antiquity* 3(3):221–39.

Stark, Barbara L., and Kevin M. Johns. 2004. Veracruz Sur-Central en Tiempos Teotihuacanos. In *La Costa del Golfo en Tiempos Teotihuacanos: Propuestas y Perspectivas*, Ed. by Ma. E. Ruiz Gallut and A. Pascual Soto, pp. 307–28. INAH.

Stein, Gil J. (ed.). 2005. *The Archaeology of Colonial Encounters: Comparative Perspectives*, SAR Press, Santa Fe, NM.

Stirling, Matthew W. 1943. *Stone Monuments of Southern Mexico*. Smithsonian Institution, Bureau of American Ethnology, Washington, DC.

Stocker, Terrance, and Michael W. Spence. 1974. Obsidian Eccentrics from Central Mexico. In *Studies in Ancient Tollan*, Ed. by R. A. Diehl, pp. 88–94. University of Missouri, Columbia.

Stoner, Wesley D. 2013. Interpolity Pottery Exchange in the Tuxtla Mountains, Southern Veracruz, Mexico. *Latin American Antiquity* 24(3):262–88.

Storey, Rebecca. 1991. Residential Compound Organization and the Evolution of the Teotihuacan State. *Ancient Mesoamerica* 2(1):107–18.

1992. *Life and Death in the Ancient City of Teotihuacan: A Modern Paleodemographic Synthesis*. The University of Alabama Press, Tuscaloosa.

Suárez Cortés, María Elena, Dan M. Healan, and Robert H. Cobean. 2007. Los Orígenes de la Dinastía Real de Tula: Excavaciones Recientes en Tula Chico. *Arqueología Mexicana* 25(85):48–50.

Sugiura, Yoko. 1990. *El Epiclásico y el Valle de Toluca: Un Estudio de Patrón de Asentamiento*. UNAM.

2005. *Y Atrás Quedó la Ciudad de los Dioses: Historia de los Asentamientos en el Valle de Toluca*. Instituto de Investigaciones Antropológicas, UNAM.

Sugiyama, Nawa, Saburo Sugiyama, and Alejandro Sarabia G. 2013. Inside the Sun Pyramid at Teotihuacan, Mexico: Excavations and Preliminary Results. *Latin American Antiquity* 24(4):403–32.

Sugiyama, Saburo. 1989. Burials Dedicated to the Old Temple of Quetzalcoatl at Teotihuacan. Mexico. *American Antiquity* 54(1):85–106.

1993. Worldview Materialized in Teotihuacan, Mexico. *Latin American Antiquity* 4(2):103–29.

2005. *Human Sacrifice, Militarism, and Rulership: The Symbolism of the Feathered Serpent Pyramid at Teotihuacan, Mexico*. Cambridge University Press, Cambridge, UK.

2013. Creation and Transformation of Monuments in the Ancient City of Teotihuacan. In *Constructing, Deconstructing, and Reconstructing Social Identity—2000 Years of Monumentality in Teotihuacan and Cholula, Mexico*, Ed. by S. Sugiyama, S. Kabata, T. Taniguchi, and E. Niwa, pp. 1–10. Cultural Symbiosis Institute, Aichi Prefectural University, Japan.

Sugiyama, Saburo, and Rubén Cabrera. 2007. The Moon Pyramid Project and the Teotihuacan State Polity: A Brief Summary of the Excavations in 1998–2004. *Ancient Mesoamerica* 18(1):109–25.

Sugiyama, Saburo, and Leonardo López Luján, (eds.) 2006. *Sacrificios de Consagración en la Pirámide de la Luna*. INAH.

Sugiyama, Saburo, and Leonardo López Luján. 2007. Dedicatory Burial Offering Complexes at the Moon Pyramid, Teotihuacan. *Ancient Mesoamerica* 18(1):127–46.

Sullivan, Kristin S. 2005. *Making and Manipulating Ritual in the City of the Gods: Figurine Production and Use at Teotihuacan, Mexico*. FAMSI.

2006. Specialized Production of San Martín Orange Ware at Teotihuacan, Mexico. *Latin American Antiquity* 17: 23–53.

2007. *Commercialization in Early State Economies: Craft Production and Market Exchange in Classic Period Teotihuacan.* PhD diss., School of Human Evolution and Social Change, Arizona State University, Tempe.

Taube, Karl A. 1983. The Teotihuacan Spider Woman. *Journal of Latin American Lore* 9(2):107–89.

1986. The Teotihuacan Cave of Origin: The Iconography and Architecture of Emergence Mythology in Mesoamerica and the American Southwest. *Res* 12:51–82.

1992a. The Iconography of Mirrors at Teotihuacan. In *Art, Ideology, and the City of Teotihuacan*, Ed. by J. C. Berlo, pp. 169–204. Dumbarton Oaks, Washington, DC.

1992b. The Temple of Quetzalcoatl and the Cult of Sacred War at Teotihuacan. *Res* 21:53–87.

2000a. The Turquoise Hearth: Fire, Self Sacrifice, and the Central Mexican Cult of War. In *Mesoamerica's Classic Heritage: From Teotihuacan to the Aztecs*, Ed. by D. Carrasco, L. Jones and S. Sessions, pp. 269–340. University Press of Colorado, Boulder.

2000b. *The Writing System of Ancient Teotihuacan.* Center for Ancient American Studies, Barnardsville, NC, and Washington, DC.

2003. Tetitla and the Maya Presence at Teotihuacan. In *The Maya and Teotihuacan: Reinterpreting Early Classic Interaction*, Ed. by G. E. Braswell, pp. 273–314. University of Texas Press, Austin.

2011. Teotihuacan and the Development of Writing in Early Classic Central Mexico. In *Scripts, Signs, and Notational Systems in Pre-Columbian America*, Ed. by E. Boone and G. Urton. Dumbarton Oaks, Washington, DC.

Tolstoy, Paul. 1958. *Surface Survey of the Northern Valley of Mexico: The Classic and Post-Classic Periods.* Transactions of the American Philosophical Society, Philadelphia, PA.

1989. Coapexco and Tlatilco: Sites with Olmec Materials in the Basin of Mexico. In *Regional Perspectives on the Olmec*, Ed. by R. J. Sharer and D. C. Grove, pp. 85–121. Cambridge University Press, Cambridge, UK.

Torres Sanders, Liliana. 1995. *La Población Teotihuacana del Sector Oeste (Estudio Osteológico de Materiales Procedentes de Unidades Habitacionales).* ENAH.

Tozzer, Alfred M. 1921. *Excavation of a Site at Santiago Ahuitzotla, D. F. Mexico.* Smithsonian Institution, Bureau of American Ethnology, Bulletin 74, Washington, DC.

Trigger, Bruce G. 2003. *Understanding Early Civilizations: A Comparative Study.* Cambridge University Press, Cambridge, UK.

Turner, Margaret H. 1987. The Lapidaries of Teotihuacan, Mexico. In *Teotihuacan: Nuevos Datos, Nuevas Síntesis, Nuevos Problemas*, Ed. by E. McClung de Tapia and E. C. Rattray, pp. 465–71. UNAM.

1992. Style in Lapidary Technology: Identifying the Teotihuacan Lapidary Industry. In *Art, Ideology, and the City of Teotihuacan*, Ed. by J. C. Berlo, pp. 89–112. Dumbarton Oaks, Washington, DC.

Umberger, Emily. 1987. Antiques, Revivals, and References to the Past in Aztec Art. *Res* 13:61–105.

Urcid Serrano, Javier. 2003. Las Urnas del Barrio Zapoteca de Teotihuacan. *Arqueología Mexicana* 11(64):54–57.

Uruñuela, Gabriela, and Patricia Plunket. 2002. Lineage and Ancestors: The Formative Mortuary Assemblage of Tetimpa, Puebla. In *Domestic Ritual in Ancient Mesoamerica*, Ed. by P. Plunket, pp. 20–30. The Cotsen Institute of Archaeology, University of California, Los Angeles.

    2007. Tradition and Transformation: Village Ritual at Tetimpa as a Template for Early Teotihuacan. In *Commoner Ritual and Ideology in Ancient Mesoamerica*, Ed. by N. Gonlin and J. C. Lohse, pp. 33–54. University Press of Colorado, Boulder.

Vaillant, George C. 1930. *Excavations at Zacatenco*. American Museum of Natural History, New York.

    1931. *Excavations at Ticoman*. American Museum of Natural History, New York.

    1935a. *Early Cultures in the Valley of Mexico: Results of the Stratigraphical Project of the American Museum of Natural History in the Valley of Mexico, 1928–1933*. American Museum of Natural History, New York.

    1935b. *Excavations at El Arbolillo*. American Museum of Natural History, New York.

    1938. A Correlation of Archaeological and Historical Sequences in the Valley of Mexico. *American Anthropologist* 40(4):535–73.

von Winning, Hasso. 1987. *La Iconografía de Teotihuacan: Los Dioses y los Signos*. Two volumes. Instituto de Investigaciones Estéticas, UNAM.

Wallerstein, Immanuel. 1974. *The Modern World-System I: Capitalist Agriculture and the Origins of the European World-Economy in the Sixteenth Century*. Academic Press, New York.

Wallrath, Matthew. 1967. The Calle de los Muertos Complex: A Possible Macrocomplex of Structures near the Center of Teotihuacan. In *Teotihuacan. Onceava Mesa Redonda*, pp. 113–22. Sociedad Mexicana de Antropologia, Mexico City.

Weigand, Phil C. 2000. The Evolution and Decline of a Core of Civilization: The Teuchitlán Tradition and the Archaeology of Jalisco. In *Greater Mesoamerica: The Archaeology of West and Northwest Mexico*, Ed. by M. S. Foster and S. Gorenstein, pp. 43–58. University of Utah Press, Salt Lake City.

Wheatley, Paul. 1971. *The Pivot of the Four Quarters: A Preliminary Enquiry into the Origins and Character of the Ancient Chinese City*. Aldine, Chicago.

White, Christine D., Michael W. Spence, Fred J. Longstaffe, and Kimberly R. Law. 2004a. Demography and Ethnic Continuity in the Tlailotlacan Enclave of Teotihuacan: The Evidence from Stable Oxygen Isotopes. *Journal of Anthropological Archaeology* 23: 385–403.

White, Christine D., Michael W. Spence, Fred J. Longstaffe, Hilary Stuart-Williams, and Kimberly R. Law. 2002. Geographic Identities of the Sacrificial Victims from the Feathered Serpent Pyramid, Teotihuacan: Implications for the Nature of State Power. *Latin American Antiquity* 13(2):217–38.

White, Christine D., Rebecca Storey, Fred J. Longstaffe, and Michael W. Spence. 2004b. Immigration, Assimilation, and Status in the Ancient City of Teotihuacan. *Latin American Antiquity* 15(2):176–98.

Whittaker, Gordon. 2012. The Names of Teotihuacan. *Mexicon* 34(3):55–58.

Widmer, Randolph J. 1987. The Evolution of Form and Function in a Teotihuacan Apartment Compound: The Case of Tlajinga 33. In *Teotihuacan: Nuevos Datos, Nuevas Síntesis, Nuevos Problemas*, Ed. by E. McClung de Tapia and E. C. Rattray, pp. 317–68. Instituto de Investigaciones Antropológicas, UNAM.

——— 1991. Lapidary Craft Specialization at Teotihuacan: Implications for Community Structure at 33:S3W1 and Economic Organization in the City. *Ancient Mesoamerica* 2(1):131–47.

Widmer, Randolph J., and Rebecca Storey. 1993. Social Organization and Household Structure of a Teotihuacan Apartment Compound: S3W1:33 of the Tlajinga Barrio. In *Prehispanic Domestic Units in Western Mesoamerica: Studies of the Household, Compound, and Residence*, Ed. by R. S. Santley and K. G. Hirth, pp. 87–104. CRC Press, Boca Raton, FL.

Winter, Marcus, Cira Martínez López, and Damon E. Peeler. 1998. Monte Albán y Teotihuacán: Cronología e Interpretaciones. In *Los Ritmos de Cambio en Teotihuacán: Reflexiones y Discusiones de su Cronología*, Ed. by R. Brambila and R. Cabrera, pp. 461–75. INAH.

Wright, Lori E. 2005. In Search of Yax Nuun Ayiin I: Revisiting the Tikal Project's Burial 10. *Ancient Mesoamerica* 16: 89–100.

Wright, Rita P. 2009. *The Ancient Indus: Urbanism, Economy, and Society*. Cambridge University Press, Cambridge, UK.

Wylie, Alison. 2002. *Thinking from Things: Essays in the Philosophy of Archaeology*. University of California Press, Berkeley.

Yates, Robin D. S. 1997. The City-State in Ancient China. In *The Archaeology of City-States: Cross Cultural Approaches*, Ed. by D. L. Nichols and T. H. Charlton, pp. 71–90. Smithsonian Institution Press, Washington, DC.

Yoffee, Norman. 2005. *Myths of the Archaic State: Evolution of the Earliest Cities, States, and Civilizations*. Cambridge University Press, Cambridge, UK.

York, Abigail M., Michael E. Smith, Benjamin W. Stanley, Barbara L. Stark, Juliana Novic, Sharon L. Harlan, George L. Cowgill, and Christopher G. Boone. 2011. Ethnic and Class-Based Clustering through the Ages: A Transdisciplinary Approach to Urban Social Patterns. *Urban Studies* 48(11):2399–2415.

Index